CITY OF SPEED

LOS ANGELES AND THE RISE OF AMERICAN RACING

JOE SCALZO

MOTORBOOKS

Dedication

For Johanna, Anneke, and Annie
Three dollfaces in one.

Library of Congress Cataloging-in-Publication Data

Scalzo, Joe.
  City of speed : Los Angeles and the rise of American racing / by Joe Scalzo.
    p. cm.
  ISBN-13: 978-0-7603-2720-3 (hardbound w/ jacket)
  ISBN-10: 0-7603-2720-3 (hardbound w/ jacket)
  1. Automobile racing—California—Los Angeles—History. I. Title.
GV1033.S33 2007
796.7209794'94--dc22

2006035318

On the cover: 1950s-vintage road race poster.

On the title page: Midgets being prepped to race. *Greg Sharp collection*

On the back cover, left: Another illustrious Watson was the *Bill Forbes*, later to be the *Weinberger Homes*, here undressed. *Bob Tronolone*

On the back cover, right: The International Race of Champions began at Riverside Raceway in 1974. Porsche provided RSRs for that first year's series, but IROC switched to identical Z28 Camaros in 1975. These came equipped with electronic rev-limiters so that the hero drivers couldn't blow them up. But for any hero driver who knew anything about cars—and there were a couple who did—it was a snap to short-circuit the limiters and then over-rev to victory or destruction. All you had to remember was to throw the offending wires out the window afterward. *Bob Tronolone*

Editors: Zack Miller and Kris Palmer
Book design: Kou Lor
Jacket design: Tom Heffron

Printed in China

CONTENTS

CHAPTER ONE	MILLERMANIA	4
CHAPTER TWO	PISTONHEADS	32
CHAPTER THREE	DUNG BEETLES, JUNKYARD HOUNDS, POISONOUS VIPERS, BIG CUCUMBERS, AND JUMPIN' JUGHEADS	48
CHAPTER FOUR	BATTLEGROUNDS	78
CHAPTER FIVE	BATTLERS	96
CHAPTER SIX	SUGAR DADDIES	116
CHAPTER SEVEN	SALT SHAKERS	128
CHAPTER EIGHT	ARTSY-CRAFTSY	140
CHAPTER NINE	BALLYHOO MERCHANTS	154
CHAPTER TEN	$$$$$$$$$	166
CHAPTER ELEVEN	SCHMOOZIN' AND BOOZIN'	178
	INDEX	191

CHAPTER ONE

MILLERMANIA

We got earthquakes, rattlesnakes, milkshakes,
heartbreaks, and everything that's good.

—Jack Sheldon,
Los Angeles jazz trumpeter, songster, laugh-riot

L.A. racing, epicenter. *Greg Sharp collection*

Throughout the adrenaline-splashed century of roaring and careening race cars that's just been put to sleep, racing's one almighty city of speed was . . . the megalopolis of Los Angeles.

Hilarious Los Angeles, lair of freaks and glorious eccentrics that all the rubes in the saphead sticks love to hate! Goofy Los Angeles, holy oasis for the radically enlightened, where the endless sun and finely poisoned smog invigorate the mind. Cool Los Angeles, where soft currents fan across the blue western ocean, massaging the soul. Dangerous Los Angeles, whose red devil winds kick in the hormones, jump-speed pulses, and spiral brain-revs off the tach!

Opposite: Harry Armenius "Father" Miller, is the indispensable Los Angeles speed merchant. And forever reigning as the most successful racing engine in America annals is his iconic Miller/Offenhauser/Meyer-Drake/Drake bazooka.
Ludvigsen Library

Yes. The racing millennium was erupting right along the Pacific shore. Straining with vitality, L.A.'s big and belly-laughing family would ride out the twentieth century mingling and networking like a pack of frenzied lab rodents set loose in a wild think tank of speed. Hundreds—thousands—of go-fast addicts toiling in harmony and creativity, our explosive multi-generation counterculture comprising geniuses, legends, clairvoyants, witch doctors, struggling artists, nervous small businessmen, sugar daddies, doomed playboys, and war heroes; plus romantic fools, tragic villains, joker screwballs, blacklisted victims, tax deadbeats, deranged alcoholics, sad suicides, and disgraced bankrupts; hard-asses, dumb-asses, and pain-in-the-asses; danger-junkies, epiphany-seeking berserkos, desperately crazy kidnappers, and knife-crazy carvers; doll faces, sirens, divas, pinups, and mobster molls; silver-tongued devils, public-relations shills, ballyhoo merchants, world-owes-me-a-living elitists, money-grubbing stock-market soothsayers, and battling impresarios; muckraking publishers and yellow journalists; drop-dead

The over-talented manpower of Harry A. Miller. Most of the elite staff got burned when Father stiffed them of back wages. *Greg Sharp collection*

handsome Hollywood idols, million-dollar babies, and boy millionaire recluses. All right up my alley.

Nobody has ever quite figured out all the reasons why, but L.A. was racing's pulse, the planet's most imitated tribe of racers. Our addictive and cutting-edge brand hurtled along years ahead of racing anywhere else.

We were the most advanced speed swarm going.

But shouldn't we be raising not just L.A.'s own but *all* American racing? And instead of keeping them to ourselves, shouldn't we be generously sharing our discoveries and inventions and secrets and people and handiwork with all the clueless Babbitts beyond our boundaries? Hell yeah!

It took time. At first we were content merely to make the Indianapolis 500 the Los Angeles 500 and, for six decades, to joyfully and sadistically observe our products and men pound the Hoosiers like bongos. But inevitably we took command of the unenlightened racing hinterlands in general, plus both sides of the equator

The abiding paradox of pale and sickly little Leo Goossen: how did a kind-hearted, meek little draftsman manage to blueprint the savagely powerful racing mills of the twentieth century? *Greg Sharp collection*

Jimmy Murphy, whom the San Francisco earthquake had made an orphan, was already a hero—former holder of the Land Speed Record, first Yank to win a Europe Grand Prix—when he captured the 1922 Indianapolis sweepstakes in a Miller, the first big Miller score. Jimmy's Miller was like a horse of Troy. Other Father Miller projectiles followed it, and strangling Miller dominance of the Brickyard was at hand. Millers of various titles and guises won six of ten 500s in the 1920s, eight of ten in the 1930s, four of five in the 1940s, ten of ten in the big cucumber 1950s, five of ten in the 1960s, and five of ten in the 1970s.
IMS Photo

and many a distant backwater land at the other end of the world.

The last reckoning: Wherever on earth Los Angeles products, philosophies, and radical personnel came parachuting in, hysteria, fright, and enlightenment followed.

And shakily presiding over this nascent, seething empire of hot-bloods with trick names and risky toys was one incredible and mysterious man, Harry Arminius "Father" Miller.

Patron saint of the city, he was also racing's largest legend and most formidable and creative genius-in-residence. And, ultimately, the most disgraced and ruined L.A. citizen ever to finish up dying bankrupt in horrible exile.

Everything that ever happened out here sprang from Father. He was of Prussian stock, born Mueller and, upon switching to Miller, he declared himself namesake and manufacturer of the twentieth century's shock race cars. Millers are still the most difficult, eccentric, elegant, over-engineered, ingenious, and successful warheads ever to explode minds.

Geniuses have strange ways.

Not at all surprisingly, Father happened to be in possession of additional choice L.A. bona fides. Tapping into the village's busy occult front, he flourished also as an extreme clairvoyant. Midnights were when he awaited the arrival of the faithful mystery voices whispering the

Winner
Frank Lockhart-Miller Special

Outside of L.A., big-hair prodigy Frank Lockhart was such an unknown in his rookie 1926 Indy 500 that he couldn't even find a sponsor's name for his Miller. Lining up 20th, and totally inexperienced in the art of working traffic, he had six rows of enemy race cars to wade through. Gaining momentum with every lap, Frankie had picked off 15 outclassed opponents in seven miles and was rocketing along in fifth. Manipulating the big steering wheel and pouncing on rival iron every mile, at 50 miles he was sitting a close second. Then rain struck and the race was red-flagged for an hour. Come the restart, Lockhart lunged straight into the lead and won the 500 by two laps. *IMS Photo*

speed instructions and inside dope he depended on. "I don't do these things," Kenny Purdy quoted Father, "I get help. Somebody is telling me what to do."

MILLERMANIA AT THE BRICKYARD
Across the sprawling checkerboard that was the Los Angeles basin, existence was experienced at top speed, and the headlong rip torched my childhood, adulthood, and would surely be burning down my fast-approaching geezer semesters now, except the twentieth century ended first.

Exhilaration was waking up in the a.m. and going to work scooping the other newspaper and magazine hacks by hitting all five counties of greater L.A. to track down the coolest news and top-secret gossip, then passing the p.m. typing up my scores. Ordinarily I did my own

sleuthing, but enemy wordsmiths like Purdy, Griff Borgeson, and the barrister/author Mark Dees were also toiling the L.A. beat. Almost everything I know about Father Miller, I stole from them.

Pillaging admission out of the way, I can relate that Father was born, apparently in 1875, in Menomonie, in western Wisconsin—a benighted address that he had the smarts to abandon quickly so he could get in on the beginning of the automobile age and adventures with the young Henry Ford, Barney Oldfield, and the Duesenberg brothers, Fred and Augie.

Next came the several wandering tours back and forth across the continent, more racing adventures, the finishing up in Los Angeles, the grand opening of the Harry A. Miller Inc., Products Company, and paradise. It was the

With six toes on his throttle foot, and a chronometer for an ass, steady Louie Meyer won his first of three 500s in 1928. His name would later appear on the Miller engine block. *IMS Photo*

first 20 years of the century, a most fertile time. The village truly was cooking and blooming with sects, fakirs, swamis, saints, messiahs, seers, faith healers, food faddists, nudists, and the first movie stars. La la land indeed. About all that was missing was a high-end race car emporium operated by a mystic convinced he had extrasensory perceptions and was hard-wired telepathically to the spirit world.

Fasten your seatbelts. Boiling over with victories and glory, as well as destruction and too much gore, here are the runaway tournaments of Millermania:

1920: Turning up at the doorstep of the Miller hut on 2625 Long Beach Avenue is pale, tubercular Leo Goossen, barely 20 years old, but already draftsman extraordinaire. Father puts him to work. By trade Leo's

a draftsman, a common pencil pusher paid to draw up blueprints. He doesn't even like going to races—perhaps because blinding speed is built into every Miller, and he can't bear observing their vicious collisions and pastings. Yet with his genius for eloquently capturing on paper Father's concepts and visions, Leo is far more than a simple sketcher and more properly an engine designer himself. But no one will ever unravel the riddle of how such a frail and kindly little cat (Leo's perhaps the one gentle-natured soul in all of turbulent L.A.) should have in his meek makeup the shocker genes enabling him to leave his fingerprints and paternity all over the blueprints of every powerhouse Miller and, later, the ponderous, and maybe hoodooed, ballistic bull Novi V-8.

No. 2, Lockhart's shock Miller of 1927, was the projectile that achieved Indy's original 120-mile-per-hour time trial average. Following Frank's demise at Daytona Beach the following year, the fantastic chariot, in various hands, went right on establishing impossible speed records—smothering Indy 500s and collecting seasonal national titles; and once or twice apparently even surviving trips out of the Brickyard ballpark. *Neil Nissing*

The Hoosier bricks of Indianapolis were not the only racetrack surface where Millers came to flower. High-walled lumberdomes, "toothpick tracks," such as Culver City and Beverly Hills, brought on average speeds of 125 miles per hour—a comeuppance of 25 miles per hour over Indy. *Neil Nissing*

THE COUNTERFEIT FRENCHMAN CARPETBAGGER

Parlez-vous francais, M. Duray? Hell, no, the fake doesn't know a word of it! Leon Duray, born George Stewart, was hacking taxicabs around either Detroit or New Orleans and took a fare to the city dirt track. The fare happened to be J. Alexander Sloan, a mountebank impresario who ballyhooed racing's unknown into celebrities through flimflam. Offering Stewart a test hop in a race car, J. Alexander refined Stewart into Leon Duray, Gallic champion and decorated hero of the Great War. Working fast, the newly minted Duray remained with Sloan long enough to earn $15,000, sufficient mazuma to buy a Father Miller supercharged front-drive. For five consecutive Indy 500s he sat on the front row. And in 1928, he took dazzling jet black No. 4 around the joint so fast that his qualifying record lasted six seasons. By 1929, with castrating engine rules looming for the United States, Duray moved his act overseas by shipping himself and two Millers to France. Nothing went right. First, "Monsieur" Duray's inability to utter one word of the mother tongue was unfavorably remarked upon. And following Duray's spectacular series of Miller speed runs at Montlhéry, there was quite a stir among irate French pistonheads—who, it appeared, had never forgiven Father Miller for his earlier rip-off of design features from the Peugeot. Upon retreating to Italy, Duray discovered the climate there equally treacherous—he slayed both his Millers at Monza. To

IMS Photo

secure first-class passage home, he turned his cripples over to Ettore Bugatti. In what amounted to a reciprocal act of international copycatting, Bugatti had Duray's Millers dragged back to France, where Bugatti paid Father Miller the enormous compliment of plagiarizing their cylinder heads. Returning on a second loony carpetbagging mission a couple of campaigns later, Duray's risks continued at Monza, where his Miller broke anew. After his starting money was withheld, Duray, to get home, renegotiated the dollar-to-lira rate, got richly swindled, and returned to America under protest in steerage.

1921: Father has his whispering voices and he has Leo, but engineering, constructing, and customizing an internal-combustion tomahawk for Indianapolis is pricey. Father lacks the old do-re-me. Then, seemingly on cue, the winning driver of the season's 500, Tommy Milton, unexpectedly appears with some banks: among them the scion of the founder of General Motors, the other Father's old pal Henry Ford. They help cut the fat check that enables Father to run up the invention that will rattle Indy and all of racing. The piece is a weird brew—typically L.A.—of high-tech sophistication married to vast reservoirs of old-fashioned raw blasting horsepower: eight slamming pistons, arranged all in a row, displacing barely 180 ci (subsequently reduced to 122, then to a pygmy 91, plus supercharger). Everybody's happy and impressed with the prize mill except Tommy, who possibly believes his name instead of Father's should go on it. The Milton ego is suffocating.

Father Miller. He clearly was obsessive in the racing sense. Obsessive enough to put himself at the mercy of race drivers, the wreckers of race cars; to depend on rich patrons, who dumped him and turned off the tap when the 1920s tanked; and to trust the agents of the Indy 500, who drafted foul rules emasculating his work. Well . . . good for Father. Everybody in L.A. is obsessed with something. *Greg Sharp collection*

World-class artist and human being Sal Scarpitta—here atypically irate—grew up in 1930s L.A. absorbing the passion and iron of Legion Ascot Speedway—experiences still informing his work today. *Neil Nissing*

Besides mastery of numbers and chemistry, Tommy claims ownership of the English language, which he uses as a weapon. "I am the one who made Harry Miller!" terrible Tommy will complain for the rest of his days. And: "Harry Miller couldn't build a rat trap without someone's help!"

1922: At the debut of Father's made-in-L.A. hot rods, Indianapolis is stunned. One of two breaks the track record and qualifies fastest, leads for 155 of the sweepstakes' 200 laps; sets another speed mark winning, and earns its chauffeur a bundle. But the winner isn't Tommy's first-string Miller, it is the backup of Jimmy Murphy, once Tommy's closest friend and protégé, suddenly his most bitter enemy. Detonating heavily at the injustice of Jimmy winning instead of himself, Tommy lets fly a thesaurus of abuse.

1923: Tommy's revenge. He shatters the old Jimmy time-trial standard by 8 miles per hour, then easily blows off everybody in the 500. Two Indy skunkings in a row for Father.

1924: Jimmy's Miller crashes and kills him at Syracuse. Tommy at last reins himself in. He had jump-started the Murphy career, and he had suffered for it, but now he keeps a last lonely vigil over Jimmy's coffin on the long train trip from New York back to L.A.

1925: Swarms of scrambling, red-lining Millers, pungent with castor oil and bristling with loud wailing superchargers and other trick and terrifying touches, create the Brickyard's new and intimidating franchise sound. Each Miller is a gunmetal-blue masterpiece, a marriage of only the most costly and prime materials finished in delicately machined, shimmering steel and

1935. The first 500 score for one of cautious Fred's little Offenhausers. Kelly Petillo, the criminally dangerous grocer's son, broke Leon Duray's old records in time trials, but was disqualified on a technicality. Then a connecting rod snapped on the second qualifying try and he was barely 22nd on his third and drop-dead attempt. Winning anyway, Kelly the Shiv established still another new Brickyard speed mark. *IMS Photo*

burnished bronze. One fully cocked-and-ready rear-drive costs 10,000 iron men; a front-drive 15,000, which is a lot. Binge-building beauties for his favorite sugar daddy patrons—the big-spending playboy Billy Durant and the union racketeer Mike Boyle with his umbrella—Father is growing filthy rich.

At home, his environment grows esoteric. He adds birds and beasts, opens a private zoo, and turns wild-animal baron. His private estate near Malibu, the quirky Bohemian colony in Santa Monica canyon, becomes populated with howler monkeys, foxes, possums, deer, ducks, chickens, and stone quail, which he is licensed to breed.

All this will be far-reaching. With or without historical acknowledgment, certain L.A. lighthouses of the future will be in agreement with Father that an animal is

merely a higher form of human being: Carroll "Ol' Shel" Shelby, ex-manure-kicking poultry farmer, will name his sporty car spoof after a serpent; Bill Stroppe will open his own compound for homeless critters; the pioneer black driver Rajo Jack will have a mascot Dalmatian; Eddie "Isky" Iskenderian an aquarium of tropical fish; hot rodders Max and Ina Balchowsky their symbol a Golden Retriever; Bob Sorrell will house his infamous Sorrell Special—destined to be forever entombed underneath Riverside Raceway—in the same barn where he generates flocks of fowl; etcetera, etcetera . . .

1926: From fragile Leo to terrible Tommy Milton, the new Miller Manufacturing Company continues attracting the hairpins. All crazed white eyes and big hair, just in from Dayton, Ohio, where he soaked up some science from his neighbors the Wright brothers of Kitty

The incredible Chickie Hirashima. *Bob Tronolone*

Hawk fame, is Frank Lockhart. Young Frank is part internal-combustion-scientist-without-portfolio, part silver-tongued devil—what a personality! In spite of only spending minimal time in T-buckets, he is already a monster race driver. So much does he make the Miller works his home that in May, when Father decamps for Indy, Frank gets to go along. The first couple of weeks he's lost in the crowd, just another cocky character out of hated L.A. But when Father permits Frank to shake down one of the house cars, Frank, with zero education on bricks, threatens the lap record. Afterwards there's nothing to do but provide him a ride for the 500. Lined up 20th and totally inexperienced in the craft of working traffic, Frank scraps and curtsies and sends salaams to all of his experienced betters, then kicks them up and down the Brickyard for 200 terrible and humiliating laps. He conquers his novice 500 by a winning margin of 5 miles.

1927: Frank tap-dances around the Speedway at better than 120 miles per hour—the first time it's been done—and parks on pole position. But a connecting rod snaps and he disappears at 300 miles. Fourteen of Father's thoroughbreds remain in the hunt, and aboard one of them, Louie Meyer—on his way to becoming yet another L.A. hero—is risking his neck as an Indy debutant. After one of the veteran Miller busmen had stopped to confess that he was exhausted and needing a break, somebody tossed Louie a helmet and told him to get his

Twenty-first-century teams in the 500 still fail to equal Lou Moore and his Los Angeles team of Blue Crown Spark Plug specials. Their front-wheel drives pulled them through the Brickyard's accumulating surface oil and rubber goo. In 1947, the Blues took first and second; in 1948, first and second; and in 1949, first and third. *IMS Photo*

Three generations of hoo-dooed Novi V-8s took turns trying to overcome both the Offenhauser and the Meyer-Drake. It was an unwinnable fight. *Bob Tronolone*

butt out there. And Louie, it turns out, has natural gifts for going round and round in circles for four hours. With a chronometer for a rump, plus six toes on his extra-sensitive throttle foot, he collects a close fourth.

1928: Frank has already taken his show to Indy's bricks; he has also cleaned everybody's clock up on the looming velodromes of board-track racing. The last surface left to conquer is sand; so, two months before the 500, he applies finishing touches to a matched pair of blown Millers, affixing them to a hobgoblin streamliner intended for hunting really big glory—the Land Speed Record. But it's not the record that falls. The Lockhart mini-monster cracks up twice; the second one cashiers Frankie. One month before the 500, six-toed Louie gets a telegram from the Duesenberg brothers, begging him to come back and race for their almost bankrupt team; but skullduggery is lurking everywhere, and some antagonist sugar daddies purchase the Duesie out from under Louie to give to another driver instead. Two weeks before the 500, Louie discovers his own sugar daddy who buys him a Lockhart Miller that Louie subsequently time-trials to a superstitious 13th. Louie lines up near the

caboose, then wins the 500 anyway. Eight Millers finish in the top 10 positions. Six months later, the *Chromolite Special,* yet another Miller, is loaded on the liner, *Vestris,* bound for Argentina and some below-the-equator hippodroming. Instead, it pits permanently on the Atlantic seabed when the *Vestris* goes down off Cape Fear. So ends a feel-bad/feel-good campaign.

1929: The stock market blows. The greed-gut 1920s are finished. The United States goes broke.

DEPRESSION DEMENTIA

1930: "Racing is madness," pontificates Griff Borgeson. You said it, Griffith. All along, Father has been cold-crazy to entrust pedigree heaps to erratic race drivers like Murphy and Lockhart, who proceeded to destroy them; barking-mad to put himself at the financial mercy of his fickle customers Billy the playboy and Umbrella Mike, who now abandon him; and certainly certifiable to leave his destiny in the unsteady hands of the masterminds operating the Indianapolis Motor Speedway, who, to mitigate the Great Depression and save their 500, initiate a lunatic junkyard formula. It is a sad and sordid thing.

COLOSUS

With Father mainly missing from Indy during the Depression 1930s, the most interesting man alive, also from Los Angeles, was Art Sparks. Ex-Hollywood stunt man, wing-walker, T-bucket racer, bill collector, schoolteacher, and Legion Ascot force, Art campaigned a much-modified Miller named "Poison Lil," in honor of a pretty but infamous widow whom all drivers feared because both of her race-chauffeuring spouses had perished while in harness. Art's only problem was an inability to keep his deadly trap shut. Once made to stand before a kangaroo court because of something he said, he got blacklisted from Indy and for two years could not even purchase a pit pass. But he overcame the blacklisting by returning to the Brickyard in 1937 with the most complex and powerful race wagons anyone had seen since Father Miller—six purebred cylinders, maximum supercharging, the works. For financing he'd mortgaged his home, gone to the shylocks, and done a deal-with-the-devil involving mad Joel Wolfe Thorne. The Sparks "Big Six" was such a monster that it broke the Brickyard time trial record by five miles per hour. But it also so intimidated the Indy rulemakers that a formula change to cripple it arrived the same year.

IMS Photo

Immediately obliterated are Father's godly Model 91s and 122s, and their replacements are passenger-sedan-based econo–race car eyesores so morbidly fat and gruesomely ugly that they repudiate everything Father, Leo, and the mystery voices love.

What few Millers remain get chopped up and dressed down with widened coachwork to accommodate a revived species long believed out of fashion—riding mechanics. Combat wages of 3 to 5 percent of the winnings is all that a riding mechanic will ever be able to squeeze out of a typically tightwad Indy driver; yet, for the real junkie of danger, the riding mechanic rewards are sublime; ringed by killer walls, and sitting there like a petrified lump in the shotgun chair, he gets to dig the hurtling sensations and vistas of wire wheels buckling, balloon tires bulging, and suspension components heaving. Brain-frying stuff. One of these fascinating creatures is Spyder Matlock—a black widow tattooed across his gut—whose Los Angeles night job is mixing Mickey Finns at the gin-mill of the century, the Club Rendezvous, bossed by Al Gordon—a fire-eating wheelman in the most concentrated daredevil form. But perhaps an even stronger example of the strange breed is the incredible Takeo "Chickie" Hirashima, a 5-foot, 100-pound

The Hoosier rulemakers twisted the 1952 powerplant rules to permit this big and ungainly supercharged diesel barge to qualify on pole position. But the Meyer-Drakes swarmed all over it and the strain caused it to malfunction in fewer than 200 miles. *Bob Tronolone*

teen trading up to hot times after all the wasted hours of bitter boredom clerking at a fruit stand.

1932: Second only to the Brickyard, the hippodrome with the greatest mystique and most Millers is L.A.'s own Legion Ascot, five-eights of a mile of gleaming fast macadam on the otherwise barren heights just east of downtown. Ascot is part finishing school for future Indy 500-winning drivers and their mechanics; part abattoir; and full-time muse of 14-year-old artist-to-be Salvatore Scarpitta. Classes at Hollywood High School, supposedly intended to teach Sal math, instead become not-to-be missed opportunities for the drawing and sketching of Ascot's choicest Millers. Yet the sketching isn't the issue—Millers also require sound effects. So, Sal's teacher gets bounced out of her chair whenever Sal vocally recreates Ernie Triplett's red No. 4; and because Sal is by no measure the school's only Ascot addict, somebody from the other end of the class is sure to reply with the

blast of, say, Al Gordon's black No. 5. This earns Sal and co-conspirators many visits to the principal's office.

1933: Louie Meyer and his half-dozen digits win their second 500. But it has been such an embarrassing bloodbath that the ruling Hoosiers punish him by cutting the purse by 40 percent. And the "winner's banquet" is conducted out on the sidewalk where Louie and the rest of the survivors are paid their stipends and told to get lost. This is the Depression's worst year. Back in L.A., the Miller house is steadily becoming the Miller morgue. Father's really up against it. With ideas he's blessed, with finances he struggles and fails. Somehow, he's got to get hold of fistfuls of dollars; angry creditors are lining the doors. Finally, there's nothing to do but shut down, abandon his loyal retinue to financial disaster, and run to dull Detroit where, in ghastly banishment, Father will discover no L.A. sun, no enlightened L.A. minds, no wild beasts, no mystery voices.

INDIANAPOLIS MOTOR SPEEDWAY, 1947
DUKE NALON

Following the World War II armistice, rugged new competition for the Meyer-Drakes arrived from Nazi Germany via—naturally—L.A. This Mercedes Benz Silver Arrow turned up in Czechoslavakia and was purchased as war plunder by L.A.-man-about-town and car collector Tommy Lee, who lived in his own goofy Lee Castle out in the remote Mojave Desert. With perhaps double the horsepower of the truck-engine Meyer-Drakes, the doubly supercharged Benz time-trialed fastest in 1948 and should have ended up finishing better than third. But this time not even the L.A. geniuses could unlock the key to make it run properly. *IMS Photo*

1935: Father, the asshole. As collateral fallout from his runaway, expensive misery rains down on fragile Leo, who loses his home. Still another poor slob getting screwed over is Ralph "Hep" Hepburn, the long-time pal of Miller who had affectionately named him "Father." Not now or ever will Hep see the costly consignment of Miller paraphernalia he's paid for in advance. Incredibly, all isn't lost. Shop foreman since 1925, and the only reasonable human being in the entire Miller family, Fred Offenhauser—a nervous small businessman merely trying to ride out the Depression—runs a huge gamble. His modest four-cylinder may be the Miller catalogue's most banal piece, but it's also the most uncomplicated and economical. Slapping his own name on it, nervous Fred tosses out a few, then sweats blood offering them up for market.

The very first Offenhauser goes to Kelly "the Shiv" Petillo, a blade-happy grocer's son and L.A. menace. Outside a race car Kelly may be a hazard to himself and everybody around him (he'll later draw hard time for carving a girlfriend), but he can really race the Brickyard. For his first time-trial qualification he gets disqualified on a technicality. On the second try he tosses the new Offy. On his third and drop-dead try with the motor rebuilt, he lands back on the seventh row. And clear from 22nd starting hole he zaps to victory.

1936: The demise of Spyder Matlock and Al Gordon and the coronation of the six-toed one as the 500's original triple winner. In January the two-man Indy wagons hit Legion Ascot for a novelty meet. Spyder and Al are in and out of first place the whole race. But the outcome is messy. For its final rubber and refueling stop, their Offy

Alberto Ascari, Italy's hottest shoe since Tazio Nuvolari, arrived at Indy in 1952 loaded for elephant with a V-16 Ferrari Grand Prix car of multi gears. It was the most dangerous foreigner since the pre-war Wilbur Shaw Maserati, two-time 500 champion. Downshifting for all four corners every lap, Al was giving the Meyer-Drakes more fight than expected—up from 19th to 7th in just 40 laps—until Enzo's car pitched a wheel. *IMS Photo*

hits the pits with a thrown tire and riding on a brake drum. During the repairs, Spyder, who has had enough of Al's chauffeuring, tries to abandon the race but is restrained. Al himself can't resume battle until somebody finds him a replacement shoe for the one he's lost. He's wearing the replacement when he and Spyder sail out of the ballpark clearing their final crash wall.

Five months afterward, it's Memorial Day and the Hoosiers are sick of Los Angeles Louie winning their clambake. So they decide to jam him up with a fool's formula restricting all 33 cars to fuel loads of but 37 gallons. A pair of Offy cylinder blocks split, and Louie works all night overhauling his last one. In the morning, he lines up 28th and no 500 champion has ever started so far back. Chronometer rump and surplus tootsies cook anew. Fuel-restriction idiocies notwithstanding, Louie conquers the 800 turns and sets another new speed record.

1939: Ever since losing his shirt four 500s earlier in a short-lived and farcical partnership with Father Miller, Henry Ford has avoided Indy. But it's Louie's good luck that Henry attends this one. Trying too hard to become the first four-time victor, Louie uncharacteristically fails a wooden fence. His car heaves into a brutal rollover. And while he's limping to a cot in the first-aid infirmary, he bumps into Henry, an old friend, who pledges to find Louie armed forces contract work in the coming war if Louie promises to give up race-driving. Louie promises.

Far from prestigious Indy and its golden 500, out on the boondock bowls of the Midwest, Emory Collins mounted double-step knob runners to his made-in-L.A. Curly Wetteroth sprint car. And then, to blast through the heavy sod, Emory enlarged crankshaft and piston dimensions to jack up a 270-inch Offy to a hard-hitting 318. *Joe Scalzo collection*

Biceps, cajones, ice-cool nerves, and a wailing 220 Meyer-Drake were all mandatory equipment if your deal was taking a flyweight sprint car around the top lanes of high-walled Midwestern hill tracks like Salem, Winchester, and Dayton. *Joe Scalzo collection*

Campaign after campaign, intimidating 270- and 255-cube Meyer-Drakes powered every dirt-track championship brute, like Jimmy Bryan's all-conquering Dean Van Lines. *Joe Scalzo collection*

1941: The Japanese Navy sinks half the U.S. Fleet at Pearl Harbor. World War II erupts. Racing stops.

BLACK ARMBANDS

1942: The incredible Chickie Hirashima and the majority of Pacific Coast Nisei get tracked down, rounded up, and shipped to the High Sierra where they are locked away in the frozen detention gulag of Manzanar.

1943: Still stranded in benighted Detroit and living in shame, Father Miller, who once held all racing in his mitts, turns up dead and alone. This is one of the things wrong with the world.

1946: The first Indy 500 since the Armistice. The winner for once isn't an Offy but a downsized Art Sparks six-cylinder—another Los Angeles car, hastily renovated inside an abandoned nightclub. Its two-man team of caretakers comprises just the sort of off-the-wall squad only L.A. can muster. One co-chief mechanic is the

Fred Offenhauser's great racing contribution was his elegant, overhead-cammed 110 Offy for midget-car racing. It was a buzzing thoroughbred mill that gave midget racing a touch of class unknown previously. From its invention in 1938 clear up to its fall in the 1970s (when L.A. desert off-roaders finally topped it with their radical VWs) it was everybody's engine of choice. *Joe Scalzo collection*

never-smiling Sicilian-American Joe Petrali, or "Smokin' Joe," the motorbike multitasker champion of marathon timberdrome competitions, flat-track sprints, Daytona speed blasts, and hill climbs up the face of perpendicular cliffs. Additionally, Smokin' Joe is best boy to America's most famous king loon, the wacko Howard Hughes. The team's second co-chief—needing to reinvent himself now that the riding mechanic era has played out—is the incredible Chickie Hirashima. He looks older than anybody can look, and no wonder. After the year's incarceration at Manzanar, Chickie got hooked up with the all-Japanese 442nd, a high-risk U.S. combat squad whose members got their tails shot off at Anzio, then fought across the blood-soaked mountains of Italy and France, pushing Nazis clear into Berlin.

1947: Nervous Fred Offenhauser has taken early retirement and half of the consortium buying him out is none other than Louie Meyer, back from his wartime contracts. The second is Dale Drake, inventor of a ragamuffin but sensational midget car engine and, once upon a time, Louie's 500 riding mechanic. Louie and Dale assume responsibility for the production of all Meyer-Drake Engineering Indy, midget, and sprint-car warheads. Fragile Leo remains as brain-in-residence.

1948: Henry Ford dies. Ditto Hep Hepburn.

1953: The half century comes into focus. A blast-furnace sun gives Indy the works and roasts its combatants without mercy. Almost two dozen drivers fall out of their seats; one dies of heat exhaustion; seven are in and out of the infield infirmary; and 16 or 17 different relief

At Indy in 1955, good guy Manual "Yo Yo" Ayulo went out to practice at noon, crashed in the afternoon, absorbed enough fractures to terminate five men, and passed in the evening. In the autopsy, it was determined that poor Yo Yo had divined the concrete because he'd been up all of the previous night preening his Meyer-Drake and neglected to install a cockpit seat belt. He was one of a new wave of L.A. sharpshooters devoted to over-developing the Meyer-Drake. The morning after his death, the Speedway honored him by calling ten respectful minutes of silence in the racing pits. But after eight minutes somebody got antsy, a Meyer-Drake fired prematurely, and pretty soon all Meyer-Drakes were roaring like animals in the zoo. Yo Yo would have understood. *IMS Photo*

Horsepower warlock Frank Coon, half of the celebrated "Traco" duo, looks apprehensive in 1954 while assembling his and Jim "Crabby" Travers' third-string Meyer-Drake. Their chauffeur, deity Billy "Vookie" Vukovich, had already exploded two previous versions practicing, hence Frank and Crabby were suspicious that this M-D, too, might be a hand grenade. So on race morning, after firing it up then immediately shutting it down, the two petrified mechanics beseeched charger Vookie to please, please go gentle with it in the 500. Then Frank and Crabby stood back to observe Vookie pound the pedal so hard for almost four hours that he set a new speed mark while lapping the field. *Greg Sharp collection*

chauffeurs get pressed into emergency duty. The heat burns on, everybody is searching for an excuse to stop the suffering by red-flagging the race, but there's no way. Thanks to the independent R&D being carried on by a Meyer-Drake league of heavies—including Sparks and his forged pistons; Gerry Grant and his cylinder rings; Stu Hilborn and his injector stacks; and obsessed L.A. chief mechanics Clay Smith, Frank Coon, the impossible Jim "Crabby" Travers, and the equally impossible Herbert "Herbie Horsepower" Porter—all of the Meyer-Drakes are tomahawks so damn mighty that they refuse to cooperate and continue roaring regardless! The strongest racing engines in the world! Mighty deep-breathers of such colossal power that when shut down for corners the four enormous cylinders gasp so desperately for breath that it's a form of braking! And 'bout the only way to stop all those invincible Meyer-Drake innards from flailing savagely up and down would be to tear off the engine block and cylinder head to grab hold of 'em!

1954: A crashing Meyer-Drake dirt car invades the signaling pits at Du Quoin, Illinois, and carries away Clay Smith.

1956: To streamline the bodywork as well as mitigate 500 miles worth of oil, rubber, and engine roar splattering drivers' faces and ears, L.A.'s race car constructors run

The way the Meyer-Drake Offy occasionally rose up to decimate its greatest proponents was frightening. Like Yo Yo Ayulo, Clay Smith also fell to it, getting struck down and killed by a flipping M-D that invaded the signaling pits of a dirt track. Godly Clay, himself ironically fondling a bent-eight, may have been the ultimate Offy guru, once explaining, "To cut it in the Offy league, you have to sense and feel every quirk of that basic powerplant. And this creates a vast backlog of widely shared information. And also a breed of gung-ho, stand-on-it-and-turn-left race drivers who keep bearing down on the throttle through terrifying vibration periods and still say, 'Wind, wind, you son of a . . . !'"
Greg Sharp collection

up Meyer-Drake roadsters, big cucumbers on wheels, which drop drivers deep inside cockpits. This becomes a cool idea. Indy is in the L.A. stranglehold. L.A. cucumbers will win the next eight Memorial Days in a row; establish incredible speed records; and fight epic and sometimes crazy duels, none crazier than this one, marked by all the Kurtis-Krafts, Watsons, Kuzmas, Lesovskys, and Epperlys lapping so fast on the paved-over surface that they outrun their rubber. Eight different roadsters blow out Firestones and clobber crash-walls, including one after the finish and four during a yellow caution. The longest period of sane racing between all the yellows is only 21 minutes. Mishaps

nearly park positions second, third, fifth, and sixth. Ace of the cucumber age will be A. J. Watson, who lives to win races and create big front-engine Meyer-Drakes for he-man shoes to wrestle wheel-to-wheel in start-to-finish battles. Quality time.

1962: Unhappy Tommy Milton, still upset with Father Miller after half a century, suicides himself with a double dose of shotgun buckshot to the chest.

1963: *Cherchez la femme.* After collapsing under the spell of a hot and sexy Italian socialite who really digs racing, Henry "Hank the Deuce" Ford II takes the family factory into competition on a worldwide scale. For Indy, Ford Motor Company dramatically appears with a

The Traco-prepped, L.A.-based *Fuel Injection Special*, winner of the 500 of 1953 and 1954, kicked off the Meyer-Drake roadster, or "big cucumber," era. *Bob Tronolone*

set of coffins-on-wheels Lotus-powered-by-Fords (i.e., gussied-up Fairlanes). One of them kicks off the lamented switch to rear-engines by finishing a controversial runner-up to the great Parnelli Jones. FoMoCo is in racing in a large way. Not long afterward, a Lotus Ford takes first place at Milwaukee. A team of factory engineers next orders a Meyer-Drake to study. But Father Miller designs can be tricky, and the engine's arrival is followed by a panicky phone call to Meyer-Drake saying the engineers don't know how to disassemble the damn thing. So, on Ford's nickel, the incredible Chickie Hirashima—now on his third racing life as a witch doctor of the Meyer-Drake—gets on a jet to teach them how. Miller cylinder-head secrets get plagiarized and incorporated in FoMoCo's own nifty new four-cam V-8.

1965: Smashing the Meyer-Drake monopoly, Fords at Indy finish first, second, third, and fourth. FoMoCo now develops plans to put its four-cammer and screaming bagful-of-snakes headers on the racing market, in

direct competition with Meyer-Drake. The Meyer-Drake partnership snaps. Louie jumps ship to run the FoMoCo program.

1966: An L.A. judge sends Kelly Petillo away for a long time—more reported knife work. Kelly and I are the only persons in the bleak courtroom aware that Kelly is a crucial piece of Millermania—the carver who got scared Fred's Offenhauser its first Indianapolis scalp.

1968: Following two more Indy losses to Ford, Dale Drake, fragile Leo, the incredible Chickie Hirashima, a wild aerospace engineer named Bob DeBischop, and a few other unsung heroes, like John Miller (no kin to Father), roll the dice and complicate matters by ramming into the Meyer-Drake—now called the Drake—a violent dose of fast-spinning aviation compression. Radical turbocharging should bring on the death of so old an engine. Yet not only does the Drake tolerate it, it thrives on it. The greater the goosing, the better it responds. A turbo Drake wins the 500. FoMoCo eventually constructs

1960: This all-business front-row trio of Watsons were named the Dean Van Lines, the Ken-Paul, and the Leader Card. They pitched in and put on the grandest, most-disputed 500 of the big cucumber age. At the hard-pounding end, the Ken-Paul conquered it. *Bob Tronolone*

a 0-for-5 losing streak. It is neutralized. A skeleton outfit of old men and an old engine has taken down a Fortune 500 corporation.

1970: Kelly the Shiv dies.

1972: Creating a sensation at one of the world's great art shows—Venice's Biennale di Venezia on the Piazza San Marco—is a recreated Miller: Sal Scarpitta's red Ernie Triplett No. 4.

1973: It has taken nearly 60 seasons for Indy cars to push their speed averages beyond 170 miles per hour. But now, within a spectacular binge of 15 months, suddenly they're racing across the frontiers of 180, 190, and,

at L.A.'s Ontario Motor Speedway, in excess of 200. One explanation for this is that the new Eagles coming out of Dan Gurney's All-American Racers consortium are the first U.S.-constructed rear-engines that drivers like. Another is that the hot dogs have their Drakes coming off the dynamometers packing as much as 1,100 ponies. In any event, Indy speeds are way too fast. A disaster is coming. It occurs right at the start. Vehicles are out of alignment and randomly going too slow or too fast; some turbochargers are kicking in, others not. A riot begins back on the sixth row and a Drake car goes on its top, spraying fuel and fire. Other burning wrecks are

Nobody constructing a big cucumber could agree about where to put its heart, the Meyer-Drake, 345 righteous pounds of hardenend steel, brass, bronze, and aluminum. Conservatives like A. J. Watson mounted it straight up and down. Radicals like Quin Epperly and Eddie Kuzma laid it over on its right or left side. And then along came Lujie Lesovsky with this "bent-engine eight ball" angling everything left to right. *Greg Sharp collection*

ricocheting off the inner and outer walls. Eleven drivers are involved, and nine spectators in the grandstands suffer trauma. Then, during the restarted 500, a pit man is knocked down dead by a fire truck charging in the wrong direction to another big fuel blaze that kills L.A.'s Swede Savage. Punitive new restrictions are drafted, limiting fuel cargos and curbing turbo boost. This will leave the Drakes strangling for air.

1974: Following the earlier passings of nervous Fred, Dale Drake, and fragile Leo, Drake Engineering, missing

its wisest minds, seems to lose its way. Quality control falls. Its hyper-expensive products now either vibrate parts onto the track or experience fatal cases of mechanical indigestion. Mutinying, major teams like Vel's Parnelli Jones take the extreme step of inventing the turbocharged V-8 Cosworth—in L.A., naturally.

1977: The Cosworth is dominant, but just when the old sucker and its quartet of cylinders are on their last legs, hall of fame mechanic George Bignotti, son-in-law

continued on page 31

Fifth at Indy in 1965, and the last big cucumber Meyer-Drake to exchange serious licks with the redcoat rear-engines, was the Weinberger Homes Watson, driven by Michigan funding and a terrific Michigan wheelman, Gordon Johncock. *Bob Tronolone*

The saga of the overpowered, turbocharged Drake—subsequent champion of half a dozen Indy 500s—began with the prototype engine bolted inside an old Watson roadster. Bob DeBischop, shown here, and Herbie Porter were the brains behind the enterprise. *Joe Scalzo collection*

Above and below: Air. Have you ever noticed that it's the crucial thing human beings and race cars share? We need it to survive, and, similarly, the more air a race car inhales, the better its health and speed. Once the turbocharged era hit, every serious L.A. team with a Drake had to employ its own turbocharger witch doctor. All-American Racers, Dan Gurney's squadron down in Orange County, a hotbed of Indy activity in the 1960s and 1970s, hired the best screwhead that money could buy—Johnny Miller (no known relative of Father's). Johnny's race day engines were built to last for 500 miles, but his time-trial-day bombs—first to crank out a 200-mile-per-hour average—were ballistic warheads, so overstressed they were good for four laps and ten miles, then kiss them goodbye. *Bob Tronolone*

Above and below: Déjà-vu all over again. After spending nearly 70 years powering winners and sometimes entire Indy 500 starting fields, L.A. is back in the engine game in the twenty-first century. This time it's with Cosworth Engineering, which equips every car in the Champ Car tournament; with Toyota Racing Development, winner of Indy in 2003; and now American Honda, shown here, presently powering everything in the Indianapolis Racing League. Leasing one of these babies for one 500 brings a five-figure tab. *Joe Scalzo collection*

A. J. Watson was another of L.A.'s multi-talents, or perhaps quadruple threats. Besides throwing off the big cucumbers that won four Indy 500s and serving as chief mechanic in two of them, he was one of the sharpies who scaled down the tall-block Meyer-Drake from 270 cubic inches to a more manageable 255. *Greg Sharp collection.*

L.A.'s triple Indy 500 champion Louie Meyer—here embracing Lujie Lesovsky—was one half of the old Meyer-Drake tandem, and longest-lived of all original Millerites. *Greg Sharp collection*

In the 1980s Indianapolis was experiencing the dawn of the Cosworth and the gloomy twilight of the Miller/Offenhauser/Meyer-Drake/Drake, great battle-ax that it had been through three-quarters of the century. Bucks-down Indy car squads unable to afford the new Cosworth were blowing their old Drakes to smithereens trying to keep up. Enter the innovative crisis-manager Howard "Tilt" Millican, a fiery Albuquerquian who spent lots of time in L.A., and who proceeded to demonstrate to the sad-sack Drake troops how to machine off a pair of blown up blocks, bolt them together, and still race. Charging a fast and cut-rate $500 per job, he and his talented spouse Anita Millican earned enough to travel to Costa Rica and purchase their own coconut plantation. *Bob Tronolone*

Continued from page 26
of six-toed Louie, sets out to find if the Drake's gasping-for-breath four cylinders can be re-born yet again. Just before his death, fragile Leo has contributed one last great set of blueprints and George uses them to modernize everything from the crankshaft up. Art Sparks is also involved. The resulting Drake-Goossen-Sparks proves structurally stronger than the Cosworth, but its poor fuel mileage dooms it. Bignotti orders his mechanics to slap on black armbands in mourning, then joins the Cosworth contingent.

1980: The incredible Chickie Hirashima expires.

1981: Indy's longest era ends. Not a single Miller, Offenhauser, Meyer-Drake, or Drake is among the 33 starters.

1984: Art Sparks departs.

1993: Mark Dees announces the Los Angeles publishing of a revised edition of his weighty opus, *The Miller Dynasty*, triggering a revival of Millermania.

1994: Mark exits in a head-on smash between Visalia and Oxnard on death trap Highway 118.

1995: Louie Meyer, last of the original Millermaniacs, the oldest living 500 champion, leaves us. This is the great Louie Meyer who, prewar, was winner of three Indys and four seasonal racing championships; and who, postwar, carried on the heavy legacy of keeping Father's wonder creation the most famous and successful racing engine of all time. No matter under what aegis, it won 6 out of 10 Indy 500 sweepstakes in the 1920s; 8 out of 10 in the 1930s; 4 out of 5 in the 1940s; 10 out of 10 in the big-cucumber 1950s; 4 out of 10 in the 1960s; and 5 out of 10 in the 1970s. During one unequaled span of 18 Indy 500s, nothing else won. Yet after all this, and even after living to the tremendous age of 91, when it's time for his obituary, the Indianapolis Speedway's "official biography" trivializes L.A. Louie as the 500 winner who inaugurated the practice of drinking milk in Victory Circle. Freakin' Hoosiers.

CHAPTER TWO

PISTONHEADS

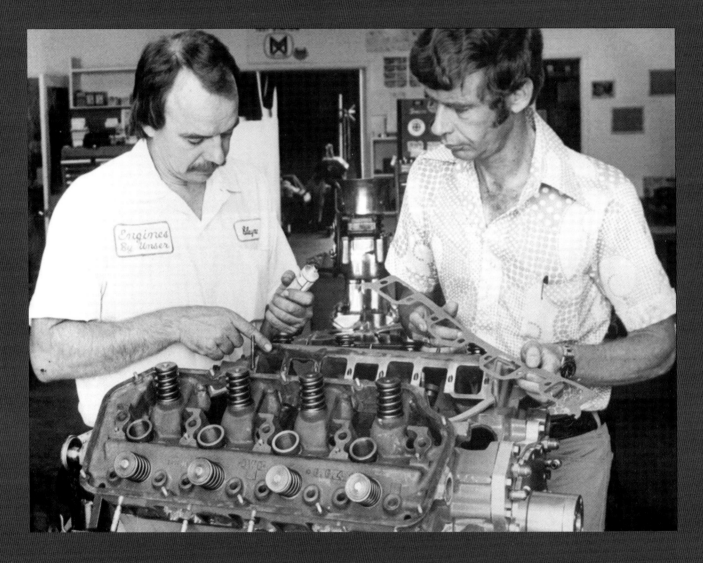

The people who run Los Angeles are the Babbitts.

—Louis Adamic, rabble-rousing firecracker

The tremendous *Gilmore Special* No. 2, Legion Ascot's most mighty Henry car. Although Eddie Winfield did the prep work, No. 2's actual owner was another wild dude named Paul Fromm, later to work with Art Sparks on Art's Big Six. Prior to the Winfield Special, Paul had dipped into his aviation background—he was an aircraft machinist—to split a Hispano-Suiza engine in half and jam it into an Ascot sprinter. But it went too damn fast and subsequently was banned from Legion. *Neil Nissing*

Father was the grandmaster—his Indy dominance speaks better than any other testimony—but L.A. talent runs deep, and as racing caught on and grew in classes and venues, many of the best-known names in speed emerged from the City of Angels. This band sealed L.A.'s legacy, wrenching, scheming, straining their minds and machinery to leave all track challengers wondering what missile from hell was pulling the leading racers off the front of the pack.

None of the opponent constructors of L.A. race car engines who came after Father Miller claimed to be

Opposite: Creative cats can be moody and crotchety, and L.A. engine men were among the worst. An exception was Louie Unser (right), namesake of Louie Unser Racing Engines, a wonderful friend and fine person. Here he and his associate Blaine Smith bring to life yet another L.A. hammer, this one Chrysler-based. *Laverne Unser*

clairvoyants served by dark occult tongues. Yet the majority of them aped Father's egotistical practice of naming their horsepower inventions after themselves. Shining examples are such commodities as the Winfield, McDowell, Utzman, Black, Navarro, and Pink. And all by itself, Eddie Cole's Chevrolet turbo-fire V-8 launched a raft of names, including the Bartz, Unser, Faulkner, the exalted Traco, and Shaver.

A twenty-first-century Shaver is a 410-cubic-inch, 13:1-compression, fuel-burning, 860-horsepower jackhammer of a sprint car mill made out of steel, aluminum, rubber, Teflon, magnesium, bronze, cork, and asbestos. And all of its choice raw guts represent the most up-to-the-instant custom speed hardware coming out of the classic L.A. speed houses—Donovan, Moroso, Cosworth, Manley, Brodex, Mondello, Iskenderian, Brownfield, Carillo.

Assembling one of the monsters takes 60 man-hours, with a Shaver Specialties staff of 10, including Ronnie

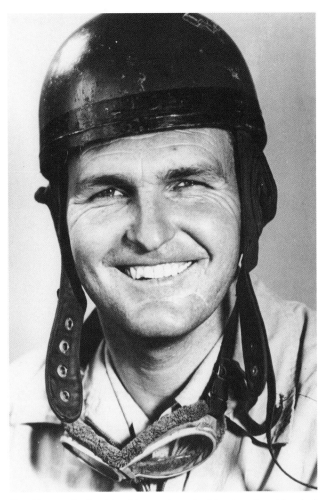

Rex Mays, who besides his great work at Legion Ascot landed on Indy's front row six times and on four occasions sat on the pole, seemed to catch all the oddball race cars—everything from the Fromm Hisso, to a Count Drivio Alfa Romeo, to the Novi, and of course the wildest chair of them all, the Winfield Special. *IMS Photo*

The big Novi V-8, here in Santa Monica at the Grancor shop, was a horsepower bully, its learning curve steep, and the difference between spectacular speed and a spectacular crash was oh-so-slight. *Greg Sharp collection*

Shaver, the guru, performing the heavy lifting. When purchasing a Shaver, bring along a cashier's check in the amount of $44,000.

With the Shaver, L.A. struck again—another example of how a killer piece gets created here; gets exported to the backwater hinterlands; and proceeds to flood, conquer, and drown the market. For a quarter century now, the Shaver has been the ax of choice in the wedge winged sprinter tournaments of the World of Outlaws, champion of better than 1,000 main events, not just in California but Arizona, New Mexico, Texas, Oklahoma, Georgia, Florida, North Carolina, Tennessee, Arkansas, Kentucky, Maryland, Pennsylvania, New Jersey, New York, Ohio, Indiana, Illinois, Iowa, Nebraska, Missouri, Wisconsin, Minnesota, Colorado, and South and North Dakota. Plus Mexico and Australia.

Among masters of the racing mill residing in the village, Ronnie Shaver is atypical. True, he relishes horsepower and the sound a mass of it makes. True, getting too close to all the fierce roaring of his namesakes has deadened his sense of hearing. True—and despite the auditory loss—he maintains he is able to discern the yodeling of his big pounders above all the other marques. All of the perfectly normal likes, damage, and conceits of the Los Angeles pistonhead.

What makes Ronnie unique and different is that he's not a paranoid hermit or bitter misanthrope. Against impossible odds, he appears to be a nice guy. A genuinely nice guy. Amazing.

L.A. pistonheads of my acquaintance generally have been, well, objectionable people. No fun at all to hang out with. A bunch of surly and hugger-mugger curmudgeons convinced any person striking up a chat is only fishing for secrets. A bunch of grouches who have been profoundly suspicious that I was out to embezzle all their tricks and spread them.

Eddie Winfield, genius, was undoubtedly the deity who was the source of all the anti-sociability.

"THE EXHAUST PIPE POINTING LIKE A RIFLE BARREL"

Prior to doing his strange "Howard Hughes" in the 1980s and, for whatever reason, vanishing into Las Vegas and its fake glitter, Eddie used to bivouac himself and his high-tech laboratory up on L.A.'s mountainous extreme north

Traco's Jim Travers, left, and Frank Coon, right, bookend the Howard Keck crew at the Indy 500. Their sled—forerunner of their all-conquering Fuel Injection Special—is a front-wheeler developed by L.A.'s Norman Timbs, who also did the Blue Crown Specials. At the wheel is triple 500 champ Mauri Rose, an on-again–off-again L.A. resident. This photo is from 1950, a 500 of madness. Lining up on the front row, Mauri discovered he had $3 in his trousers; being a tightwad, he gave it to Travers for safekeeping. The $3, every stitch of Travers' clothing, and nearly Mauri himself, were all almost incinerated in an inferno sparked by a botched refueling stop. Rose resumed the 500 anyway, as did the nude Travers in the pits—after somebody finally brought him fresh threads. Mauri subsequently finished a close third.
Greg Sharp collection

end, among the far nudist colonies. Reasons why: the population there numbered in the low hundreds, those human beings who did exist out there were reclusive, and L.A. proper was a fair distance away.

Among many great Winfield decades, the 1930s in particular were years when Eddie had lots of fun. Depression days were raging, but so were Wednesday-night sprint car meets at Legion Ascot, where hardly a Miller in the pits lacked the benefits of the ingeniously complicated Winfield carburetors or the magic-tinged camshafts. As a consequence, many a customer who owned a Miller made the long trek out to Eddie's seeking an audience, perhaps even an invitation to enter the tiny lab to catch the reclusive great man at work. But hardly anybody ever gained entrance. Rajo Jack may have earned an invite or

two, but only because he arrived bearing gifts in the form of fresh eggs from his poultry farm down in Mud City.

What all Miller squads were desperate to uncover—so they could rook the Legion Ascot rules and outlaw them—were all the dangerous secrets sprouting from Eddie's dumbfounding Winfield Special. Outwardly just another glittering L.A. vehicle (west of Indianapolis, Legions were the country's most gorgeous race cars), this unsophisticated Winfield's unexpectedly violent wham came courtesy of nothing but an innocuous-looking banger straight off the Ford Motor Company assembly line.

Nothing but a crude lump of iron among all Legion's hand-wrought Millers, it was a deliberate in-your-face insult to Father Miller and all his clients. Even a joke, at first.

"This baby's a runner!" *Bob Tronolone*

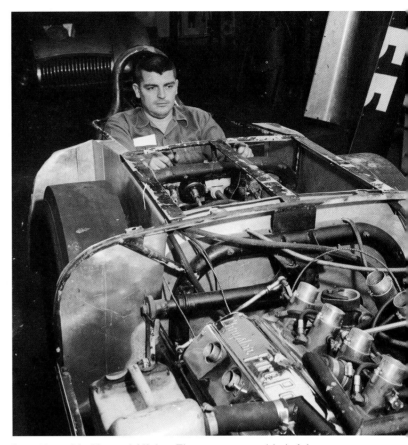

Love those big Mopars! Mickey Thompson, arguably L.A.'s ultimate hot rodder—and perhaps ultimate racer—surely did. This is one of his dry lakes and Bonneville toys. *Greg Sharp collection*

Yet following countless man-hours twisting, tweaking, fussing, refining, porting-and-polishing, and over-head-camming, Eddie forced something incredible to happen. He became the witch doctor who turned his lethal Winfield into the Legion Ascot vampire, which came out on Wednesday eves to slay all Millers and drink their blue blood.

It became a gory massacre. Six Legion Wednesdays in succession, Millers went down to agonizing defeat, everything highlighted by the fantastically embarrassing evening the Winfield Special was wounded and missing fire on a cylinder, yet continued dominating anyway. And those half-dozen maulings became the most brutal the mobs of Father Miller ever suffered.

Which was the whole point, of course. All L.A. geniuses harbor suspicions of each other, and Eddie was of the strong opinion that, as a genius, Father was lacking and just didn't rate all that high. Even if Father was a genius, Eddie once cuttingly pointed out, he was a minor genius, one "who let Leo Goossen do the work."

Eddie invented the Winfield to put Father in his place.

Crediting Eddie with being the first innovator to divine and tap into all that vast, untapped go clever Henry Ford had packed into FoMoCo's sensational 1932 model line is tempting. Only it wasn't Eddie. It was Johnny Dillinger.

Johnny, Public Enemy No. 1, was the criminal visionary who realized that the days of running the law ragged on hot-blooded stallions were over, and that the really modern bank robber must loot by auto. He went gaga over the very first Model B flathead he stole. It could accelerate and jam through the gears, stop on a dime, and back up going 40 miles per hour.

Following an orgy of brigandage, random killings, and top-speed getaways, Johnny had the law agencies of Florida, Missouri, Kansas, Minnesota, and Illinois all chasing their tails trying to nail Johnny's flying Model B. Once they at last captured it, in downtown Chicago during a heat wave, the bulls took no chances, and Johnny got shot dead on the spot. So it sometimes goes with visionaries.

Dillinger's well-deserved apocalypse occurred in 1934, the summer of Eddie's own rampage across

Professional sports car racing was blooming in the 1960s and 1970s, and Crabby and Frank got in on it. Every Can-Am vehicle in this picture is powered by either a bonafide Traco or something dreamed up by an ex-Traco employee: billet-steel Carillo connecting rods, Art Sparks' pistons, Isky camshaft, Aviad dry-sump oil systems, and all the other speed city accoutrements.
Bob Tronolone

Legion's shiny, lethal macadam. Two very different winning pilots were involved in the Winfield's care and chauffeuring: good boy Rex Mays and bad boy Kelly Petillo. Rex was smooth, Kelly the Shiv so ragged that his jittery throttle foot pounded dents in the floorboards.

Yet so pristine-appearing was the Winfield when its latest owner Kenny Howard trailered it to Legion Ascot in 1985 for a photo shoot that everything had been smoothed over. There was no sign of Kelly's old pounding. Ten years of Kenny's life went into the immaculate restoration. Decaying in a ruined barn when he'd first stumbled upon them, the Winfield's precious remains had passed the prior 10 years rotting out in the open. Now everything was Legion Ascot choice again.

So here the Winfield was, bristly with l930s' technology, wondrous and primitive. I studied its Miller-bullying mill closely. Between heat races at Legion, Eddie used to swaddle everything in army blankets. Was it a case of the old paranoia of the pistonhead? Or was it because he wanted to pamper all the vital and secret organs by keeping them warm and toasty?

Probably the latter, because the almost suicidally stressed-out Winfield used to eat a whole crankshaft every two Wednesdays—power pushed to the brink of oblivion. Yet long after Legion shuttered and Eddie became busy on other projects, one of L.A.'s journeyman racers, Bayless Leverett, upped the Winfield's steroids so it could continue raging well into the postwar 1940s.

The 6-foot-long exhaust barrel, tuned and chromed, mesmerized me: the Winfield is reputed to be one of the most joyous-sounding heaps ever to race. I lusted to hear it.

Kenny Howard wasn't cooperating. The Winfield was his trailer queen; he had no intention of lighting it off.

All wasn't lost. There was another way to learn of the Winfield's legendary bark. I piled into my sled and sped through Gardena, Compton, Bellflower, Norwalk,

Mickey also crammed one of the giant hemis into his quarter-mile slingshot, a radical design he is commonly championed with inventing. *Greg Sharp collection*

Whittier and didn't stop until hitting El Monte in the sun at the end of the old Santa Fe Trail. The tumbledown compound of Joe Gemsa was, as ever, chockablock with extremely valuable vintage racing treats and peculiarities. In all L.A., only Vince Conze's collection used to be comparable. Behind the Gemsa barbed-wire fencing, the various impressive-looking locks, the loud-screaming siren alarm, and the ragged pack of snarling and vicious guard dogs that tolerated nobody but their master, stood Joe Gemsa himself—ex-wheelhouse man, walking and talking racing encyclopedia, patron of all dead and gone L.A. race cars.

"Tell me about the Winfield Special," I urged.

Smiling with delight, Joe started unspooling the fantastic Gemsa memory.

"Last time I saw it race," he began, "was up at Oakland. Nineteen forty-eight. I was following Bayless Leverett with that great big Winfield exhaust pipe pointing at me like a rifle barrel. And just then Bayless hammers it, really hammers it. I watch flecks of flame turning from orange to yellow to blue, followed by a *blam!* And out rolls this huge fireball all swirling and loud. Fantastic.

"Ed Winfield was a genius."

SIREN SCREAM

A genius, yes, but brains run wild in that family, and a gifted younger Winfield brother, Bud, similarly contributes his own made-in-L.A. fowling piece. The season is 1941. Bud's big, bad, rogue elephant of an Indianapolis motor depends on two crucible components: a shrieking supercharger and a flailing club of a crankshaft yoking together what appear to be a matched set of scared Fred's Offenhausers. Double the pleasure, double the fun. Bud's larger-than-life creation is both alarming and expensive. So, to obtain the necessary lettuce for its development and maintenance, Bud surrenders the right to call it a Winfield and instead permits his sugar daddy—a free-spending Indy 500 acolyte and crony of old man Ford—to name it, oddly, after the Detroit township of Novi.

Left and below: Black and Pink, the hues of the two witches of the blown Chrysler, Keith Black and Ed Pink. Between them, they built a wicked smorgasbord of supercharged nitro mills, supercharged gasoline mills, supercharged alcohol mills, normally aspirated nitro mills. . . . *Greg Sharp collection*

The Novi. A moniker that will long give other teams in the 500 the heebie-jeebies. Its firepower is perhaps twice that of an Offenhauser or Meyer-Drake. Its technology is ahead by a decade. And one Novi or another will be fastest qualifier in five Indys, four of which will be in a row. Three Novis will start from pole position. Yet what should be a saga will instead be a disaster.

For all the rolling thunder and blower shriek, and despite staying active from 1941 through 1966—the hexed team will last for 25 crisis-filled years—no Novi ever wins the 500. The ungodly power brings with it ungodly problems. Novis devour tires at the rate of 28 per 500; annually keep the Brickyard groove oiled-down by throwing a quart or two of 50-weight every 100 miles; and need a warlock's brew of benzene and explosive nitromethane to soup up and cool down all those 16 frantically sparking-plugs, eight hard-pounding pistons, and even harder-pounding rods, plus 24 whirring and buzzing valves . . .

Horsepower-harnessing attempts with front-wheel drive, conventional rear-wheel drive, and even four-wheel drive fail: three decades of Novis in all three versions clobber Indy concrete, and frequently flame-out.

To Greg
Best wishes
Ed Pink

In 1940, just three model years after its introduction, old man Henry Ford killed the V-8-60; the little engine just wasn't selling. Yet to those owners of midget open-wheelers too financially pinched to afford a pedigree Offy, the V-8-60 was a delightful alternative. You needn't even visit a Ford dealership to acquire a "jiggler"; for as little as $25 you could drag a V-8-60 out of a boneyard. And then, with judicious primping and preening, porting and polishing, boring and stroking, the cast-iron little flathead took on the qualities of a giant. One hundred and twenty-five horsepower V-8-60s weren't unknown, and that equaled the output of the hottest Offy. This fantastic Dutch Hurd V-8-60, raced by Allen "Knothead" Heath, won a 500-mile marathon around Riverside International Raceway. *Joe Scalzo collection*

"Hoodoo wagons?" Perhaps they truly are. Belting out its supercharged lyrics, an unlucky Novi seems alive with macabre spirits rising up and swirling around it. Each year of its existence, the Novi renewed promises unfulfilled the year before, stringing the faithful along for a quarter century before they wrote off the sophisticated brawler as unmanageable. Examples:

1963: Three fast-pedaling warriors put a trio of Novis in the big Memorial Day show. One leads the opening lap but is disqualified for oiling. The second grenades its engine. The third creams the concrete.

1959: A Novi is taking practice miles when, without warning, all dashboard lights flash and the truncheon crankshaft rips free of its moorings. There is a cataclysmic unloading. Spraying debris and flaming engine oil, the beast pirouettes off two different walls, and its faithfully flailing crank blows out the bottom of the cylinder block, bludgeoning a deep furrow in the surface of the track several football fields long.

1956: The first time a Novi starts in the 500 since the death of its chauffeur, the L.A. antediluvian, Chet Miller. Down on the home straightaway it joins a trio

A double overhead camshaft STUDEBAKER? Only-in-L.A. maverick Willie Utzman, who dated clear back to Legion Ascot, came up with his huge innovation in the 1950s, aiming it toward the Indy 500. It was as incredible and promising as Barney Navarro's ill-fated, turbocharged, stock-block Rambler a decade later. Unfortunately, back at the Brickyard, Willie's brilliant four-cam Stude developed a ferocious appetite for starting shafts, which it kept breaking in two. But apparently nobody thought of a push start. Consequently, Willie's trick Stude was deprived the opportunity of turning the needed development laps.
Greg Sharp collection

of Meyer-Drake roadsters in the middle of a leaders' dogfight. With a standard Novi war whoop, it rips past all three. But 11 laps later, still leading, a right-rear shoe disintegrates and—again!—it's concrete city.

1950: The croaking of its creator Bud Winfield in a highway crack-up contributes to the kicking in of the superstition that the Novi is hexed.

1948: Its two assigned drivers are intransigent about getting their set of Novis up to speed, so the team cans both of them. And out in L.A. the past catches up to retired Hep Hepburn, who receives an invitation from the desperate team to get his butt back inside a Novi

wheelhouse. Hep first had had his mind blown by the original Novi back in 1941. Then, in 1946, he and the Novi together authored sensational speed records in time trials. So now in 1948, Hep dutifully arrives back at the Brickyard still carrying the heavy charisma of being the one man unspooked by the Novi. But Novi charisma is lethal: Hep is up all night making adjustments, and the following morning the familiar supercharged aria rings out anew as he zaps to peak revs—and the killer speeds straight into the wall. Hep dies, and it will be his replacement Novi drivers, and their replacements, who will suffer after him.

The dry lakes and Bonneville Salt Flats were L.A. hot rodder territory. Although off the beaten path, they had a mystique that was theirs alone. Weird and wonderful things happened there, particularly with FoMoCo flatheads. Just float the valves and go for it! *Greg Sharp collection*

How much good life and raw energy Bud Winfield's deadly invention has plowed under. All to no avail. And maybe all because of that Novi siren scream.

AHRAHARAHAHRAH!

"LISTEN TO THAT ENGINE. THAT'S A TRACO."

General Motors' breakthrough small-block Chevy of 1955, created by chief engineer Eddie Cole, was among the first mass-produced motors capable of extracting one horsepower for every cubic inch of displacement. Inside the engine houses of Los Angeles was where it became really fast. And where it probably jump-started more L.A. pistonhead careers than anything else.

Addicting was the ear-burning bellowing of Cole's bad stovebolt, a clamor just as angry as the temper of the impossible Jim Travers, properly called "Crabby," who with Frank Coon was co-sovereign of Traco—the mightiest engine house of postwar L.A.

A Traco V-8 was fully tricked-out and ready for market when it was bellowing away on the Traco dynamometer in Culver City and could be heard clear to Loyola Marymount University, 3 miles distant. Responding to that runaway bellow, his highness, A. J. Foyt, took delivery of a Traco for his personal sprint car, then, in 1963, enjoyed one of his best tilts ever. Encomiums from Tex being rare, Crabby and Frank framed and mounted and relished A. J.'s autographed photo of his rampaging sprinter: "To Frank and Jim. This baby's a runner!"

Having exclusive access to a world-class client like A. J. opened up Traco to the envy of all L.A.'s opponent mill houses. But jealousy was nothing new to Crabby and Frank. Pre-Traco, they'd hit the jackpot as the coddled racing employees of Howard Keck, wealthy oil baron and Bel Air sugar daddy supreme. What set Mr. Keck apart from other racing sugar daddies with a stable of fast race cars was that he was totally hands-off: in effect, Howard was telling Crabby and Frank, "I'll buy you guys anything you want. I'll pay every bill. I'll never complain. Just make my iron win."

Such noninterference, combined with all Howard's green, made Crabby and Frank the despised "Rich Kids" of L.A. wrenches, freeing them to concentrate on the one meet that mattered to Howard, and everything else then: Indy. Twice in succession they and their personal discovery, Billy "Vookie" Vukovich, won it for Howard.

They quit being the Rich Kids the day Howard's oil-well secretary telephoned to tell them they were fired. Howard, it seemed, was resigning from cars to pursue other appetites, including thoroughbred racing—one of his new wife's temperamental ponies subsequently won the Kentucky Derby. But after that, everything plunged. Howard's selling Superior Oil for $5 billion was followed by a high-profile divorce so acrimonious it was juicy even by Bel Air standards. Then in his last late years, Howard became a philanthropist, doing much good work, and sought further posterity by having his name planted on whichever building, boulevard, library, or museum would have it. Ultimately, he had to be satisfied with an observatory and telescope on the side of a young volcano out in the old Sandwich Islands.

As for the suddenly out-of-work Crabby and Frank, new racing careers were available if they acted fast. Peter DePaolo Engineering, FoMoCo's shadow outfit in the Deep South, harbored them until it folded. Back in L.A. they put on the blue-and-white livery of high-end Reventlow Automotive until the Scarab project, too, collapsed.

Fortunately for them, Eddie Cole's missile of a V-8 was just beginning to take off. Traco rose with it. From the late 1950s and well into the 1970s, Tracos routinely won every sports-car and single-seater road race worth mentioning. They won the Can Am, the Trans-Am, the Formula 5000 series. They won the 24 Hours of Daytona, Speed Weeks in the Bahamas, the *Los Angeles Times* Grand Prix of Riverside. Not to mention every dirt track from Williams Grove to Ascot Park, where A. J. fielded that runnin' sprinter.

It was, however, a lucky thing that Howie Keck had been such a hands-off sugar daddy and was seldom around the house, because he'd never have gotten along with Crabby. Hardly anybody ever did, unless it was Frank, and he had the sympathy of all. A riff that broke out between Crabby and his former partner Stu Hilborn, the innovator of fuel-injection, turned so horrible it lasted for 25 years, until romantic Kirby Avant reunited them. And Smokey Yunick, himself no shrinking violet, once visited from Daytona Beach to assist Traco in the preening of a Trans-Am Camaro. After Smokey finished the safety wiring, Crabby went around cutting with clippers everything Smokey had wired, lecturing Smokey that he'd done the job backwards.

I'd have paid money to have witnessed the explosion that followed. No complaints, though. I got to experience my very own meltdown with Crabby.

One day in 1963 I was paying my first trip to Traco—my last trip to Traco—and, before gaining entrance, was subjected to Crabby's fierce grilling. Cursing and moaning and bitterly blaspheming, he suffered tortures demanding to know what I was doing there. What the hell did I want to know? Why was I putting him through such unbearable misery?

My explanation that my readers were curious about Traco and wanted to learn more about it must have deepened his suspicions. Now Crabby was certain that the true purpose of my visit was to pilfer and spread all his and Frank's deepest confidences!

Once inside the building, my rubbernecking tour terminated immediately. Because I'd been led to believe that Traco was merely another engine shop and not an aseptic hospital, or a holy temple, I made the mistake of butting a Lucky Strike on the cement floor. Crabby freaked.

"You did *that*?" he demanded, pointing at the butt, eyes narrowed to slits.

"Sorry," I said, "I . . ." That was as far as I got. Next thing I knew I was being forcibly ejected from the premises.

They say that Crabby has gone off to spend his late seasons far from humanity, off in remote northern Utah, equipment maintenance man for displaced beasts. Yet another of L.A.'s myriad animal lovers.

"LIKE THE ATOMIC BOMB GOING OFF"

Los Angeles invented organized drag racing in the 1940s and 1950s, and then the sport appeared to get lucky in the 1950s when Detroit let loose a parade of its biggest ballbusters ever, 350-plus-cubic-inch Pontiacs, Lincolns, DeSotos, and especially hemispherical combustion head Chryslers—raw chunks of huge V-8 muscle. Quarter-mile supermen going big-game hunting in the Top Fuel

dragster class gyrated to those series 300 Chryslers. They were built the strongest and had the best bore-and-stroke ratio and, of course, those slippery hemi-heads.

After first opening up the Mopar package to a volatile 450 cubes, L.A.'s best digger boys, like Ed Pink and Keith Black, loaded up monstrous 671 superchargers lifted off GMC 18-wheelers, doped everything up, and spectacularly exploded horsepower to a monstrous 2,200. Whereupon everybody stepped back and, somewhat apprehensively, waited for speeds to rocket and elapsed times to tumble.

Which promptly happened, so that 200-mile-per-hour velocities suddenly were routine, as were 6-second ETs. Such numbers may now sound puny, but they were more than sufficient to get the chauffeur of a sling-shot digger bumped off in the 1960s.

Lefty Mudersbach perished at Irwindale when either a tire blew or a braking parachute malfunctioned. And Mike Sirokin bought it at Lions when his two-speed clutch blew apart and cartwheeled him. Platoons of other heavy dudes caught it, too, but why rub it in? In point of fact, the blown Chrysler Hemi was vicious. Under the violent pressure of its 2,200 horses, it was prone to flinging its wailing steel intestines straight back into the driver compartment.

Throbbing connecting rods threatening to blast grenade holes through the cylinder block . . . the Jimmy blower preparing to backfire and burst free of the block . . . crankshaft journals flexing . . . pistons making ready to disintegrate . . . savage arguments threatening to break out between pumping rods and thrashing valves . . . the overworked electronic ignition going bananas searching for the cylinder it didn't like so it could burn it down . . . searing exhaust gases blending with flickering yellow alcohol fumes. Inside a supercharged Hemi was a hideously dangerous place, heaving with mayhem and destruction. Especially when you goosed, gagged, and radically stressed out everything with that 95 percent load of nitromethane.

For the unlucky digger driver, there was very little warning. One instant he was hauling the mail at 200 miles per hour. Then suddenly there came the roar of pistons shattering, cylinders shifting, and then the whole slingshot shuddered as a massive internal explosion ripped through the engine and the driver was savaged by a hellish rain of molten metallic fragments, scalding coolant, and quarts of boiling oil.

I never knew many digger men, compared to sports car and circle-trackers, but one I did know, Johnny

Mulligan, had already lived through such a nightmare, skidding backward through the timing traps, burning, at 200 miles per hour. Then there was an anxious wait while track firemen, a full quarter mile away, took a long time coming to his rescue.

Johnny was a man of few words, but still remembered the incident: "The mill made a noise deep down in its gut like I never heard before," he told me. "Like an atomic bomb going off. A 15-pound chunk of engine hit my helmet and split it in three pieces. Knocked me koo-koo. Afterward I said, 'OK, this is it. Build me a rear-engine before this thing kills me.' But that was a year ago. Nothing bad has happened since then. And we've won the Winternationals."

It was summer of 1969. Johnny was absolutely out of this world at tire-hazing when the Christmas tree went green—the best in the business at opening up a one-length advantage out of the hole. His 6.43 ET allegedly was fast time of the decade. He and his big Top-Fueler had, indeed, just conquered the Winternationals at the Los Angles County Fairgrounds. Now he was preparing to depart for another big fueler meet, the Summernationals at Indianapolis.

Johnny was short, chubby, 25 years old with a big round face and double chin, and he smoked small cigars. I liked him. At his small garage in Huntington Beach, called "the Cave," I asked him if I could sit in the digger. Tight fit. My legs straddled the differential, my feet bumped against the throttle. A butterfly-shaped "wheel" worked the steering. A small handle fired the parachute. There were no dashboard instruments of any kind. Leaning back in the bucket seat and looking straight ahead, all I could see was that formidable hunk of Hemi with its gargantuan belt-driven Jimmy windmill.

"How do you see out of this thing?"

"You don't," Johnny replied. "You sort of look down the side of the car and guide yourself by the white line or the guardrails at the side of the strip."

Two years later, drag racing embraced rear-engine diggers at last, saving lots of lives . . . but not Johnny's. He dressed in flame-proof socks and boots and a full fire suit, but they weren't enough to save him when he experienced a second atomic bomb explosion during the Summernationals.

"JAN OPPERMAN CUT HIS HAIR."

Shaver Specialties is one Los Angeles shop emitting much of the old twentieth-century roar. After a visit there during a cold morning in 2006, I walked past the old Vel's Parnelli Jones facility and museum next door, then crossed the street to Cosworth Engineering, once the corporation of Brits, to check out the jolly dude's building, servicing, leasing, and assembling Cosworths for one of the big ground-sucker series that runs internationally. Had anybody there ever heard of Jan "Opp" Opperman? Nobody had. Disgraceful.

No matter. The curious tale of Opp and how he added to the L.A. legend by indirectly putting Cosworth in the game remains potent, even if unlikely.

In May 1974, following season after season of blissful existence among wild bikers, stoned hippies, werewolf spiritualists, obsessed holy rollers, and other fascinating freaks and long-hair nonconformists, Jan Opperman at last abandoned his remote Nebraska farm to go direct his fervid attentions toward the biggest automotive contest of all, Indy. There really was no choice. It was now or never. At 34 years, he was certain that advancing age was eroding his reflexes and skills. And the 80 yearly starts in sprinters—more than anybody else—were one fine day sure to waste him.

His arrival rattled Gasoline Alley, and no wonder.

There Opp was, holding hands with his five-year-old daughter Krystal, and all dolled up in torn and faded jeans, moccasins with holes in them, a motley orange T-shirt from a celebrated but bankrupt speed shop, and an outrageously old cowboy hat. Plus, he was sporting the standard Opp regalia: the Christian message buttons "Jesus is LORD" and the frightening "Your Choice: Jesus or the Lake of Fire" . . . the necklace with the bear tooth gifted him by his deceased younger brother, a racing casualty . . . the zodiac bracelet . . .

And following his crashing of Gasoline Alley's gates, he proceeded to invade the garage and suites of the wealthiest, most imposing team on the premises—the first to use an 18-wheeler transport, Vel's Parnelli Jones, the over-talented squad of 500-mile champions. Delivering his pitch, Opp practically dared VPJ to throw hippie-rebel and daughter out the door.

On the condition that he cut his hair, VPJ handed him the keys to one of its most savage wagons, a turbocharged Drake-powered Parnelli with the kick of a mule. With zip for Brickyard smarts, Opp had to work hard. He barely time-trialed at all, next to last.

He was facing Indy's usual 32 formidable boy scouts, 21 of whom he overtook in 215 miles and, in the process, he also put all his fellow rookies a lap behind. Then a rear Firestone punctured, spinning him out of the show. His postmortem? Indy was an anticlimax. Just another one of his ecstatic adventures. No more, no less.

He unfortunately headed out for additional sprint-car campaigns of 80-starts-per-season—and he was proven right, ultimately the experience destroyed

THE WINFIELD SPECIAL

Right up to his passing in 2005, Winfield Special restorer Kenny Howard continued making fascinating discoveries about his little trailer queen, including the fact that Rex Mays got away with twisting the vibrating overhead to 7,000 rpm; that its real speed secret wasn't so much the beautifully polished cylinder heads but its custom-tuned exhaust; that Eddie Winfield made a mistake with its first camshaft, which sprayed raw Gilmore gasoline everywhere; that Eddie, who had himself raced at Legion in the 1920s, did the original testing not on a racetrack but out in the dry gulch vineyards near his home; that the violently high-strung little mill refused to idle at anything below 2,000 revs; that smooth Rex could get two or three Wednesday Legion features out of a crankshaft, but the ragged Kelly Petillo required new parts every time; and that for a long time the Winfield's ignition system wasn't quite

Neil Nissing

right—it was dropping revs because of a high-speed miss. While the Winfield was in the middle of an East Coast barnstorm, the head mechanic of the bus company of New York City identified the source of the glitch as a too-small condenser.

him—and his entire Indy caper might well have been forgotten except for one incident.

One of VPJ's stable of 500-mile champions had followed Opp around the Speedway for enough miles to afterward raise unholy Hades about that squirrelly hippie's being a faster Drake than his own!

Opp's weapon had been the work of one Larry Slutter, then unknown. Larry was a Pennsylvanian who'd wandered west to L.A. in the 1960s to apprentice with six-toed Louie, when Meyer was assembling all of FoMoCo's four-cammers. Larry had no special standing at VPJ—just a third-string pistonhead.

But VPJ—then in the midst of a wasting argument with Drake Engineering over six-figure price tags coupled with zero reliability—was about to take the extreme step of inventing its very own Indy warhead. Thanks to the fallout about Opp, Larry got called up to lead the project.

No existing domestic powerplants had the proper goodies, so Larry was given his choice of one of two hammers of Formula 1: the Alfa Romeo pancake or the DFV Cosworth, owner of half-a-dozen world championships, the first engine to be an integral part of the race car chassis, but seven long seasons old. Neither one was designed to race flat-out for 500 nonstop miles or accommodate the indispensable dose of brutal turbocharging. Larry went with the Cosworth.

Inside the VPJ compound, Larry got to work repeating the successful formula of old genius Eddie Winfield and the Winfield Special: exercising the privilege of utilizing a hunk of equipment for an incorrect racing purpose.

Compared to a turbo Drake's four simplistic cylinders, the Cosworth's eight made for an intimidating handful, awash with 1,825 separate components. Courtesy of VPJ's formidable war chest, Larry was free to dispense the big

State-of-the-art dynamometer testing at Toyota Racing Development in Orange County's Costa Mesa. *Joe Scalzo collection*

bucks creating stouter pistons, revived camshafts, mightier con rods, longer bore, and shorter stroke.

The Cosworth era struck in 1976. A VPJ entry won a wild 500-miler not at Indy but Pocono. Success breeds imitation and, over time, Cosworth turbos—not always belonging to VPJ or serviced by Larry—captured eight Indys in a row.

Just like Bud Winfield, Larry never got his name on the engine, but he did for a time become a chief of Cosworth Engineering, the redcoat-scented outfit across the street from Shaver Specialties, which by the 1980s was marketing Cosworth's own DFS (later the XB).

Those racing 1980s were almost as money-wild as the 1920s: the looting of Indy by Brits generally was at hand; Indy car teams were playing merry hell keeping up with the dollar-to-pound ratio; and throughout the dizzy decade, Cosworth purchases were going at the rate of 70 a season.

Perhaps, in retrospect, Cosworth was no Miller/Offenhauser/Meyer-Drake/Drake. But still, for its revs to zap along at a hard 10,000-plus for 500 miles, and for its 47 inches of turbo boost to successfully overcome the terrible handicap of a modern Indy chariot's pavement-sucking ground-effects underwear, the Cossie surely had to be some sort of special piece. With 155 victories in 10 years, this tweaked Brit mill indeed proved it was.

And, basically, it was on account of the missing Opp—who would have hated all of it. Appalled is what he'd have been for indirectly helping Los Angeles gain still more glory via Larry's Cosworth, for Opp was certain that all of us out in L.A. existed in one vast sinkhole of evil. Nobody abominated Los Angeles more.

And not necessarily without sound reason, either, because whenever Opp showed his face at Ascot Park to race his sprinter, our local heroes bounced him off corner plankings and made his eyes cross. Prior to that, aboard his Harley hog, it was equally bad—the Friday-night flat trackers piled him up on the back straight.

"Get out, good people! Get out!" he implored his L.A. acquaintances. But we ignored him.

"Jan Opperman cut his hair" has come into some small cult usage as a phrase meaning nothing is scratched in stone, that everybody is free to switch beliefs.

CHAPTER THREE

DUNG BEETLES, JUNKYARD HOUNDS, POISONOUS VIPERS, BIG CUCUMBERS, AND JUMPIN' JUGHEADS

Forget it, Jake. It's Chinatown.

—spoken to Jack Nicholson in *Chinatown,*
the noir flick about the dangerous riddles of L.A.

Originally intended to flee L.A. and give a rough time to all Ferraris and Maseratis on the European continent, the Scarab instead dominated all North American racing from Riverside to Nassau. *Bob Tronolone*

He wrote up two weeks' worth of attack essays, he took them to the printer, and in October 1955, *Motoracing*, his Los Angeles tabloid (15 cents Cheap), rolled off the presses. He—Gus V. Vignolle, hellfire reporter—called it a racing newspaper, but *Motoracing* was really an assault weapon, forever primed and ready to go off.

Whoever invented the exclamation mark was thinking of *Motoracing*. Red may have been perfect for L.A.'s Ferraris and Maseratis, but it was also the color particular to *Motoracing* headlines. And everybody taking *Motoracing* fire soon learned what the "V" of Gus V. Vignolle meant: vitriol.

Things Gus loved: scribbling, tracking down and breaking sensational news exposés, getting grogged out of his head, and reading the hairy-chested garbage of Ernie Hemingway.

Opposite: In all its lovliness—the original Ol' Yeller.
Bob Tronolone

Things Gus abhorred: authority figures, sacred cows, the very rich with their privileged and coddled lifestyles, and, especially, the common hoi polloi—all the clueless peasantry of L.A. in whose honor Gus directed the all-purpose smear name "Babbitts."

Effeminate, limp prose also lit the Vignolle fuse, as when Lance Reventlow and Max Balchowsky, two classically opposite personalities of the 1950s and 1960s, were profiled in a rival L.A. rag. "Together," the rag rhapsodized, "they would make a *lovely* team." *Motoracing* gagged. "Now isn't that sweet, ducky?" Gus riposted.

Gus was dead wrong. Lance—Mr. Scarab—and Max—Mr. Ol' Yeller—would truly have made quite a twinning.

Corporate or sugar daddy capital is what funds racing enterprises in Los Angeles. So Lance, heir to a great department-store fortune, used his seemingly limitless mazuma to maintain vaunted Reventlow Automotive, whose Scarab sports cars and Formula 1s were constructed from only the most costly, high-end materials and components; and were designed, quality-maintained, and raced by the brightest bunch of minds and talents all together

Semi-undressed, the Scarab still bristles with glamour and pedigree. *Bob Tronolone*

under one roof since the fat days of Father Miller's salon. Max, on the other hand, gathered up a potpourri of blasted parts and miscellaneous ugliness to create his spectacular chain of Ol' Yellers, allegedly the most repulsive backyard wrecks ever to bamboozle L.A. racing.

Lance's golden childhood was mostly spent in the utterly worthless company of all the cads, gigolos, rogues, bounders, Lotharios, and free-loading studs forever swarming around Lance's mom, the Woolworth millionairess, Barbara Hutton. One celebrated member of this floating and ever-changing male harem of international ding-dongs was a Dominican rake, who, so it is claimed, ignited the early Reventlow's passion for fast wheels and racing. Barely 17, Lance was already in possession of his first Merc SL gullwing. Aged 24, he had Reventlow Automotive up and running.

As has been widely and even endlessly chronicled, Reventlow Automotive planned on spreading the L.A. message all across Europe by having its Scarabs win the world championship of sports car racing, as well as ambush all the foreign heaps on their home turf.

If you were in L.A.'s motorhead hall of fame, Lance and Reventlow Automotive, out on Venice Boulevard by the beach, wanted you. The whole congregation was there. Emile Diedt, ex-Miller, beat tin and shaped slinky Scarab coachwork. Drag racer Tony Nancy worked the upholstery. Von Dutch pinstriped. Crabby Travers and Frank Coon, Traco, subjected the Scarab stovebolts to highly advanced PhDs spreading the battle cry of Eddie Cole's V-8. The gifted duo of Troutman-Barnes tooled up De Dion rear-ends, performed delicate suspension dialing-in, and set camber and caster. Chuck "Charlie" Daigh, ex–dry laker and Mexican Road Race tough, was Scarab first-string shoe and Lance himself—when he wasn't scaring himself—the second.

Nineteen fifty-eight, that first and best RA campaign, swung hard.

In roughly eight months, Charlie and Lance and their Scarab legions had hit the biggest races on both coasts twice, occasionally dropped in for a match in the Midwest, and even had made a winter detour to sunburst Nassau, where the baffled Babbitts of the

BLUES FOR CRAZY JOEL

Lance Reventlow's racing playboy predecessor was fellow L.A. inhabitant, and aviation victim, Joel Wolfe Thorne. There are good reasons why a lot of romantic playboys like Lance and Joel don't live very long. They try to squeeze 100 hours into every day: they over-live, over-drink, and become over-traveled, over-stimulated, over-sexed, and over-destructive. Joel Thorne, with a fat rail and banking inheritance, hit the ground running. He sped a motorcycle through the lobby and up the stairs of the Waldorf-Astoria. He challenged the Rocky Mountains towing a race car with no trailer brakes. Back in L.A., he cracked up a motorcycle and broke his head at Hollywood and La Brea. He turned barfly and got his jaw broken by a drunken doll face and a burly nightclub bouncer on the Sunsent Strip. And finally, during an unlicensed joy ride in an un-inspected old airship on a misty L.A. night in 1955, he suffered the concluding

Thorne at the wheel. *IMS Photo*

catastrophy of his supercharged existence when he crashed headlong into a Burbank bungalow apartment, taking with him three innocents on the ground.

Bahamas stood 10 deep digging Charlie and Lance and the Scarabs putting the moves to Blind Man's Curve during Speed Weeks. Result? Something like 8 Scarab triumphs in 13 attempts, and all import iron dashing for cover.

Now RA's all-star personnel readied for the conquest of Europe. Only everything got sabotaged.

After looking over and listening to the Scarabs and their 380 horses, the Europeans panicked and said, "No, thanks." Then the international sanctioning body pulled a fast one by running up a change in the global engine formula. RA was stopped cold. Reeling from this international reaming (but only briefly), Lance, unquenchable, responded by selling off the sports cars and turning out a line of Scarab single-seaters for a 1960 go at Formula 1. An allegedly tip-top aviation engineer came aboard as chassis designer; fragile Leo, on temporary leave from Meyer-Drake, contributed a witty engine of desmodromic valve design.

Everything crashed. It was one of the few times L.A. mojo failed. First, the Scarabs of Charlie and Lance became continental laughingstocks with their dead-as-a-dodo front engines. Then Leo clashed with Crabby and Frank about cam timing, and the desmo was a disaster. Charlie scuffed up some ribs crashing at Silverstone, and Lance's own passion cooled upon checking in at Spa-Francorchamps and discovering that deathtrap Masta and des Carriers corners were expected to be negotiated flat out.

As Reventlow Automotive limped home to L.A., ass well kicked, its sheepish all-stars discovered that in their absence Max and Ina Balchowsky and their odious Ol' Yellers had been having their usual high old time.

"Ol' Yeller" was the canine handle that Max and his inseparable spouse Ina looted from a popular 1950s movie about a terrific yellow cur. First they applied it to their own bitch retriever, later to all of their doggy yellow boneyard bombs. Which reminds me of my own bow-wow story.

Master alchemist Max Balchowsky, inventor of Ol' Yeller, hit Los Angeles mainly to escape the Pennsylvania Appalachians where a lot of his ancestors were in the coal business—burrowing into mines deep underground to dig for it. Once, as a young man, Max tried hauling illegal hooch. But he did it only once. He had no appetite for crime, and besides, he almost got caught. It did teach him about rocket driving, though. *Bob Tronolone*

During the 1980s (hardly a great decade) and years after Gus folded *Motoracing* and Lance had gone down in a private plane deep in the Aspen Rockies—and long after Ina and the Balchowsky family yellow pooch also had exited and the legend of Ol' Yeller was no longer potent—and Max himself was out of racing and busy rigging movie chase cars for Steve McQueen, I, too, was missing from the L.A. bubble.

Journalistic responsibilities had dispatched me to the rebel backwoods, chasing and writing up the wedged-wing sprint car tramps, and their $44,000 Shavers, from the World of Outlaws. It wasn't a bad job. Every August was the Knoxville Nationals, a mammoth melee conducted in the center of Iowa on a big black dirt track in the dead of night. And this one summer, for whatever reason, Knoxville was going buggy

Short-lived Scarab meister Lance Reventlow was a halfway decent shoe—he once won a Memorial Day feature at Santa Barbara—but delivered greater value as celebrity team owner. Peacocking around the racing pits with sexy movie starlets, surrounded by the beautiful people and what looked like cruncher bodyguards, he was even more dazzling than his Scarabs. And his privileged bearing and dough empowered him to pitch temper tantrums and even haul off and kick one of the Scarabs when things went against him. *Bob Tronolone*

with mutts. Down in the jam-packed infield pits, mixing nicely with the usual hundred-odd glittering wedged-winged eyesores and all Knoxville's spic-and-span sugar daddies, drivers, and mechanics, were dozens of pedigree poodles, adorable Chow Chows, huggable Shih Tzus, and soft and sweet Samoyeds . . .

It might have been show time at Madison Square Garden, for God's sake. But not quite. Acting as counterpoint to all the shiny chromed machines and beautiful beasts was a wonderful gang of hostile and spectacularly dirty-looking specimens out of Kansas City—unshaven and dirty-looking males, dirty females, and one truly terrible, dirty wreck of a sprinter. The cynosure of all eyes, though, was their dirty pet pooch, a mixed-breed brute so large and violently dangerous, it had to be chained. Silently it lurked in the shadows, on guard should anything get too close, and at that point—all fierce snarls, bared gums, and pointed teeth of hatefulness—it would charge without warning or quarter.

Superb animal, and what a refreshing relief from all that other nauseating cuddliness! And so evocative of Ol' Yeller—and how it scandalized L.A. sporty car racing.

Hilarious scene: on all those incredibly blue-skied Memorial Day or Labor Day racing weekends of the late 1950s, everybody is up in Santa Barbara and the Goleta airfield, 90 miles north of L.A., digging the majestic arrival of all the well-heeled teams for the season's two biggest

"Everybody told me Buicks were no good!" complained Max Balchowsky. So, being Max, he became enamored of them. First he installed a straight-eight in a '32 Ford highboy, but that was a hot rod, not a sports car. So he tried a Buick-powered Doretti, but the Doretti wasn't American and was too pretty. In 1955, serendipity mixed with disaster kicked in. He came into the possession of the blasted remains of a backyard bomb with six-cylinder Plymouth go that had just crashed upside-down on its rollbar-free back at Torrey Pines, extinguishing "Pete" Pritchard, fastest femme pilot of the period. Performing a fast rebuild, Max ditched the Plymouth flathead for a Buick nailhead, then sprayed everything blazing yellow. Ol' Yeller was born. *Bob Tronolone*

BRAINS BLOWN OUT

First-string Reventlow Automotive Scarab pilot was Chuck "Charlie" Daigh. Hairy career! Charlie and his brother Harold first did the postwar hot rod number at El Mirage: 200-mile-per-hour runs in their flathead FoMoCo belly tanker weren't uncommon. Then Charlie's ability with engines caught the attention of Clay Smith and Bill Stroppe, who needed bodies to assist in the construction of their clandestine squad of leviathan Lincoln luxo-sleds for the Carrera Panamericana. After three years of serving as navigator, ballast, and problem solver to the Smith-Stroppe squad of Indy 500 gringos, Charlie decided he could drive just as fast as they could and began his own racing career. L.A. sports car racing was just being born. Much like Max Balchowsky, Charlie wasn't drawn to Ferraris or Maseratis but to backyard bombs, of which Los Angeles had a glut. Among Charlie's first was a dreadnought Kurtis-Kraft whose Chrylser powerplant unleashed a rolling ball of flame through its four-barrel, causing Charlie to duck with every up- or downshift. He changed his orientation and got into the Troutman-Barnes Special, a famous rig. This was followed by his all-winning Scarab years, plus an unsuccessful shot at Formula One. He concluded his career in the mid-1960s, his card full. The task of being a racing mechanic was a far higher

Joe Scalzo collection

calling than being a race driver, he concluded. "A race driver," he explained cryptically, "is just a mechanic with his brains blown out."

sports car weekends: purebread Ferraris, Masers, and even Scarabs up the yin-yang, all of them pampered and rolling in aboard custom trailers.

But then beautifully blasting all across tony Santa Barbara comes a familiar deep-down groaning rumble of an unmuffled behemoth Buick; and suddenly bursting into sight before anybody can yell "It's Max!" comes gloriously shabby Ol' Yeller, with Max, Ina, and even the goddamn dog, all bundled together inside as usual, having commuted up from L.A. The worst mongrel mutant among all the Santa Barbara thoroughbreds, Ol' Yeller is

also the sole sled licensed for the highway and packing Idaho (!) street plates (14 898 Famous Potatoes).

Following the dramatic arrival, nothing is left but for Ol' Yeller to line up for the main event, and for Max—dressed down not in a hero-driver's suit of lights but common garage-man coveralls—to take his place in the raunchy wheelhouse. With offbeat race cars come offbeat senses of humor. If Max is feeling mischievous, he'll next fake a fast case of the epileptic shakes, or the jumpin' d.t.s, for the benefit of all the confused and horrified nabobs and wallahs lined up in Ol' Yeller's wake.

More Lance. Like Joel Thorne's, his own demise in a private aircraft was a great loss to the ranks of exotica. *Bob Tronolone*

Moment of fun over, the green flag drops, mongrel Ol' Yeller disappears, and Max—his Near Eastern kisser a mask of flat indifference—blows off all the cosseted and high-strung import crap by the numbers.

It is hard saying who is having the most fun, his bright yellow (a 1955 Chev truck shade) Ol' Yellers, or Max himself, whose odd taste for the nailhead Buick has made him the common man's hero and a hate object of racing snobs.

Babbitt knowledge held that each Ol' Yeller was a foul brew of scrap, everything shakily held together by worn-out components that Max, on a junkyard scavenger hunt, had filched off old Pontiacs, Studebakers, and, naturally, Buicks. The square and sleazy yellow bodywork was cobbled out of old Pepsi-Cola boards.

Many replica Ol' Yellers make the rounds at twenty-first-century car shows. Pity there are no replicas of Max and Ina. *Neil Nissing*

Carroll Shelby, Ol' Shel, the one and only. *Bob Tronolone*

And what was this Max Balchowsky? He was a barmy Balkan and penny-pinching miser who was too tight-fisted to buy a trailer for his Ol' Yellers and who lubricated their worn-out nailhead innards with used motor oil and who foraged in garbage cans for discarded spark plugs. And who took Ol' Yellers into battle on cheesy recapped white sidewall rubber.

No one today remembers who started all this. It could have been the voluble photographer Lester "Ye Old Road Tester" Nehamkin, who loved Max, Ina, their hound, and spreading the legend of Ol' Yeller to the very end.

And that end came out on the Pomona fairgrounds in 1961 when one of the yellow juggernauts at last turned rogue and charged the crowd. A spectator died. And then a giant lawsuit (later dismissed) was brought against Max and everybody else involved for the crime of "permitting a defective vehicle to race." It was proof positive that shysters, too, had bought into the spurious legend of Ol' Yeller.

Certainly there was nothing whatsoever junkyard about the roaring heart of every Ol' Yeller. The Balchowsky nailhead was a tremendous piece of goods—all radically bored and stroked with half a dozen Strombergs and also benefiting from genius Winfield camshafts that Eddie Winfield gave to Max and nobody else. Perhaps

A Cobra's big-horsepower and full-race FoMoCo mill overwhelmed its wonky AC Bristol suspension, making for a dysfunctional, hang-out-the-ass-end steering technique. Hard on drivers, but great viewing for spectators. *Bob Tronolone*

One of the rare Cobra coupes of young L.A. stylist Peter Brock—now worth millions, if you can find one for sale.
Joe Scalzo collection

Ol' Yeller reminded Eddie of his own Winfield Special, blue-collar terror of Legion Ascot? Whatever the reason, Eddie came out of semi-retirement to work with Max.

Every Ol' Yeller was licensed for the boulevards because Max had no dynamometer except Angeles Crest Highway, 10,000 feet above the sea, where he knew by memory every kink and hairpin, and many a midnight sent Ol' Yeller hurtling across the San Gabriel Mountains.

Frequently he removed himself from the Ol' Yeller saddle and, as an act of charity, came to the assistance of such temporary out-of-work winners as Dan Gurney, Ronnie Bucknum, Carroll "Ol' Shel" Shelby, and Bobby Bondurant. Max's driving instructions were concise: always have Ol' Yeller well and truly pointed before you dropped the hammer and the throttle cracked wide open; additionally, remember to hold onto your ass (figuratively) with both paws, because otherwise all that nailhead ordnance would rip you a new one. Almost all of these guys won matches with various Ol' Yellers.

Additional differences between Mr. Scarab and Mr. Ol' Yeller: Lance had a short-lived marriage with a movie starlet whom he later had a damnable time evicting from the family manse. But the Balchowskys, Max and Ina, together lived one of the great automotive adventures, including having Max's Studebaker President straight-eight on the highway to Nogales to start in the inaugural Mexican road race before breaking down in the Sonora desert instead. Ina was as good-looking as Ol' Yeller was bad. The claim that she, instead of Max, was the real brains behind Ol' Yeller was more apocrypha, but she could change, swap, and completely rebuild the axle center section off Ol' Yeller in under 30 minutes, as well as assemble it in the first place. She was also deft at keeping the books for Hollywood Motors, Max's demon hop-up parlor on Edgemont Boulevard. And faithfully she shielded him from questions whenever her husband was experiencing the mental hell of synchronizing Ol' Yeller's six-pack of Strombergs.

The professional sports car racing circus of 1963 was a great one for Davey MacDonald and King Cobra. The duo won both the prestigious 200-mile Monterey Grand Prix at Laguna Seca and the *Times* Grand Prix at Riverside Raceway. *Bob Tronolone*

Also, Max was such a maniac of an irresistible personality that ultimately he won over even the snobs. Yet Lance, for someone so young, had a natural gift for making enemies, many deadly.

One was fumbling desperado Cal Bailey who, under the pretext of purchasing Lance's gullwing Benz, was actually hatching a plan to kidnap Lance for ransom.

Another was Johnny von Neumann (not the Hungarian number cruncher), the L.A. Ferrari distributor. Eight opponent Ferraris were facing the Scarabs at Riverside International Raceway for the inaugural *Los Angeles Times* Grand Prix, a fantastic extravaganza won by Charlie Daigh. Lance, by comparison, didn't even make it to the second turn before suffering a sodomizing from Johnny's personal prancing stallion, after Johnny overcome by rage at the vista of the blue-and-white keister of that hated dung beetle leering just ahead; not only did Johnny manage to disable Lance, but himself as well.

And Lance even had Gus Vignolle and *Motoracing* coming at him on a rampage. Gus was a new kind of trouble that Lance didn't need.

Roughly 1,000 Cobras are said to have been built. After they pulverized L.A.'s hapless Corvettes and E-Jags, Shelby carried his amazing reptiles to Europe and watched them do ditto to works Ferraris. *Bob Tronolone*

Quiet Quin Epperly was another member of L.A's great quintet of big cucumber creators. Laying the Meyer-Drake over on its side was Quin's great fetish. *Greg Sharp*

The firestorm began when *Motoracing* got hold of, and Gus naturally published, the original drawings of the still-top-secret F1 Scarabs, and Lance counterattacked by siccing on *Motoracing* the white-shoe law firm of Mullin Richter Balthis & Hampton, which zapped Gus with a harsh letter talking lawsuit.

He was lying paralytically bombed when the missive arrived, but its contents were so venomous and threatening that reading it sobered up Gus and he became enraged.

After printing the letter—surrounded by red borders and typically exploding exclamation marks—Gus ordered Lance to prepare for hell because *Motoracing* was coming after him.

Unrelenting *Motoracing* abuse began storming down. First came the harpoons belittling Lance's abilities as a race driver. Then the deflating accounts concerned with Lance's frequent temper tantrums. Fierce epistlcs also deplored the corrosive effects of inherited wealth (the old Gus prejudice). And finally the savage

Whether rocketing around the Brickyard at full stride or sitting silent in a neighborhood of houses, the big cucumber Watson was an elegant thing to see. *Greg Sharp collection*

print lynchings of all of Lance's beautiful and preening sycophants, henchmen, and parasitic male and kowtowing female flunkies alike.

In the end, however, Lance and Reventlow Automotive got taken out not by Cal, Johnny, or even Gus and *Motoracing*, but by the IRS, the same implacable foe that had just finished jumping on and liquidating the vast scuderia of L.A.'s ultimate sugar daddy, Tony Parravano. IRS bandits permit the writing off of racing losses for only so long. Reventlow Automotive's time had run out.

Still, life remained exciting inside the old Scarab house on Venice Boulevard. The whole joint subsequently got leased to Carroll Shelby, chicken plucker and snake charmer, who had his own ambitious plans for taking L.A. race cars to Europe. Providing, of course, he could discover some friendly sugar daddy to underwrite them.

"A BASEBALL BAT'D BE QUICKER"

Three o'clock in morning probably isn't the best time to be barreling along at 100 miles per hour across "Blood Alley"—the deadly dark California 46—towing a priceless and irreplaceable Shelby King Cobra on an open rail

Above and below: Eddie "Kazoom" Kuzma, whose big cucumbers were distinctive, yet never won an Indy 500. *Greg Sharp collection*

Indianapolis was near its peak during the big cucumber seasons of 1952–1964 and Lujie Lesovsky's iron was prominent in the brawling. *Greg Sharp collection*

trailer lashed to the bumper of a dangerously overloaded station wagon. If there is a best time.

Yet I had no choice. It was the month of October 1963. I had to be at Laguna Seca Raceway on the Monterey Peninsula by dawn. Between the raceway and myself were 10 towns, two counties, five speed traps, and perhaps 200 miles. I had three hours. The speedo needle nudged toward 110.

Two years earlier, back at Santa Barbara on the Labor Day weekend, I had for the first time heard a four-pipe Honda RC6l screaming its head off in top gear. All my horizons shifted. Ol' Shel, somebody I really admired, was among the first people to learn that I was forever finished with trying to become the new Kenny Purdy and was instead setting out on a fresh career as Grand Prix motorbike road racer.

His response was not as enthusiastic as I'd wished.

"Scoop," he suggested, "a baseball bat'd be quicker."

Himself a master of blunt-force trauma, by the time Ol' Shel finally concluded his own race-driving career he was a medical basket case. A tumbling Healy from the

Mexican road race had pretzeled one of his arms. While attempting to leap-frog a Parravano Ferrari 4.9 over the tops of cars ahead of him, he'd bruised liver and spleen on the start at Palm Springs. Getting made whole again after stacking up a Maserati 4.5 at Riverside had required a fresh set of choppers and the services of a plastic surgeon to construct him another face. Le Mans and its 24 wasting hours ruined him and reduced him to such a state of physical exhaustion that forever afterward he was popping tabs of nitroglycerine—sometimes while racing—to cool his angina. Poor Ol' Shel.

Out in L.A., whenever my hero was staying busy wheeling and dealing and working that plastic surgery grin of his, he was the ultimate snake charmer. Oozing the east Texas charm, Shelby was both wildly beguiling and wildly underfunded.

So he bewitched Goodyear out of a rubber dealership for the 11 western states. He had L.A.'s most generous sugar daddies lining up to offer him killer Ferraris and Masers. And when Max Balchowsky next did the same thing with Ol' Yeller, Ol' Shel sweet-talked Max into

Above and below: Another illustrious Watson was the *Bill Forbes*, later to be the *Weinberger Homes*, here both undressed and dressed. *Bob Tronolone*

Big cucumbers out of L.A. won twelve out of thirteen 500s—a dozen in a row—and also cranked off the first and vaunted 150-mile-per-hour lap. This is George Salih's 1957–1958 winner, the *Belond*. *Bob Tronolone*

hauling Ol' Yeller back to a big professional Grand Prix in distant Wisconsin at Road America, the mastodon Buick's one and only start east of the Rockies.

What a mesmerizing spectacle that proved to be. Disbelieving Babbitt spectators had never imagined anything like it; mobs of them came spilling and overflowing onto Road America's grassy pits to trample each other, digging the never-to-be-seen-again L.A. tableau of Ol' Shel dressed up in his chicken-plucker overalls, Max in

his trademark coveralls, and Ol' Yeller. Came the Grand Prix, Ol' Shel popped yet another nitro pill, got moody with Ol' Yeller, and split. He was still leading when the crank sawed in two.

Done with race-driving, Ol' Shel had a new, seemingly impossible, goal: the invention of a high-performance sports car he could name after himself.

Suddenly everything jelled. Hank the Deuce and his Italian socialite girlfriend were in the process of

Gasoline Alley, Indianapolis Motor Speedway, the great L.A. home away from home. *Bob Tronolone*

floorboarding FoMoCo back into racing, so Ol' Shel got the corporation to come across with serious change and several 260-inch V8 Fairlane M 260 V-8 mills, as well as lease money for the old Reventlow Automotive digs, where the Fairlanes received the Shelby Cobra treatment, including aluminum flywheels and transmission housing, roller-tappet cams, exhaust headers of lightweight steel, four-throat Webers . . .

Next Ol' Shel flew to the United Kingdom, getting hold of lots of engineless bolides from AC Bristol. Each AC chassis was decades old, and had been designed for a Bristol's 100-plus horses instead of a Fairlane's 350. But the coachwork was great-looking, and so were all the groovy Cobra scoops, louvers, fins. So what was the big deal?

Those were good days. I was beginning to collect trophies with my Honda 305 Super Hawk. And after building some 30 to 50 Shelby Cobras, Ol' Shel had embarked on yet another charmed offensive and, against all odds, bilked the Sports Car Club of America into certifying the Shelby Cobra as standard production-line iron. In short order, it collapsed all the Corvettes.

At the same time, the bustling Shelby American conglomerate outgrew the old Scarab hut and shifted headquarters to a huge airport hanger outside L.A. International. For as long as the FoMoCo money lasted, Ol' Shel stayed busy hiring all the city's racing luminaries—he himself

Above and top right: Among big cucumber constructors pitched out of the Indy 500 by the ascendant rear engines was the blacksmith's son, Frank Kurtis. He took it the hardest. This was his take on all the redcoat race cars. *Greg Sharp collection*

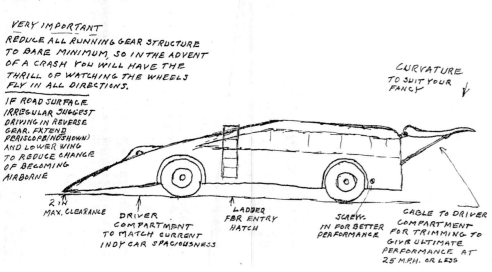

SUGGEST, TO CONTACT GOODYEAR TO SUPPLY 29 IN. WIDE SLICK TIRES AND MAG WHEELS, BY EXTENDING ABOUT 18 INCHES OUTSIDE THE BODY, YOU WOULD BE IN STYLE.

A FRANK KURTIS DESIGN

WITH APOLOGIES TO
COLIN CHAPMAN
DAN GURNEY
McCLAREN
A. J. FOYT
LOLA
ETC. ETC.

VERY IMPORTANT
REDUCE ALL RUNNING GEAR STRUCTURE TO BARE MINIMUM, SO IN THE ADVENT OF A CRASH YOU WILL HAVE THE THRILL OF WATCHING THE WHEELS FLY IN ALL DIRECTIONS.

IF ROAD SURFACE IRREGULAR SUGGEST DRIVING IN REVERSE GEAR. EXTEND PERISCOPE (NOT SHOWN) AND LOWER WING TO REDUCE CHANGE OF BECOMING AIRBORNE

CURVATURE TO SUIT YOUR FANCY

2 IN MAX. CLEARANCE

DRIVER COMPARTMENT TO MATCH CURRENT INDY CAR SPACIOUSNESS

LADDER FOR ENTRY HATCH

SCREW. IN FOR BETTER PERFORMANCE

CABLE TO DRIVER COMPARTMENT FOR TRIMMING TO GIVE ULTIMATE PERFORMANCE AT 25 M.P.H. OR LESS

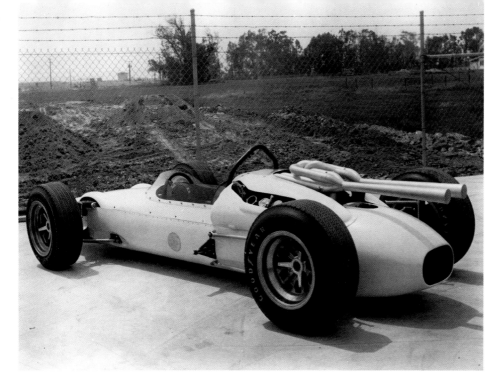

L.A.'s first rear-engine funny car, the ill-fated *Shrike*, came out of Halibrand Engineering. With its monocoque construction of multiple light alloy castings, it may have been ahead of its time. Its involvement with a wild-card Mickey Thompson creation in Indy's horrendous crash-and-burn of 1964 got it off to a bad start. But by season's end, the *Shrike* seemed to put the notoriety behind it by winning the Phoenix 200. Come the 1965 500, several *Shrikes* were entered but gears from another supplier failed and there were no more *Shrikes*. *Bob Falcon*

turning into a sugar daddy—from Formula 1 world champion Phil Hill to Indy 500 winner Parnelli Jones, and even the reluctant warlord of the sideways Corvette, Davey MacDonald.

Winners in Europe at Le Mans, Shelby Cobras revenged all the bitter losses of the Scarab F1s.

Shelby American went right on hiring. One day the dollface racer Kirby Avant showed up at the door needing to buy a new Goodyear for her bug-eye Sprite. Ol' Shel proposed not a new shoe but employment as secretary and model.

Better still was Ol' Shel's hiring of a pair of motorcycle people I knew, Jim Culleton and Bruce Burness. Jim I

well knew from his own racing days, when the cylinder walls of his Puch used to dry out, locking the pistons and tossing him over the handlebars. And Bruce I knew even better because he'd done something to the combustion chamber of my Super Hawk that had made it the fastest Honda in the entire American Federation of Motorcyclists.

Sugar Daddy Vel Miletich and Parnelli Jones contributed the Indy 500's "super" team of the 1970s. It fielded the fastest cars, best drivers, and best chief mechanics and crews, introduced to racing the original 18-wheel transport; and operated out of a then-huge 15,000-square-foot emporium in Torrance with $4 million worth of inventory, 35 workers, and a $65,000 monthly payroll. It even had its own Formula One team. Yet it still could produce the occasional lemon. This ungainly 1972 "dihedral car" got its wings clipped even before taking to the Brickyard. *IMS Photo*

Three of the jolly—not looking so jolly here—blokes who ran L.A. out of Indy: left to right, Colin Chapman, Graham Hill, and the unearthly Jimmy Clark. *Bob Tronolone*

Following six decades at the mercy of L.A.'s engine men like Father Miller, Fred Offenhauser, and the partners Louie Meyer and Dale Drake, Indianapolis was taken over by ground-suckers and suddenly the 500 was governed by the wind. This Pontiac-powered, ground-sucking Eagle from All-American Racers was one of the last L.A. cats to start the 500. *Bob Tronolone*

Promotion was rapid at Shelby American. When the team packed up for Sebring, Jim had become chief mechanic to Phil Hill, and Bruce to Dan Gurney.

I felt slighted that Ol' Shel had never offered me some sort of a job, too. I did, however, have the run of Shelby American. Which put me there at midnight when Jim and Bruce—following 24 sleepless hours spent assembling the second of only two rear-engine King Cobras—pronounced themselves too exhausted to drive and unexpectedly informed me that I must drive them, their toolboxes, and the King Cobra to Laguna Seca. And that Shelby would have their asses if they hadn't arrived when 7 a.m. sign-ins started.

The station wagon was a FoMoCo loaner with tall gearing and the police package, and even though overloaded it wanted to fly. Making the journey in seven hours seemed a snap.

But Jim and Bruce had barely piled into the back to go to sleep, and I hadn't even gotten out of the L.A. freeway system, when I made the discovery that the rail trailer holding the King Cobra was one of those 45-mile-per-hour, look out! rigs. And at 45 miles per hour, we'd never make it.

Then I remembered a conversation about towing I'd once had with Davey MacDonald, Shelby-America's most reluctant employee. In those sunny seasons before Shelby flew him to races first class or by corporate jet, and while he still was blissfully racing his Corvettes, Davey used to tow his infamous No. 00 on an unruly rail hooked to his personal Nomad wagon. Both of us were then living in the San Gabriel Valley, and I couldn't figure out how we'd leave for races at the same time, yet Davey regularly arrived an hour or so ahead of me, 45-mile-per-hour rail notwithstanding. He explained he always blasted straight past 45 miles per hour and well beyond; at such blinding tempos the rail came to its senses and behaved.

So, with some nervousness, I stood on the gas hard, and station wagon, trailer, and King Cobra got to trotting.

And I never lifted.

So there I was on route 46 at three in the morning, looking out for the spirit of Jimmy Dean while booming through Turnupseed crossroads at a fantastic 110 miles per hour, when there was movement in the backseat and a terrific yowl went up.

Jimmy Culleton had semi-awakened and was sitting up staring at the pegged speedo.

"God *damn it*, Scoop!" he complained. "How long have you been driving like this?"

"Not long," I replied. "Just a couple of hours. We're going to make it."

"Jesus," he moaned, tumbling back into exhaustion.

We made landfall at Laguna Seca with an hour to spare.

Two days later, it was Monday morning along coastal Highway One, and we were on the way home to L.A. via the Pacific route. I had been relieved of steering wheel responsibilities. Near Big Sur a serene ocean vista rose up in front of us, but on the trailer behind us, the King Cobra was a total wreck, looking like it had been dropped off a bridge. Its clueless driver, not L.A. talent at all, had run into everything but the pace car. And he would have done that had there been one. But the second King Cobra had won its second Grand Prix in two weeks. It was raced by Davey MacDonald—attacking the wheel with pipe-stem arms to make everything get

sideways while his head reared back and his jaw tilted upward like a flag. His career was streaking.

Repairing the mangled King Cobra meant more heavy triage for Jim and Bruce—a rough deal, but that's what mechanics do. I, on the other hand, was contemplating being back in L.A. for another Indian summer, always racing's high season. Some smorgasbord it was going to be. Ahead were two Saturday nights' worth of Indy 500 drivers racing sprint cars at Ascot Park; a dash for cash put on by the AFM at Willow Springs; a full-blown national sanctioned by the Sports Car Club of America, also at Willow; Ascot's Thanksgiving Grand Prix for midgets and their 110 Offys at Ascot; plus the opportunity to watch Davey get all sideways again, this time in a taxicab, at Riverside Raceway's Golden State 400.

What a life!

R.I.P., BIG CUCUMBERS

During a prerace ceremony honoring the Meyer-Drake big cucumber roadsters at 1992's bitterly cold Indy 500, the gray morning was so frigid, and the old Meyer-Drakes

Sales of this L.A.-based Corvette-powered "Cheetah" fizzled, perhaps because of its nasty handling. Still, you hadn't lived if you hadn't seen racing's wildest editor of a sports car magazine, Jerry Titus, getting rough with his. *Neil Nissing*

Above and top right: Many an L.A. racer who returned from World War II with a sound body and undamaged brain found his horizons shifting: bombs, bullets, high-explosives, rockets, and other weapons of mass destruction sure were interesting! And so were war-surplus belly gas tanks off fighter aircraft, just the size and shape to make an aerodynamic race car. Weighing in at barely 230 pounds, with the right high-tweaked V-8 and running gear, one was easily capable of exceeding 200 miles per hour on the lakes. Literally in a class by themselves were Alex Xydias and the SoCal Speed Shop 'tanker. *Greg Sharp collection.*

so grumpy about having to swallow so much frozen air, that many of them at first refused to light off at all. But amid much belated trumpeting and righteous Meyer-Drake war-whooping, light off they did, and they were the sounds my heart raced to through three Indy decades when 33 of them used to explode in stampede.

Then came a sudden swirl of gray or balding heads and of crow's feet and pot bellies. Arriving was a crush of the last living Meyer-Drake drivers, the vast majority out

of L.A, including some who hadn't been inside the cockpit of a big cucumber for better than 35 Memorial Days. Next came the haunting motorcade lap.

Then we segued to the 500 itself. Miserable. First of all the imported redcoat ground-sucker rear-engines couldn't warm up their fat tires on the freezing track surface. But the marathon's incompetent gang of ne'er-do-wells, green-card foreign devils, pampered progenies riding the coattails of famous fathers, hobbyists acting

Left and below:
Two long-lived L.A.
sprint cars from
Ascot Park that
regularly hung it on
one and all: the
Offy-powered No. 3
Tamale Wagon, and
the Kenny Worth
small-block Chevy,
ditto No. 3. *Joe
Scalzo collection*

out their dangerous fantasies, and ride-buying hustlers took the green anyway. Even with the assistance of radio-control spotters on the corners telling them when to turn, they made a mess. The pole car spun out and crashed on the pace lap, and it was all downhill from there.

A Meyer-Drake big cucumber roadster would have eaten any of these charlatans alive.

There were seven sound reasons why the reverse-weight big cucumbers of Los Angeles should not have been able to win as often as they did: (1) they were so long, overweight, and heavy-gauge that to maintain momentum throughout a 500's three-and-a-half hours, they had to be hauled around without drivers touching the brakes, yet when cucumbers squeezed themselves down onto the smaller, meaner miles of Milwaukee and

The classic Corvette road racer of L.A.'s late 1950s and early 1960s. Before Ol' Shel's Cobras kicked the life out of it, the L.A. 'vette was BAD. *Bob Tronolone*

Trenton, no braking system was sufficient to whoa their hurtling deadweight of tonnage; (2) they were constructed out of cast-off war-surplus hardware (the drivers even raced in tanker goggles) from the bomber aircraft plants of Los Angeles, employed primitive locker rear ends without differential gears, and of course their engine of choice was the Meyer-Drake, a dinosaur a third of a century ancient; (3) their very tall and thin tires came to the helmet tops of their drivers, and the stressed-out cucumber canvas might, without warning, "grow hair" and ferociously blow out; (4) their constructors—Kurtis Kraft, Eddie Kuzma, Quin Epperly, Lujie Lesovsky, and A. J. Watson— were an underfinanced and unlettered fraternity working in tiny crowded garages, making great race cars without blueprints or, of course, computers—Watson, the coolest cat among them, marked out wheelbase dimensions in chalk; (5) their custodian chief mechanics were underpaid, overworked, jacks-of-all-racing-trades assisted by a skeleton staff of stooges and gofers; (6) the sugar daddies bankrolling them were a high-spirited and go-for-the-gusto gang of everything from wagon masters of 18-wheeler fleets to peacocking pig farmers going racing not for business purposes at all, just strictly for the hell of it; and (7) the hardest and fastest big cucumber gun of them all, Parnelli Jones—first to cut Indy's subminute lap—never attended a race-driving school except the "Jalopy Derby," a gritty staple of L.A. culture starring battalions of ruffians leaning on and pounding each other in iron junks.

Yet out of barely 100 constructed, one big cucumber or another won 12 of 13 Indy 500s—an incredible 11 in a row—and cucumbers remain the most successful Indianapolis stagecoaches of all time. Just another Los Angeles success.

L.A. drivers in L.A. cucumbers developed an L.A. style of racing that saw them humping wheel-to-wheel around the Brickyard Indian-file, every cucumber busy nibbling the rump of the next one, every driver performing the whole strange cucumber tap dance of backing off, avoiding the brakes, then applying the wham to the throttle.

And what with all Meyer-Drakes being identical, everybody was perfectly matched. Consequently, lead changes occurred by the dozens. And while L.A.'s brilliant boys and their brilliant big cucumbers were busy working the Speedway and each other, L.A chief mechanics with all-L.A. crews of refuelers and tire-busters were busily perfecting the sub-30-second pit stop.

They were good race cars. In a wreck they did not automatically blot a driver to extinction or reduce him to charcoal.

Dazzled by the yearly spectacle, awestruck Hoosiers wandered about in a daze afterward, babbling about Parnelli, J. C. "Aggie" Agajanian, Dean Jeffries paint jobs, crash helmets striped by Von Dutch, cast-magnesium Halibrand center-sections, Joe Hunt magnetos—the whole big cucumber nomenclature and panoply.

Los Angeles already had owned Indianapolis for half a century now, so cucumber Indy was afire not with racing

Ol' Yeller wasn't the only one: sports car racing in the 1950s at Palm Springs, Paramount Ranch, Hansen Dam, Pomona, and Riverside Raceway was overloaded with other lumbering backward-built bombs as ugly as gargoyles. Your typical malevolent monolith had no status, however, without an imaginative handle, and L.A.'s were the best: *Reynolds Wrap Special*, *Batmobile*, *Eliminator*. Mundanely named the *Thompson Special*, this is one of the least lovely of them all, Mickey Thompson's short-wheelbased Caddy-powered Kurtis, just let out of its cage. Dig the Mick's crazy tanker goggles—more war surplus. *Greg Sharp collection*

alone but with customary City of Angels' camaraderie and gusto. Taking soundings, an entourage of L.A. happy faces hit 16th Street to visit and discard all its motley diners, grim dumps, and seedy dives, before anointing shabby Mate's White Front, next to the rusted railway trestle, best gin mill in town. Mate's, accordingly, became the great Los Angeles haven. Race drivers, chief mechanics, stooges, and even slumming sugar daddies comfortably mingled while bawling the L.A. jive.

And although unaccompanied by L.A. doll faces—greatest in the world—nobody was lonely. Faithfully working the fences ringing Gasoline Alley was the daily riot of convivial Hoosier dollies flirting and passing notes to anybody flying the L.A. colors.

Great race cars, great personnel, great races, great times. The reign of the Meyer-Drake cucumber roadster at Indianapolis should have lasted longer than 1952–1964, barely a 10th of the twentieth century.

The end started unexpectedly. At the beginning of the 1960s, Rodger "the Dodger" Ward, second-ranked only to Parnelli among L.A. cucumber chauffeurs, traumatically hit 40. And as collateral fallout he immediately declared himself worn out and too much of a geezer to get physical with a big cucumber anymore.

So, searching for a softer Indy ride, Rodger the Dodger turned cucumber copperhead by inviting to Indy the English. Previously, the United Kingdom's brightest boffins had been kept too busy dominating Formula 1 to take much notice of the 500. And thanks to Colin Chapman, they'd just finished shafting six perfectly healthy decades of race car design by concocting

the rear-engine—in effect, giving all existing front-engine race cars a suppository.

Brit rear-engines subsequently proved bad; you couldn't even dig a driver working his steering wheel anymore.

But Rodger heartily endorsed the little dingbats anyway. So even though he subsequently never got to race a decent one, the pandemic he'd started spread.

Nineteen sixty-three, the season when rear-engine flu really caught hold, Hank the Deuce spent lots of his FoMoCo's jack entering in the 500 a matched set of flimsy fiberglass bathtubs filled with gasoline and covered with stressed-skin. Of course, these Lotus-powered-by-Fords were the brain strokes of Chapman, and wherever

Late-model taxicab racing was a long time catching on in L.A. Yet whenever the cabs raced, it was a spectacle. Scotty Cain's T-Bird mauls and knocks down another fence. *Joe Scalzo collection*

Constructed in L.A. in 1961, then raced two seasons, the Troutman-Barnes-built Chaparral, financed and campaigned by Jim Hall's oil money, was last of the fast front-engine sports racers. Owner Jim Hall is behind the wheel here. *Bob Tronolone*

Chapman went, it seemed, drivers died. His flyweight products had already made cadavers out of some of the globe's top chauffeurs; at Indy they'd almost take out a trio of 500 champions.

What wasn't equitable for jolly bloke Chapman was to set everything in motion, then not stay to see his revolution through. Yet after a his coffin-on-wheels Lotus won the l965 500, he was back in Formula 1 and pretty much out of Indy, leaving behind a mess.

Nobody wanted to race cucumber roadsters anymore, and L.A. shops didn't know how to make Lotuses. Previously godly, such L.A. constructors as Watson and the Scarab-masters Troutman and Barnes now had no choice but to crank up their own bogus Lotus copies, with suspension points totally screwed up and frames that flexed like spaghetti. Toe steer, bump steer, droop steer, our L.A. guys never got those equations right. Los Angeles, in turn, began suffering its first dose of bad publicity.

When a helpless race driver prostrated himself in an L.A.-manufactured rear-engine, the list of horrors he was facing was endless. Everything from neurotic understeer to snap oversteer. And everything ready to go zooming lethally out of control in an instant.

Indianapolis paid a stiff price for permitting such flaky monstrosities to replace its dependable big cucumbers. The worst thing to happen occurred in 1964. A jittery Mickey Thompson fireball masterpiece—with four-cam Ford muscle, go-kart rubber, and oversize fuel bays—got all sideways, located the concrete, then blew itself sky high in an enormous red flash of flaming gasoline and greasy black smoke. Behind the wheel of the sideways Mickey car was—you probably guessed it— Davey MacDonald. But also trapped and immolated in his L.A. Halibrand was innocent Eddie Sachs, previously one of the few luminaries from outside L.A. capable of getting a big cucumber really moving.

Frank "Duffy" Livingston—exhaust muffler magnet, possible inventor of the go-kart—decided in the 1950s to go sports car racing with a flourish. His red-and-white *Eliminator*—named after its fiery Iskenderian camshaft—came dangerously close to having a career as a dirt track hot rod roadster. But after sizing up its boxed-frame, front axle off a 1937 Ford, Halibrand center-section married to an old Cook rear-end, full bellypans, and torsion bars, Duffy decided to lay in a 3/8 x 3/8 flathead Merc and go frighten the sports cars. After the package never ran or handled properly, Duff paid a fast $20 for a Chev small-block with a scored cylinder. He carried out emergency repairs, and the *Eliminator* with its Spalding flame-thrower ignition became a monster. *Bob Tronolone*

Not surprisingly, after what had happened to Eddie, few of the remaining big cucumber names would consent to strap on an L.A. Funny Car, especially one with the violent zap of the newly turbocharged Drake. But their replacement chauffeurs from the worlds of taxicabs (stock cars), sports cars, off-road, and even Formula 1 were, almost without exception, steering-wheel challenged. Some years in the 1960s the 500 couldn't even get started until half the field wrecked while lining up. One year the pace car itself went berserk. Traveling at full speed, it entered a grandstand full of photographers, laying out dozens.

During the 1970s, certain big shooters struck back, trying to make Indy an L.A. race again. Vel's Parnelli Jones with its *Johnny Lightning* Specials captured two consecutive 500s, then lost its edge going with a radical

dihedral car called the *Parnelli*, among the most fantastic cock-ups of that whole crazy decade. All American Racers, Dan Gurney's outfit, which was actually not in L.A. at all but across the line in Orange County, had some major years with its Eagles but couldn't maintain them.

So, by the 1980s, the English were back at Indy, brighter than ever. In fact, a hero was anybody with a Beatles' accent. I panicked. After rear-engines, what might the Typhoid Marys be bringing with them this time?

It was an abomination called "ground effects": aerodynamic, beneath-the-chassis underwear that sucked bodywork down onto the track surface and cost Indy drivers their skills. No longer, in fact, are they race drivers at all, only robotic passengers. Just pump up the adrenaline, blank out your imagination, live in fool's paradise, and go slamming into corners on the far side of 200

But not all L.A. sporty cars were as oversized as the *Eliminator*. This rattletrap little Cooper-Climax had sharp teeth. At an especially bitchin' Palm Springs meet, it won by wiping out all the expensive trick stuff, including the Porsche that had just finished fifth at Le Mans. Its estimable chauffeur was kick-back Bobby Drake. *Bob Tronolone*

miles per hour believing that, thanks to its ground-effects undies, your race car will stick fast no matter what.

The Indy 500 hasn't been an L.A. race now going on 40 years, and there's nobody around to talk to about the big cucumbers because nobody remembers them. Even Mate's White Front has lost its status, replaced by a thing called the Union Jack.

Yet the joke is on twenty-first-century chauffeurs with all their technology-laden computer brains, antennae, software, hardware, artificial intelligence, and cockpit devices for measuring g-forces and heart rates. The age of the electronically controlled, driverless, zombie race car surely is coming.

BUY THE TICKET, TAKE THE RIDE

In 1960, my friend Don Hulette—an L.A. artist race driver, or L.A. race driver artist—took me for a hot lap around Riverside Raceway while I sat on the seatless floor of the same crappy old Lister Corvette he was going to destroy in a gigantic crash 'n' burn during the annual Grand Prix one week later. The memory still bites. Since there was no seat, there were no seat belts and so I may or may not have been wearing a helmet. All the same, we were rolling at better than 150 miles per hour. As Don wailed away at the steering wheel, the cockpit was pungent with high-test gasoline, hot oil was spewing everywhere, and rubber smoke from the burning tires was billowing up between the floorboards. I was in white-trash heaven! I understood how you could get hooked on this ride-along thing.

And from there it was a short step to investigating which riding mechanics among L.A.'s professional danger-junkies had gotten the biggest blast for their ride-along dollars.

Prewar, it must have been the incredible Chickie Hirashima. For his very first riding mechanic gig, he was a flyweight teenage passenger facing 200 fogbound laps in an Indy car around Mines Field, a 1930s L.A. dirt track. The maniac he was assigned to passenger was the overanimated Kelly Petillo, whose erratic pedal foot was working overtime. At one point, a windmilling Petillo elbow nailed Hirashima square on the chin, and Chickie awoke groggily on the floorboard with Petillo fiercely kicking him in the ribs to get back to work. Came the midrace refueling stop, Chickie stubbornly refused to

The incredible Chickie Hirashima as a riding mechanic partnered with Rex Mays. At Mines Field in the rainy winter of 1934—Chickie's first gig as a ride-along—Kelly Petillo's flailing elbow caught him square on the chin and Chickie ended up comatose on the cockpit floor. He and Kelly the Shiv won anyway. *IMS Photo*

Mickey Thompson's you-have-to-see-it-to-believe-it 1953 combination drags-and-lakes bolide wedded Chrysler hemi and FoMoCo flathead. *Greg Sharp collection*

quit the fog—and Kelly and his dangerous elbows—and instead chose to go down with the ship. He and Petillo won big.

And postwar, still in a class by itself, is Smokin' Joe Petrali's shotgun aviation trip as flight engineer to his boss Howard Hughes in mad Howard's monster cargo aircraft the *Hercules*. *Hercules* was its official name, but it got libeled the "*Spruce Goose*" by a Howard-baiting congressman who attacked the double-deck, eight-engined, all-wooden amphibian—as big as a 747—as a $20 million boondoggle that would never leave the water.

Came the long-awaited afternoon when Howard's big bulbous bird at last was to get airborne, its manifest consisted only of Howard, Smokin' Joe, half a dozen clueless newspapermen—and no co-pilot. None. As flight engineer, Smokin' carried no pilot's ticket of his own and was unqualified to fly. In other words, Howard

was about to demonstrate the worth of the Goose by attempting to pilot it the length of Long Beach Bay solo. Joe and the soused scribblers offered no complaint. And Howard succeeded. Had the Goose gone down, it would have been good-bye dumbbell hacks, good-bye Smokin' Joe, good-bye Howard.

You can't discuss shotgun-riding mechanics without a nod to the South of the Border. From its ragged start in the steaming jungles of northern Guatemala, to its always bloody termination five days and 2,000 miles later at Juarez on the lawless Texas frontier, the old Mexican road race was grandfather of all riding-along gigs. And brave but soft-hearted Bill Stroppe's personal favorite.

In Mexico, Stroppe was conscripted to construct and maintain FoMoCo's factory squadron of Lincoln door-slammer town cars, the biggest and heaviest race cars in

To Grey
Fellow Race Buff
Ak Miller

Ak Miller's mighty horse of iron in the Mexican Road Race was an inspiration of parts and pieces that only a crack L.A. hot rodder like Ak could imagine and assemble: Ford, Chrysler, Nash, Caddy, and Oldsmobile! *Greg Sharp collection*

the world. Yet he was expected to perform far more than routine prep and detailing. He also got dragooned into traveling along as navigator and ballast to Team Lincoln's L.A. gene bank of Indy 500 chauffeurs: Manual "Yo Yo" Ayulo, Jack McGrath, Walt "Jack the Bear" Faulkner, Johnny Mantz, plus Vookie Vukovich out of Fresno. All of them knew what speed was, and along with Clay Smith, the brain surgeon of the Meyer-Drake and Stroppe's partner and best friend, and Stroppe himself, they comprised Team Lincoln's magnificent Mexican seven.

The unspoken rules of pulling shotgun duty in Mexico were clear. Admitting that you were petrified was a no-no, giving unsolicited advice to your chauffeur marked you as an idiot, criticizing your chauffeur's wheelmanship was the crime of crimes. Poor Stroppe once was guilty of the felony of grabbing a steering wheel out of Johnny Mantz's hands. This provoked Johnny into slamming to a stop and ordering Bill out of the Lincoln so Johnny could knock his brains all over the Tehuantepec straightaway. A mini-size steering wheel was installed on the passenger side afterward, forever marking Stroppe the ultimate lame-o.

In the 1950s, a full decade before Shelby and his Cobras got cozy with Hank the Deuce and his check-book, Stroppe and Smith accomplished the same thing. Their shared conceit was to get Lincoln-Mercury to bite on the brainstorm of sending squads of the division's Lincolns into Mexico, to persuade Lincoln that a wild road race across the savage southern tropics was an ideal advertising setting for its luxo tanks. A hard sell indeed for a pair of ambitious dry lakes kids and oil-field roughs from Long Beach, but Stroppe and Smith swung it.

Heavy Lincolns proceeded to dominate and win the thing four times in five years, and after Mexico ended, Stroppe in the 1960s and 1970s went right ahead working nonstop creating high-tonnage blunderbusses, mostly for Mercury, and many of them intended for the newest L.A. speed game, off-road racing. Bill turned out to have a real talent for this. Once he even added suspension and off-road armor-plating to a Condor Coach motor home. It was supposed to be a joke. But the joke backfired when the gigantic Coach proved itself able to outrun dune buggies.

Nobody carried the Los Angeles message further and to such extreme places as Stroppe. With a 10-vehicle Mercury Comet platoon, he lit up the East African Safari Rally. Carrying out another simple little task for Mercury's advertising sales department, Stroppe flew four Comets to Cape Horn, at the tip of South America, and ferried them across the Strait of Magellan. Then he turned them over to a Los Angeles gang of really hard men, who flogged them 10,000 nonstop miles across the equator, all up through South America to the Mosquito Coast, followed by Panama, Nicaragua, Honduras, Guatemala, Mexico, the United States, Canada, and Alaska before at last crashing, exhausted, at their final destination of Fairbanks, in just 44 days.

Stroppe additionally earned and enjoyed still more L.A. applause during the 1970s, 1980s, and 1990s for rescuing Parnelli Jones. The fastest and greatest of all Los Angeles race drivers from the second half of the twentieth century had taken early retirement from a dense and unmatched career to become top kick of his own Indy and Formula 1 stable—and to discover how to become a businessman multimillionaire, which, compared to his racing, proved easy. But his retirement had been premature. P. J. still had lots of unspent excellent racing ticking along inside him, only now he was spending far too much time wandering around uttering bilge like, "The real estate market is a little soft. . . . I need to telephone my broker to ask where bond yields are going" and was risking the loss of his chops.

He returned to racing but not to the racetrack. Choosing off-road instead, he caromed across the trackless rattlesnake deserts of peninsular Baja California's barren brown finger, with Stroppe at his elbow. Two ways to go off-roading: dune buggy rail or big truck. Big truck took more skill, so Parnelli went with that and Stroppe constructed him some terrific jumpin' jughead Bronco Fords, plus a creature called "Big Oly"— record-breaking champion of the preeminent Baja 1000. However, the spectacular victory went largely uncelebrated by off-roading's rank and file, just as Parnelli's departure from the game—at last he'd gotten racing out of his system—went unmourned. Everybody was scared to death of him, his Jalopy Derby race driving like nothing they'd seen before. And outside of the even hotter times in old Mexico, P. J. provided Stroppe his ultimate riding-mechanic money's worth.

After the Mexican Road Race, the number seven proved portentous. Six of Team Lincoln's big seven got brutally whacked: Smith died in the signaling points of Du Quoin; Ay, supposed son of a Peruvian consul, neglected to put a harness in his big cucumber at Indy and

A great ghost from the wonderful L.A. past, this replica of a Mexican Road Race Towncar Lincoln dramatically appeared at a Gilmore Roar's Again picnic. *Neil Nissing*

caught a wall warming up; Vookie—while trying to win three 500s in a row for Howie Keck, Crabby Travers, Jim Coon, and himself—was at the center of a deadly six-car spill; McGrath, Indy speed record holder, didn't change a weak axle and went headlong down the back straightaway at Phoenix; five months later, Faulkner—called Jack the Bear despite weighing 110 pounds—slipped out of his seatbelts during a taxicab roller on the third corner at Vallejo; Mantz, Stroppe's outraged playmate from the Tehuantepec straightaway, was outliving everybody until a big highway smash managed to pulp most of the bones in his body and even sever his tongue. And after narrowly surviving the seven hours of surgery it took to make him whole again, Johnny got into another road smash that finished him.

Not even Stroppe entirely escaped Mexico's sad and horrible legacy. Time after time he had his emotions well torqued acting as pallbearer at all of the celebrity funerals of his old employees and buddies. He was too kindhearted and soft for the times. Toward the end of his own life in 1995, his Long Beach shop near Terminal Island had turned into a sort of unofficial shelter for homeless members of the animal kingdom. Then there was additional hurt when he entered into a haphazard agreement with a Ford heir, lost the shop, and after a bitter fight won it back again.

From gargantuan town car Lincolns and Comet Mercurys, to the astonishing jumpin' jugheads of P. J. in the Baja 1000, all Stroppe products entered combat looking as if Bill was prepping it for a *concours d'elegance*. Bill Stroppe's legacy is that he is the Father Miller of monster iron.

CHAPTER FOUR

BATTLEGROUNDS

Los Angeles the Damned

—H. L. Mencken, Baltimore bard

Flourishing in L.A. for almost as long as anybody can remember were various racetracks named Ascot. This is Ascot Park, the last of the breed, in its lifetime the busiest stadium in America with 170 promotions per year. It was razed in 1990. An intriguing rumor has it that prior to the razing, its well-manicured track surface was dug up and trucked away to a secret place, to be stored away until the inevitable construction of the next Ascot. *Neil Nissing*

Los Angeles race cars used to go rip-assin' all across the planet, yet occasionally stayed home to make battle on L.A.'s very own fighting family of drag strips, road courses, circle tracks, dirt ovals, macadam bowls, and one lone superspeedway. Each battleground possessed its own special energy; each one hotted-up the culture of speed. There were better than 100 of them, and only three or so survived the twentieth century. Our local history is to blame. We just don't build things to last out here.

RED DEVIL WINDS AND TEAR GAS

Snake-bit Riverside International Raceway (1957–1990) got covered up by a hideous subdivision of cut-rate shacks. Lions Drag Strip (1965–1986), I think, lies

Opposite: Palm Springs, that elite desert spa, briefly opened up its airport to the sports car set in the mid-1950s. *Joe Scalzo*

beneath a freeway. After getting torn down, Ascot Park (1957–1990), the busiest speedway in the land, deteriorated into a vast and useless vacant lot atop a heaving landfill. And although opening to a California sports record audience of 180,000—*180,000* of the buggers!—Ontario Motor Speedway (1970–1980), L.A.'s circus maximus, went completely to hell. After first defaulting on a debt of $25.5 million, it next suffered the ultimate indignity of its acres and acres of grassy green infield becoming a pasture for crapping sheep. Unhappy, razed, OMS doesn't even make a decent-looking ruin. The superspeedway that was expected to make Indianapolis obsolete, finished up, just another sprawling parking lot alongside the gridlocked San Berdoo freeway.

A couple of springtimes back, during a Nextel Cup extravaganza at high-llama California Speedway (just down the block from where OMS once stood), spectators by the dozens got hammered by an unexpected scorching sun and collapsed. Pleased that I hadn't been

The International Race of Champions began at Riverside Raceway in 1974. Porsche provided RSRs for that first year's series, but IROC switched to identical Z28 Camaros in 1975. These came equipped with electronic rev-limiters so that the hero drivers couldn't blow them up. But for any hero driver who knew anything about cars—and there were a couple who did—it was a snap to short-circuit the limiters' and then over-rev to victory or destruction. All you had to remember was to throw the offending wires out the window afterward. *Bob Tronolone*

among them, I was nonetheless reminded of yet another local tradition. L.A. racetracks often succeed not only in mugging L.A. race drivers—possibly that is one explanation for Parnelli Jones and his imitators being so hard-boiled—but also inflicting terrible punishment of one sort or another on their very own paying clientele, the poor, boob public.

Take Ontario Motor Speedway's Labor Day gala grand opening. At first it appeared that the big 500 might not come off at all. By sheer bad luck, OMS rested at the base of barrier mountains that often burned and was downwind of Kaiser Steel Mill, the state's largest

source of air pollution. A giant wildfire was raging up in the mountains. So, between the foundry and the flames, there was so much steel guck and dense smoke that the 180,000-strong hooligan crowd could barely breathe. The field of 33 lined up to take the green flag, but could hardly make out Turn 1. History was going to be made. OMS's inaugural sweepstakes was on its way to becoming the first automobile race ever canceled by environmental disaster.

Not to worry. Anything can happen at an L.A. racetrack.

Sure enough, suddenly kicking in to chase out all the foul, dirty fog so that everyone could breathe and see was yet another well-known phenomenon, the Santa Ana winds. Not soft Mediterranean breezes, but red-plague currents howling at 70 miles per hour. They saved the day but ruined the 500. So much wild and destructive Santa Ana sand was sprayed between all the violently whirring turbocharger blades of the various Drakes and Fords that the track almost emptied. Only about half a dozen finishers got counted at the end.

Lions Drag Strip could surprise you by tossing into its grandstands molten, maiming material off exploding Chrysler Top Fuel diggers.

Ascot Park, meantime, was in little Gardena, a lawless, blue-collar encampment with few zoning laws and a tradition of gambling dens and trailer parks. And for the additional dose of bad mojo, just across the street was Ascot's nearest neighbor, a moldy necropolis.

Uncontrolled nighttime Ascot was where everything happened. You might be sitting in the bleachers minding your own business, when suddenly your eyes would begin watering and streaming because, strictly for the fun of it, a neighbor in the next seat over had cracked open a canister of tear gas. Heavy acts of assault and battery raged in the aisles. One Sunday eve I chanced to be at a figure-eight spectacle, digging Willie Kimbrough winning yet again, when a flying battery thrown off one of the crashing hulks made landfall in the sixth-row grandstands.

Out on the racetrack, it didn't matter whether it was sprinters, stocks, motorbikes, or even pickups packing the dirt surface smooth while simultaneously waging their own illicit races—everything at Ascot always was erupting at rocket tempo. One mad evening, while I was enjoying the drama of the battling wheel-packing pickups, a fast and really cherry Ford F-100 decided to go on its gourd and spit off windshield and rear window simultaneously. Surrounded by the half-mile oval, Ascot's race cars pitted precariously among trademark rat-infested palm trees and polluted lagoons, where one accidental wrong look could earn you a boot to the testicles.

Above: Some of the balmiest and bluest skies in the world back-lit Santa Barbara's Memorial Day and Labor Day sports car extravaganzas for Saturday-Sunday soldiers. Two Ferraris and Ol' Yeller fill the front row. *Bob Tronolone*

Still, it always was undeniably Riverside Raceway taking the most costly toll on its race drivers, spectators, and especially unlucky race cars. Just like OMS, Riverside, technically speaking, wasn't an L.A. racetrack at all. All by itself, it sat off on a barren patch of ugly and undulating real estate right on the edge of the boiling Anza-Borrego Desert, approximately an hour and a half's commute from downtown—said commute conducted in 1958 by an unexpected monster audience attracted to Riverside's inaugural *Los Angeles Times* Grand Prix.

The vast majority of this highly confused mob was to witness its very first sporty car race. They were not yet fans, merely gullible rubes unable to resist weeks of pounding Grand Prix ballyhooing published in the *L.A. Times.* Which in itself was quite a turnaround. Back in the distant 1930s, William Randolph Hearst and his vengeful *Examiner* had attacked racing as something that demanded banning because it was "legalized murder." Yet now, in the l950s, L.A. racing was savoring the ballyhooing of a friendly newspaper, the *L.A. Times,* all because a member of the paper's ruling Chandler empire was a racing fool.

Race day at last dawned. A paralyzing October sun superheated the Borrego air into the 100s. Endless lines of traffic jam locked to the distant horizon. Neither Riverside

nor the *Times* had been prepared for such a crush, or had any idea of relentless publicity's ungodly power.

The atmosphere was ugly. Smashing down fences and totally ignoring signs quaintly imploring, in capital letters, "Do Not Confuse the Ticket Takers"—an ancient tribe of geezer volunteers—tough roughneck hordes surged into Riverside without purchasing general admission tickets at all.

Chaos escalated violently. Half of the cars in the Grand Prix sickened and died of heat stroke. Half the sun-blasted spectators almost did. A steward of the Grand Prix, Egbert "Babe" Stapp, a Legion Ascot luminary there to protect drivers, instead swung on one, Lance Reventlow. Concession stands emptied of product, including drinking water. All the privies overflowed and everybody went crazy.

But next year they were all back. And for all the years after that. The Grand Prix, in fact, ended up being yet another Los Angeles triumph that set standards for all future professional sports car racing extravaganzas.

RED-DOG BLITZ

Riverside was the middle linebacker of L.A. racetracks, a vicious and kill-crazy creature charging at you on the red-dog blitz and eager to bite fingers, gouge eyes, demolish groins, and shred everything in its path. General

Ascot Park featured sprint car racing at its rawest and best. You got to see Allen "Knothead" Heath winding himself up exploiting Ascot's rim, middle, and bottom while doing impossible things with a long ton of sprinter and a hook for a right arm; or Don Hawley—buried across the street from Ascot—standing the roaring spectators of Turn 1 on their feet with his motorbike moves in Louie Senter's oversized Ford four-cam; or Ron "Yo Yo" Ellico out-racing all the other dirt-surface-packing pickup trucks with his rampaging Ellico Ford F-100. *Joe Scalzo collection*

manager Les Richter was himself a famous ferocious former linebacker. Perhaps he'd even been the quarterback-crippling prototype of all famous ferocious 'backers. Les was a homicidal maniac so invaluable that the L.A. Rams traded away half its team just to acquire him. Yet nobody was ever kinder to me than Les. For only $20 a day during the week, he'd close down Riverside just so some of us motorbiker crotch rocketeers could hone our moves.

The blood danced, the endorphins roared: those were some tremendous Riverside days! Fantastic freakin' fun was screwing it on in high gear and flying across the dangerous blind switchback esses from the bottom of Turn 1 to the top of Turn 6 without once resuscitating the throttle.

Yet another of my favorite Les stories concerns the time I was trapped in a typical financial crisis, and for

Carrell Speedway. *Joe Scalzo collection*

Anybody lucky enough to be part of the Los Angeles culture of speed knew that L.A. racetracks were bizarre and off-the-wall. Racetracks unexpectedly sprang up on city boulevards, parking lots, high school football fields, baseball parks, football stadiums, air force runways, and even out on the floor of the desert. *Greg Sharp collection*

starvation wages Les turned me over to wizard publicist Deke Houlgate, just then busy overworking himself flacking a Riverside taxicab 500-miler. To digress a bit (but not much), Deke, much later, became press agent of Roger "Unfair Advantage" Penske. And this was a true coincidence, because Riverside had been where it all began for Unfair Advantage. Everything about him in racing's twenty-first century, including his always having a better weapon than everybody else—springs from Riverside's 1962 Grand Prix. There, Unfair Advantage pulled his very first fast one by showing up for what was supposed to be a sports car meet with a single-seater Formula 1 with coachwork. Then he proceeded to railroad this mutant right past flummoxed technical scrutinizers and win and ruin the Grand Prix, starting a sleight-of-hand legacy critics have harped on ever since.

Back at the Riverside taxicab 500, Deke hadn't trusted me to do much, so instead assigned me to pull emergency duty guarding Dan Gurney, the 500's winner. This came about just as Dan was being hustled up to the Riverside press box for interviews and I heard Deke snap, "Look out."

I looked. Then looked again: Liz Renay.

Moll of mobster Mickey Cohen, who currently was locked up doing hard time, Liz was recently out of the joint herself and going for free publicity by crashing the press box to get photographed with clean-cut Dan.

"If you let her get her ass anywhere near Gurney," Deke whispered sweetly in my ear, "it'll be *your* ass."

In the 1920s, the two mighty board track domes could not have been more different. Beverly Hills' was as luxurious as its name. Culver City Speedway, here, was blue-collar and far faster. *Greg Sharp collection*

For company, she'd even brought along a pair of Cohen meatballs, and how I ever succeeded in holding off all three of them I don't remember. Liz, I remember well. What a screaming beauty—and she scared me to death.

Riverside devoured the innocent and the hard-edged alike. Speedways can do that. Two seasons after Riverside's own summer opening, clear across the country in Florida, a pair of the last of NASCAR's great dirt-tracking moonshiners stood staring in absolute horror at their own beautiful new playground, high-banked Daytona Speedway. Contemplating all the devouring miles of looming bankings, imagining the supersonic speeds required to stay on top of them, and sadly aware that the fun and craziness of dirt tracking was ended, one nervously said to the other, "*Goddamn*, Tim! I'm putting two belts in my car." Good call.

Similarly, the Saturday and Sunday innocents of Los Angeles amateur sports car racing getting dragged kicking and screaming onto Riverside for the first time realized that it was all over for them, too. The fun and risk-free weekend afternoons running neck-and-neck around parking lots or up and down airport runways were forever finished. From now on they'd be dangerously averaging almost 100 miles per hour around Riverside's three hungry miles and nine corners, any of which could eat you alive. At that very first opening meet, one of them promptly did. On Turn 6 the driver of an MG martyred himself by turning over without a rollover bar. Riverside subsequently became the first road circuit where cockpit rollover bars were mandated.

Gilmore Stadium, 1934–1950, annually hosted "Turkey Night." The name was not pejorative. It was the annual Thanksgiving evening Grand Prix spectacle for midget cars. Incredibly, the Grand Prix still continues in the twenty-first century, better than 60 editions old, now conducted at G-rated Irwindale Speedway. *Greg Sharp collection*

Say this about Riverside, the place wasted no time. Its very first corner, Turn 1, an uphill left just beyond the start-and-finish line, lay in wait to carve you immediately. Before Riverside widened 1 and made it faster and easier, automobiles and motorcycles of all velocities stacked up there. Entering it was easy; a good Ferrari or Maser could do that traveling flat out. And then wish it hadn't because the paving narrowed and confronted a hill of hard dirt.

Left: Muroc Dry Lake, dating at least as far back as the years of Frank Lockhart and Tommy Milton, eventually made way for an army base. *Greg Sharp collection*

Opposite: October 12, 1958, the Sunday afternoon big-time professional sports car competition enjoyed a riotous birth at Riverside Raceway. *Joe Scalzo collection*

Race Broadcast

The fourth annual $20,000-added 200-mile LA Times-Mirror Grand Prix for Sports Cars will be broadcast in its entirety from Riverside Intl. Raceway, Sunday, Oct. 15, from 1:45 to approximately 4:45 p.m., over radio KBIG Catalina.

Again this year veteran sportscaster Roy Storey is producer and chief announcer, backed up by announcer Ted Davis and chief engineer Mal Morrett.

Next broadcast is the Laguna Seca Grand Prix from Monterey, Oct. 22, starting at 2:00 p.m.

MOTOR RACING
and Economy Car News

6th Year—No. 25 —Los Angeles, Calif.
(Published bi-weekly except last issue of calendar year)

OCT. 13-20, 1961

25¢

Price Goes Up

MOTORACING and Economy Car News, which starts its seventh year of publication with its next issue, has finally been forced to raise subscription rates. We tried to stave this off, but the rising costs of printing, paper...and all that jazz.

Old rates were $8 for 3 years, $3 for 1 year. Effective with issue of Oct. 27-Nov. 3: $10 for 3 years, $4 for 1 year. Take advantage of old rates and extend your sub by filling out order blank on pg. 7.

Happy Happy Riverside or Togetherness at Riverside

By STAN MOTT

85

Les Richter, lord and ruler of Riverside, booked into his favorite track everything from Formula Ones to Top Fuel diggers, to motorcycles and Can-Ammers. But his wisest move was brokering dates for the southern sots-with-steering-wheels and their gargantuan taxicabs. Here a field of the broad-beamed sleds fill up the switchback esses. Bobby Allison (No. 12) and David Pearson (No. 21) set the tempo. *Bob Tronolone*

Every fool with a decent set of balls wanted to be first to attack Turn 1 at full pedal and be first to make it *all* the way around without lifting. Two of the chuckleheads attempting it were named Bob Johnson and Stanford Jay Lerner. Who made the worst job of it is open to debate.

Chucklehead Johnson was pulling the trigger on a lumbering mechanical masterpiece named after ornithologist Bob Sorrell. The Sorrell beast had a sticking throttle and for lap after lap, Johnson, going for machismo, was using his foot to pry it shut.

At last the dumb-ass got too deep into Turn 1, lost it, hit the wall backward, flipped over, and the Sorrell's magnesium gas tank—salvaged off the wreckage of a burned-out Lister-Chevy—erupted into bright hot white flame. Very, very nasty stuff, burning magnesium. Whenever you see it, either send in the Hazmat boys dressed in their Mylax suits, or run like hell.

No Hazmat squad was available, and magnesium is so toxic that if treated with water it can produce a hydrogen gas that might explode. So Riverside's fire laddies came to the conclusion that the only way to extinguish the Sorrell was to call in a skip loader, dig a hole, and bury it! Today, 40-odd years later, the burned-over Sorrell purportedly still lies out there among the tract houses, presumably ready to burst into white fire all over again should somebody mistakenly dig it up.

Chucklehead Stanford Jay Lerner, or "Eric Hauser," as he called himself, was a stocks-and-bonds guru and madman who knew how to invest other people's money. Into his possession came one of Max Balchowsky's discarded Ol' Yellers, less the Buick engine.

But the deal with Max closed so late that Eric, to make a weekend meet at Riverside, had had to lease a rat motor from a drag racer. By midnight on Friday, he

Artist-racer Don Hulette attacks Turn 6 at the top of Riverside's switchback esses. What he didn't realize was that it wasn't Turn 6, but Turn 4, that was plotting his nasty comeuppance. *Bob Tronolone*

and seven volunteer slaves and the drag racer were still working in shifts bolting and welding. They didn't complete installation until late Saturday afternoon, when Eric had had to use some of his drag as a fabulous character to get Riverside re-opened so he might log some practice laps.

You won't believe Eric's subsequent crash on Turn 1, but I'm giving it to you straight.

He traveled barely a mile when the throttle linkage partly fell off. Always the optimist, and with the engine running poorly, he now saw the golden opportunity to be first to take Turn 1 flat.

Instead, he struck the outside guardrail and the wallop took with it the brakes and much of the body-work. Then everything went airborne and, during the great flips, the borrowed mill of the drag race tore loose and got tossed in the direction of the switchback esses.

The author's Grand Prix scooter, originally an ordinary Honda Super Hawk, was, in L.A. fashion, chopped-and-diced into a spicy stew whose ingredients included S&W valve springs, ForgedTrue pistons, Harmon-Collins camshaft, Bruce Burness ported-and-polished combustion chamber, Ferodo brake linings, and Borrani aluminum wheels. On Dunlop green spot rubber, a tank full of Union 76 high-premium, and a crankcase of Castrol R, the creature—even minus a windscreen cleaned off in an earlier spill—could be coaxed into running really fast. And never more so than in June 1963. Paradise was a half-hour's worth of rocketing around Riverside with no goof, finishing in the top five, and conquering the engine class. *Joe Scalzo collection*

Lurching unsteadily toward Turn 7 in the 1962 *Times* Grand Prix comes Charlie Daigh, winner of the 1958 inaugural in a Scarab. This time Charlie is strapped into a big and crude Maser coupe that's relative to the ones that will nearly fry L.A. expatriate Marvin "Pancho" Panch at Daytona and take down the founder of Camoradi USA Lloyd "(un)Lucky" Casner at Le Mans. This Maser is a big oiler, and besides being faced with merely keeping on the road around Riverside—not an easy occupation in itself—Charlie was forced to steer with one hand and rag off the windshield oil with the other. Charlie, you're nuts! *Bob Tronolone*

Everything else crash-landed, flaming. It was Turn 1's worst conflagration since the Sorrell.

The fire crew was late. So the operator of a septic pump that had been cleaning out the same privies from the *Los Angeles Times* Grand Prix now trained his pump's contents on the blaze while Eric—totally unharmed except for a split lip—fled for cover.

A Scarab and a Lister hump along preparing to make the up-and-over jump into bad-news Turn 7. *Joe Scalzo collection*

I tried offering condolences to the poor drag racer who'd just witnessed his first—and presumably last—race at Riverside, except that he was beyond consoling. "That's my fucking mill in the dirt! That's my fucking mill in the dirt!" he went on babbling over and over, dazed and in total disbelief.

After Turn 1 came the fiercely switchbacking esses, a nasty chain of four blind bends admirably arranged to trap race cars and make them collide.

Lotuses flipped Lotuses; Ferraris wrecked Scarabs and each other; rooster-back Ford taxicabs took out winged Chrysler Hemis; turbocharged Drake mauled four-cam Fords; and one somersaulting Lister-Corvette once did much of the esses flaming. One year, right in the middle of the switchbacks, an act of thoughtfulness that went bad brought on the worst episode of them all.

Shelby in a Birdcage Maserati was having a big Grand Prix until the usual Riverside killer temps made his bum ticker scream for a soothing cap of nitro. But helping himself to an angina pill meant slowing down and steering with one hand, and Ol' Shel, observing a bottleneck building behind him, courteously pulled over to signal the first car through. By sheer Riverside bad luck, following Shel was a tiny air-pump of a yellow Porsche RS60 belonging to a plodding Hungarian count who sold bootleg luxury cars in Buenos Aires. Confused by Ol' Shel's waving him past, the poor, plodding

continued on page 92

1

2

3

4

5

6

7

Nos. 1–7: Riverside wasn't a racetrack—it was a trick! This is Turn 7, where ominous things happened to—mostly—good people. This pair of crashing Novice-class motorbikers in 1976 didn't complete one lap. *Joe Scalzo collection*

Continued from page 88
nobleman sped up, missed Turn 4, and his RS60 waltzed off into the hell's half acre of Riverside gullies and ditches where the count fatally flipped.

Race drivers, sadly, were not the only ones losing their lives at Riverside because they dropped their guards and quit paying attention. Turn 5, up in the second half of the switchbacks, even took out one of its own paying customers, an innocent spectator from San Diego.

The circumstances were enough to make one question the wisdom of ever attending a race at Riverside: this unfortunate fan arises early, commutes all the way from San Diego to Riverside where he fights his way through all the yahoos and yoyos to secure himself a choice spot for race viewing right on Turn 5's fence. Immediately behind him are a couple of bozos who've been imaginative enough to bring along a five-ton backhoe—to stand atop for superior spectating. In the excitement of the race getting flagged away, they accidentally kick the backhoe out of gear. And its five tons proceed to creep silently down the hill and run over and squash the unfortunate San Diego guy.

From the foot of the switchbacking esses to their summit at Turn 6 was a windmilling mile of hell; so, Turn 6, with its skyline of tall grandstands, was always a welcome destination: you knew you'd survived the hellish esses for another lap.

Turn 6 seemed benign—a big right-hand horseshoe easy to negotiate. Yet Turn 6, like everything else at Riverside Raceway, was always preparing the old sucker punch: Ol' Shel, for instance, ruined his Maserati 4.5 and his face there. And in a little cemetery in Norfolk, Virginia, a map of Riverside with an X-marks-the-spot highlighting Turn 6 appears on the gravestone of superstitious Joe "Little Joe" Weatherly, John Barleycorn merchant and comic. He'd arrived at Riverside on Flight 13; qualified 13th; crashed on lap 113; and was found to have 13 bucks in his wallet. His family agreed that all that explained the disaster. Little Joe was the wit who named Meyer-Drake roadsters "big cucumbers."

After Turn 6, the track fanned out like a carpet, better than a quarter of a mile or so, then zoomed over a rise to confront left-bending Turn 7 where my Honda once flew

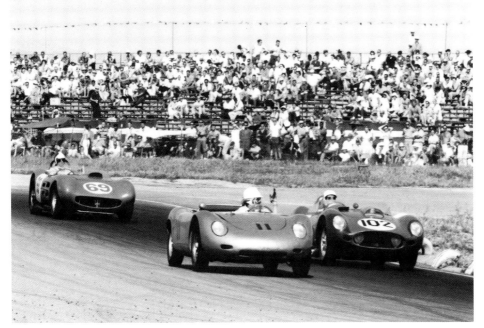

Waving faster cars past him—in this case Pete Lovely (No. 102) and Bobby Bondurant (No. 69)—was just about all that poor slug Count Pedro von Dorey could manage at Riverside's 1960 *Examiner* Grand Prix. He had utterly no business being in a professional GP and paid a terrible price by waltzing his Buenos Aires Porsche off Turn 4. *Bob Tronolone*

out of control and doubled itself around a bale of straw. Seven was odd. It weirded-out even the godly Formula 1 chauffeurs, who, finding themselves turning right instead of left, demanded and achieved the installation of an emergency signboard with an arrow pointing left. Even so, the gods still couldn't get seven right, which was one of the reasons Formula 1 drivers never returned to Riverside.

Many a Formula 5000 open-wheeler and IROC Camaro raced by an Indy 500 luminosity jumped the road at Turn 7 and ended up stuck fast in the sand. On the same weekend that they together won a *Times* Grand Prix, Parnelli and a skating King Cobra slid wide there and parked. And barely two months after his Turn 6 clobbering, Ol' Shel returned with a rebuilt face and rebuilt Maser, only to slew wide on seven and temporarily take himself off the road. He'd seemed too far behind to win, but wasn't. During his last frantic, masterful closing laps spent regaining first place, Ol' Shel had us ready to jump on the back deck of the Maser and ride along to wherever he would carry us.

Via still another quarter mile of undulating paving, corner seven connected to corner eight, Riverside's penultimate, and eight doubled back on itself to dump everybody onto a mile's worth of vast, glistening straightaway.

Relatively few products of Colin Chapman ever raced at Riverside, and those that did rarely lasted the distance; some spindly component would break and fall off first, precipitating a crash. Which is precisely what happened on Turn 8 in 1962.

Worldwide, '62 was among the most deadly of all the Lotus campaigns, with the death count hitting four in just four months. Probably the least likely statistic was

Turn 8's. The deader was one Peter Hassler, Colin's very own L.A. distributor, who'd been out for a joyride when his Model 20 formula junior decided to jump on top of him. Of course once it struck the ground and did the standard Lotus breakup, Peter had no chance. Struggling from the wreckage, he stumbled 12 feet, then fell at Turn 8's exit and was no more.

Nobody bagged the evidence for an autopsy. No post-mortem was necessary. With Chapman cars there never were: everybody knew that, whatever the wreck, it had been precipitated by something fragile breaking.

Having at last hit the straightaway after successfully negotiating eight of Riverside's nine hungry corners, a race driver had a tendency to speed down the 5,650 feet reading a book, eating a sandwich, taking a nap, and finally grabbing a breath of relief. Doing that could get you annihilated.

Out on the back-straight in 1966, Ken Miles, at 47 the oldest and most accomplished hero chauffeur of FoMoCo's entire long-distance team, temporarily dropped his guard and had something go awry with one of the works J Cars during a speed test. He was carried off. Wanting to bury the scandal of its J Car disintegrating in a straight line, and to save face, FoMoCo next decreed that its works squad no longer would employ any race driver older than 40—clearly implying that Ken, its most successful gun, had been done in by all those extra years he was packing.

What a crock. Oldest member of the squadron he may have been, but he behaved as though he were the youngest. A nonsmoker and nondrinker, all bone and gristle, he looked more like a marathon runner than a marathon driver. Off at Daytona and Sebring and Le Mans, the other team members might be copping Zs between stints at the wheel; but Ken was always so wired that he never slept for 12-, 24-, or how many hours an enduro lasted.

He was always one of L.A.'s best. A former Tommy staff sergeant who'd expatriated himself from the UK and became a citizen just when the sports car boom hit, he was right in there among the other sports car racing lions Phil Hill, Dan Gurney, Richie Ginther, Bobby Drake, and Ronnie Bucknum; his rainy-day upset win at Pebble Beach, his wild exploits in his MG flying shingle, and his shellacking of world-class names at J. C. "Aggie" Agajanian's *Examiner* Grand Prix at Pomona were classic L.A. races, classic victories.

Alas and alack, Ken the champion sporty car pilot had another side. Among many candidates, he was the most arrogant, supercilious, even repulsive (this last epithet coming from Ken himself) character in all the village. A real bad actor. He stood accused of fudging tech inspections, hoodwinking flagmen, orchestrating illegal pit stops. Once at Palm Springs he bombed his car out of the joint, almost running down a rival driver. Yet another roar of anger went up after he created a hullabaloo charging through the pits of Pomona at fantastic speed. And regardless of the stunt or punishment meted out afterward, Ken defiantly employed his pleasing personality and sweet tongue to lordly maintain he'd done nothing wrong. Nothing fazed him.

His driving didn't deteriorate with age but improved. Needing a Shelby Cobra test and development pilot for his Anglo-American anachronism, Ol' Shel chose Ken. Next, FoMoCo asked him, aged 40-plus, to give international long-distance racing a whack. And what a gas he proceeded to have manhandling those heavy-duty Mk II trucks! In 1966, he was partnered with a popular Indy car celebrity from Texas, Lloyd Ruby, also an old man in his 40s, and between them they immediately won Daytona and Sebring. With Le Mans coming up, it next seemed that FoMoCo would issue orders guaranteeing Ken, its brilliant old timer, victory in the 24 hours along with the gift of the never-before-accomplished Daytona/Sebring/Le Mans hat trick. But guess again. Things were not all that ducky between FoMoCo and Ken. He had succeeded in irritating the team managers and, worst of all, had given a hard time to some of the corporate execs. It was these fiends who made the decision to shaft Ken without mercy. Through some hocus-pocus and micromanaging, the order came down for Miles to be Le Mans runner up rather than winner.

What was dumbfounding was that Ken hadn't blown off the order and double-crossed the suits by winning Le

Mans anyway, thereby guaranteeing himself a larger place in posterity than the one he occupies. He really should have, because after Le Mans he had about eight weeks to live, until that J Car junked beneath him right on Riverside's rear straightaway.

Turn 9, Riverside's last, was also its most deceptive—one of those irritating corners where however late you left the braking or delayed the downshifting, it never felt quite deep enough. Master of 9 was George Follmer, who one afternoon arrived at its mouth going 217 miles per hour in a panzer Porsche and somehow swung it all the way around without hitting anything.

Far less fortunate was that character from the Pacific Northwest who claimed to be short-listed by the FBI as D. B. Cooper, mysterious folk-hero skydiver, scuba diver, and jetliner highjacker. Unable to whoa his barreling Indy car in time to negotiate 9, he proceeded to round off all four edges after flipping purposely to get stopped.

Screwing up at Turn 9 meant risking one of two punishments, neither recommended. One was to sail over the fencing and go completely out of the ballpark. Another was to disappear into the deep yawning canyon on the corner's inside. A Corvette-racing pal of Davey MacDonald, Mike Jones, chose the former. Clearing the wall, he pancaked in upside down and burning and barely slipped out to jump clear in time. Watching the flames rise, Mike was seized with utter panic. He was a whole 23 years old. All the money he had in the world, and more, was tied up in his now-blazing chariot, and he was still in hock to the shylocks for $6,000 worth of payments. How would he ever be able to get them off his back? Suddenly Mike felt somebody hugging him; he also heard somebody sobbing with relief about him being physically unharmed. It was Davey MacDonald himself, who always took it bad when his buddies wrecked. By the time the fire department arrived, nothing was left of Mike's Corvette to extinguish. He never raced again, and it took years to settle with the shylocks.

Turn 9's inside canyon took its own deadly toll. A retired full bird air force colonel from Houston dumped his V-8 Genie down there and never emerged afterward. And a far more famous Houstonian, A. J. Foyt, came out of Turn 9's gorge a completely different driver and person following the terrible injuries he racked up when his Banjo Matthews door-slammer blew out the binders, then plunged to the canyon bottom going 150 miles per hour.

Fifteen hundred feet of worn blue-gray banked blacktop curving around to the right toward start and finish, Turn 9 was ringed on the outside by killer railing. A poor devil in the same Red "Dead" LeGrand car that earlier had almost terminated a cousin of Jim Culleton cashed in his chips there, right against that deadly railing. Afterward, to make 9 safer, Les Richter installed stronger plating, but an Indy car driver in a taxicab promptly died catching his head on it.

Turn 9's very worst year was 1962, when the Lotus marque and Chapman were themselves having an especially blooming campaign. Not only would Lotuses blitz Hessler, the pathetic distributor, but also the boy toy champions of Canada, Peter Ryan, and Mexico, Ricardo Rodriguez.

Yet another Lotus fatality at Riverside could well have helped provoke World War III. The victim was a Pat Piggot, one of the planet's fastest in a Chapman formula car, but who during the year's *Times* Grand Prix found himself in a sports car model 23 Lotus. Accelerating at peak revs off of Turn 9, something broke and the 23 jumped out of control; upon locating the Turn 9 wall it typically broke up like an egg, and nearly an hour was consumed cutting Pat out of the tatters.

The zinger was that Pat was kin through marriage to CIA spy-catcher John McCone. And subsequently, attending his stepson's funeral almost made McCone late to the burgeoning Cuban Missile Crisis.

Above and left: Ken Miles was just as quick in heavyweight Cobras and Ford prototypes as he was in popgun Porsches. Here he stalks a clumsy and bombastic—full of song and fury, signifying nothing—clump of big bores, prior to blowing all of them off and winning an *Examiner* Grand Prix. *Bob Tronolone*

CHAPTER FIVE

BATTLERS

Don't shoot Los Angeles!

—Ogden Nash, rhyme and meter quill

Scotty Cain: "Sons of bitches, when I lean on you, you'll take it and like it." All Scotty heaps automatically came equipped with bludgeon bars. *Joe Scalzo collection*

When Parnelli Jones came home to Los Angeles after quitting racing in the Indianapolis 500 at the age of only 34, all his competitors applauded with relief. Had P. J. not quit, and if they were ever going to beat him, they might have had to learn how to race like he did. And nobody except Parnelli had ever raced that hard. Well, perhaps Ralph "Scotty" Cain had. In a race with either of them, you were going to have to race harder than you ever had in your life.

JALOPY DERBY

P. J. and Cain were graduates summa cum laude of Jalopy Derby, a chunk of L.A. life brawling every Sunday afternoon at fortress Gardena Stadium, just up the block from Ascot Park.

Opposite: To preserve his bod in ugly head-ons like this, Scotty Cain at first tied himself into his jalopies with rope. But after angry fists came raining in on him before he could untie the knots, he abandoned the practice. *Joe Scalzo collection*

Gardena Stadium was the most low-end speed emporium in the whole Los Angeles basin, and every Jalopy Derby offered up the compelling spectacle of dozens of perfectly matched junks and heaps taking each apart while the poor-white grandstands roared.

But don't be misled. Jalopy Derby was a roughhouse race driver academy of hard-knocks teaching, red-meat aggression, and various other invaluable licks. What it really proved to be was an antidote to Kenny Purdy's utter nonsense literature about a race driver being an intelligent, articulate, refined, sophisticated, and brainy gentleman. And that racing itself was a cerebral activity as difficult to perform as, say, open-heart surgery. You had to spend a lifetime developing the maturity, sensitivity, and intellect required.

Of course all that was a bunch of crap, but L.A's snobbish cognoscenti lived and believed it. Jalopy Derby, to them, was an abomination so, of course, they missed the whole point of it, with its rogue's-gallery cast perfectly led by Parnelli and Scotty. Neither was a deep thinker or full of finesse. They were a fighting breed of race driver,

Scotty flinches as car owner Bill Clinton gives him a pre-race tongue-lashing about holstering his cowardice. *Joe Scalzo collection*

guys who went into racing not for the alleged glamour and glitter, but for the danger, excitement, fun, and more danger. They lived racing raw and thrived on it.

So if Jalopy Derby was all that hot, how come Parnelli was the only race driver to break out of it, graduate to Indianapolis, and become 500 champion?

Because the only racing activity that Jalopy Derby dignitaries truly seemed fit for was . . . Jalopy Derby. They were too tough for anything else. Physically manhandling their heaps had made them wide-shouldered, thick-chested, and thin-bellied. They were punch-first-and-ask-questions-later babies. Jalopy Derbies lasted barely 15 white-knuckle miles, yet Parnelli had schooled himself to race like that for 500. From the very first time it saw him, Indianapolis was frightened of him.

And it had a right to be, because in the beginning he ran right over all competition Jalopy Derby–style. He also decked people. Luckily for him, Parnelli had for a sugar daddy Aggie Agajanian, who was emperor of his own trash business and sprawling pig ranch, a ballyhoo merchant, and, most important, the big cucumber race car owner with the most Indy juice of anybody—and the 500 is always a juice race. Besides being available 24/7 to bail him out of trouble, Aggie played Pygmalion to Parnelli, forever smoothing the rough edges and mellowing him out so he could mingle with Hoosier society.

Had Scotty Cain—the original Jalopy Derby grad to hit Indianapolis—had somebody with Aggie's drag coaching and assistance, there's no telling how far he might have gone.

Instead, Scotty's initial visit to Indy in the mid-1950s, in hopes of realizing his dreams of getting his mitts on a Meyer-Drake roadster (one of the big cucumbers), was his last. Given his one chance, Scott fucked it up most magnificently.

His reputation as a Jalopy Derby goon who, in unruly duels, "leaned" on his competition, had preceded him. Stewards of the 500 were scared of Scotty on sight. Before ever getting to turn one Brickyard lap, Scotty was rebuked by a committee of the Indy powers-that-be, which ordered him to holster his Jalopy Derby licks. And especially to knock off that made-in-L.A. practice of leaning.

Responding, Scotty gave the committee a summation of his views: "Sons of bitches," he explained, "when I lean on you, you'll take it and like it."

Which got him forever banished back to L.A., although it didn't stop him from almost winning a 500-mile race right in the homeland. Let the Hoosier Clydes keep their brink rink: on Memorial Day, 1958, friendly Riverside Raceway was playing host to its own 500 miler, a madhouse sweepstakes of eight-ball monster iron flogged by a mad multitude of bad nicknames.

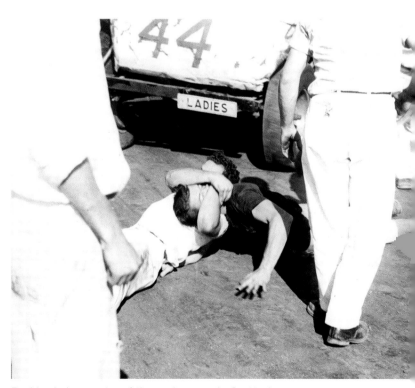

Besides being master of the sucker punch, Scotty, here on the bottom, was a proponent of professional rasslin' on television. As such, he was on familiar terms with such holds as the spoon grip, full nelson, Boston crab, Japanese arm bar, etc. Here he subdues another irate Jalopy opponent with the Indian death lock. *Joe Scalzo collection*

Laughing Harry E. Eisele used the racing *nom de guerre* "Bud Rose" to escape maternal detection. His big moment was winning a 500-mile hooligan show around Riverside Raceway, faking out Scotty in the bargain. *Joe Scalzo collection*

The starting field is oversubscribed, nearly 50 eight-balls strong. Many are real thrillers. The Purple People Eater, a big Dodge, seems to be generating the greatest din. Also handsomely acquitting themselves are assorted mastodon Chryslers, Caddys, and Pontiacs.

Spending six slogging hours going up, down, and over RIR's tricky kinks isn't going to be a sneeze for "Tiger" Valenta, "Full Race" Cummins, "Knothead" Heath, "Termite" Jones—raging sprint and midget thugs all. Their thing, usually, is turning hard left for 10 nerved-up miles. So, to mitigate the drudgery, the 500 is being conducted circle-track style, or counterclockwise. Which is thoughtful but demented. It means that Tiger, Full Race, Knothead, Termite, and friends will spend this waltz of 162 endless laps submarining their lumbering eight-balls downhill through the blind switchback esses. Plus, for an epilogue, they'll be treated to the fun of making 162 freefalling plunges off the lip of friendly Turn 1.

Quickly, though, it's apparent that rapidly coming to the front through unruly traffic and dislodging snail-stomachs from their positions is an amazing crossbreed of a mutant Kurtis Kraft big cucumber roadster with reverberating Buick audio blaring from eight festooning exhausts. This is Scotty.

You can take Scotty out of Jalopy Derby but not Jalopy Derby out of Scotty. Concerned that all these other strokers are dead-assing the 500, he decides to put on a snow.

Swing high, swing low; chop me off here, I'll lean on you there. And after Scotty has fired off his last carom shot, and he and the mutant hurtle clear of the wolf pack into the lead, the majority of other eight balls have paid the price of trying to keep up with him: they are pooping out, bleeding out, disintegrating with cases of mechanical avulsion. Scotty and his team are beginning to hallucinate about a $10,000 winner's payday.

But Scotty is accustomed to the nonstop battling, the essence of Jalopy Derbys. And, all by himself in the lead, he yearns for company.

Suddenly he finds it when the *Clark Gable Special* appears from nowhere to park on his ass. The Clark Gable Special, all thoroughbred coachwork and Meyer-Drake sound, is a famous old movie star—just about the only redeeming artifact from *To Please a Lady*, Gable's horrible Hollywood speed flick.

The catalytic agent responsible for taking a sham movie race car and turning it into the romping, raging real thing is Jiggler Gemsa. Being hip to the whereabouts of almost every worthy vehicle that had ever raced, Jiggler had known the Gable beauty had, for years, been at rest

Chrome dome bombhead Dickie Rathmann. Mr. Bad News.
Joe Scalzo collection

Rufus Parnelli Jones, aka "Ruf," aka "Parnelli." Fastest of all L.A.'s wheelhouse corps, he set race-driving standards nobody else approached. *Bob Tronolone*

inside a warehouse on a back lot of Metro Goldwyn Meyer. So he'd purchased it for the Riverside 500. Just one afternoon's worth of rehabilitation back at the Gemsa compound has made it like new.

Chauffeur of the Gable is one of Jiggler's oldest comrades in arms, "Bud Rose," also known as "Butch Rose" (not his real name either—the genealogy of L.A. race driver pseudonyms is confounding).

Jiggler is slick. Deciding playing head games with Scotty will provoke him into either blowing his mind or the Buick, Jiggler chalks up signal board messages instructing Bud/Butch to "Get Scotty."

Of course the boards aren't there for the benefit of cool old pro Bud/Butch, but for Scotty to read and get psyched out. Result: Scotty blows the line into the esses four laps in succession before the Buick gets away from him and he smears it along the Turn 6 railings hard enough to take himself out and lose his only opportunity to capture a 500-mile matinee.

Jiggler Gemsa's *Clark Gable Special* wins the 500 in a cakewalk—seven laps and 20 miles ahead of the first eight-ball runner-up. MGM subsequently threatens to drag Jiggler into court to sue his socks off for using Clark Gable's moniker without permission.

DAVEY

Guys who punch well are always interesting; and as fisticuffer and knuckle breaker, Scotty got into, and won, fights that would have killed most people.

Bombhead Dick Rathmann, also one very hard and bad baby, was among the best punchers going, not just in L.A. but probably the whole country.

After beginning to acquire tattoos at 14, he moved from teenager getting into rock fights in the dry L.A. riverbed to child race driver. Dick was always a nomad deluxe. Early on, he bailed out of L.A. to enlist in Al Capone's old Chicago and the Hurricane Racing Association, where he (and a softer younger brother, Jim) learned T-boning, short-braking, crooked scoring and rooked results—the whole lawless Hurricane menu. Lessons gleaned in that hoodlum academy stayed with Dick for life.

After participating in his first Indy 500, Dick decided that the Brickyard's meager prize money was a rip-off and ran off past the Mason–Dixon to race with the sots-with-steering-wheels and their taxicabs.

He led the South in death stares. Racing with a flat front tire at North Wilkesboro, North Carolina, he won anyway, holding off all opposition because everybody knew

Troy Ruttman, here aged all of 17. Rutt was the one Parnelli named as his inspiration and god. *Joe Scalzo collection*

he'd pound their brains soft if they dared pass him. Over time he organized his own cracker pit crew and appeared to be winning another big race, until making his final tire and gas stop and discovering his helpers prematurely celebrating victory with a demijohn of fermented corn liquor—with the cap off. They were fried. Afterward he did away with pit crews entirely. Instead, Dick invented his famous practice of stopping randomly in anybody's pit stall and threatening to beat the mortal crap out of the crew unless it serviced him with his rubber and gas.

Then he decided to depart taxicabs and parachute in on the Indy 500 once more. On various Memorial Days throughout the late 1950s and early 1960s, he had sat on pole position; become co-instigator of the biggest and most dramatic wreck in the annals of the big cucumber roadster; whacked a wall after the 500 was over; almost nailed the Brickyard's original 150-mile-per-hour lap; and once, during a stop, had his own pit crew—pit crews were his nemesis—set the race car on fire.

Dick's final Indy was the 1964. It was the final one for a lot of other drivers, too, especially all the ones barely escaping immolation in the second lap's gigantic crash and burn.

Starting the 500 at 12th, Dick, on the very first corner of the second lap, took a hard chop job off the 500's 14th-place starter, the L.A. sports car racer and Indy novice, Davey MacDonald—who was already all sideways in his red rear-engine Mickey Thompson flying bomb with sidesaddle fuel bags and tiny go-kart rubber. Then, following the chop, Dick observed Davey and the gasoline-laden Thompson continuing to go merrily about their business, throwing themselves sideways at more cars before disappearing into traffic.

Less than half a minute later, Dick rounded Turn 4 and found the front straightaway blocked by a firestorm three stories high. Braking to a safe stop, he was out of his big cucumber quickly—forget the fire, he intended to go find Davey and pound stitches into his skull as payback for the chop job. Dick, however, soon discovered he'd have to stand in line—three or four other drivers were also unhappy with Davey for racing like a sideways maniac, and wished to harm him.

However, there was no chance of more harm coming to Davey now. The instigator of the second lap mess had destroyed himself and the Thompson bomb in the raging holocaust. And he'd taken with him the poor, blameless

Dan Gurney burst onto the Los Angeles scene in 1957 and by 1959 was already rocketing Ferrari Formula Ones around Spa-Francorchamps and the Nürburgring. Danny was also one of Max Balchowsky's celebrity heroes, catching a gig racing mighty Ol' Yeller in a Riverside Grand Prix. Meaning it as praise, Gurney afterward remarked that if only Yeller had had modern disc brakes, instead of cheapskate drums, no sports car on the planet could have smoked it. *Bob Tronolone*

Eddie Sachs—he and his Halibrand-Ford out of L.A. trapped in the wrong place at the wrong time.

The following morning a sullen gray dawn broke over Indianapolis. Up and down pit road, tackle and equipment were getting broken down by silent mechanics with blank faces. Drifting among them was Kirby Avant, who'd worked with Davey at Shelby American

Nobody had ever before raced sports cars the way the Corvette swashbucklers did. Their inventory included wham-bam powerslides; roughhousing V-8 blasts; plunging swerves, slides, and desperation veers; even tattooing doughnut shaped wheel marks on each others flanks. Corvette racers played for keeps. *Bob Tronolone*

during the Cobra years, and who'd just spend a restless night without sleep. Broken by Davey's accident, and appalled by the absolute insensitivity of the business-as-usual males, Kirby passed a signaling blackboard and wrote up a remembrance:

To Davey—

I know a speedway in the sky

Where brave young drivers thunder by.

And all who love this racing game

Must know that fate may call their name.

In a perfect world, Kirb would have done well to have also remembered Eddie Sachs—taken out, after all, by Davey. Her elegy became famous nonetheless.

Back in L.A., at approximately the same time she'd been chalking it up (although the time change meant it was two hours earlier), the Memorial Day sports car races were getting flagged away at Santa Barbara. I was in Santa Barbara, and it was like being at a weekend-long wake. Santa Barbara, after all, had been one of Davey's favorite places, an airport track where the most radical member of the most far-out wing of fiberglass elephant Corvette racers tossed off at will the desperate veer, the hypnotic swerve, the shivering side-to-side plunge . . .

L.A. Corvette road racing: think Jalopy Derby with fiberglass and both right-hand and left-hand curves, plus barely 6 inches of recap rubber. Depending upon one's taste, it was either great or deplorable racing. On the one hand, all the wild men with their plastic cars and Eddie Cole V-8s deserved to be honored for making

Not only was Davey MacDonald a master of the impossibly sideways plastic pachyderm, but he knew more about what made the 'Vette go fast than General Motors itself. Travis Brown, background, and Butch Mueller, right, were his devoted aides-de-camp. *Joe Scalzo collection*

sports car racing less sissy. On the other hand, they could be slandered as a gang of hoodlums who raced like thugs.

Certainly nobody had ever road-raced the way they did: wham-bam power slides, roughhousing V-8 blasts, even tattooing doughnut-shaped wheel marks on each others' flanks when there wasn't room.

"Do you know how to fiberglass?" Davey once asked his understudy, the racing infantryman, Joe Freitas. When Joe shook his head no, Davey assured him, "You'll learn."

Charlatans around the country labored at cracking the code of racing the Corvette in the L.A. manner. And they never came close. One year I was out among the corners of Daytona's infield road course, checking out the Corvette talent, and audible above the din of all those lumbering, atrociously driven, plastic crates came an angry high-pitched buzzing sound not unlike a poisonous stinging insect. It was Jimmy Clark in his own tiny plastic projectile, one of Colin Chapman's Lotus Elite coupes. And by overdriving all the corners and passing on the outside, Jimmy was making every Corvette fool there look stupid. Great stuff, although it never could have happened in L.A. Scottish Jimmy was one tremendous throttle artist, an Indy 500 champ, world Formula 1 titlist, and fated to become Colin's biggest statistic. Yet out in L.A., Corvette guys would never have permitted him to dick around with them like that. They'd have swatted the Elite like a fly.

Davey was a shy but compelling character with crew cut, jut chin, and oversize, probing eyes staring out of a narrow face. He had pipe-stem arms and skeletal body. A bust from Dick Rathmann would have inflicted serious damage.

The bravest men on earth. No, not the Corvette daddies, but the sitting-duck corner flagmen from the Long Beach MG Club. *Bob Tronolone*

Idling at a hard 5,000 revs, any 283 Corvette with a Duntov camshaft and Bill Thomas blueprinting, porting, and polishing sounded like all the others. So friends and fans alike came to identify drivers by livery: jumpin' pumpkin orange meant Bobby Bondurant; metallic blue, Vince Mayell; gunmetal gray and black, Tony Settember; candy apple red, Rich Thorgrimson; blackjail black, Andy Porterfield; icebox white, Doug Hooper; and white and blue, master Davey MacDonald (#288), along with his protégé, the ex-infantryman, Joe Freitas. H. Dean Geddes leads here. *Bob Tronolone*

His destiny was set the day he was a high school freshman and taught himself how to jump the performance of his mother's DeSoto by rigging its heater hose to blast extra air into the carburetor.

From then on it was only a matter of locating the right set of racing wheels, and that search led to the Corvette. In the desert at Willow Springs he burst free of a torrid duel and captured one of the first Corvette shoot-outs he ever participated in.

Two seasons, countless Corvette wins, and much glory later, he began to attract the company of two sugar daddies wanting to help him. The first of them, Jim "Thanks a Million" Simpson, financed the construction of the Simpson Special, the swerving behemoth that forever established Davey's style. And the second, Ol' Shel, proposed paying Davey serious FoMoCo money if he'd abandon his Corvettes and come race the Shelby Cobra.

As a Chevrolet man and dedicated Ford hater, Davey was at first so horrified that he immediately rang his friends in General Motors high-performance to anxiously inquire if they'd equal Ol' Shel's financial offer and keep him in Corvettes. They would not. And so Davey had had no choice but to grudgingly accept FoMoCo's loot, to race the all-conquering Shelby Cobra, and over a crushing span of 14 months to have the bittersweet satisfaction of killing off the Corvettes that he inwardly wished he still were racing. During his glorious 14-month burst of almost nonstop winning, he became not L.A.'s greatest road-racer, but America's.

He won in good Cobras. He won in wounded Cobras. At Riverside for a *Los Angeles Times* Grand Prix, he was given custody of a King Cobra rear-engine that he liked even less than the standard Cobra front-engine. Its temp gauge pegged on its first lap. Continuing to hold his

Davey MacDonald winning a Grand Prix at Riverside. His rampaging King Cobra pegged its temperature gauge on the first lap and never got any hotter. And Davey lapped the field anyway. *Bob Tronolone*

throttle foot down anyway, Davey thought to himself, "This is easy. I'll get out of racing the fucker by letting it blow up." The rest of the field didn't know what hit them until he showed up and lapped them, molten mill notwithstanding. Sometimes I wonder if Davey drove Mickey Thompson's car the way he did on the opening lap of the 1964 Indy 500 in hopes of quickly blowing it up, too.

The Sunday following Riverside he won the Grand Prix at Laguna Seca as well. Yet despite all this, Davey never was fully assimilated in the Shelby American clan. He made Ol'Shel nervous. Never losing his hatred for the products of FoMoCo, the Cobra in particular, Davey was forever telling people that, compared to a Corvette, a Cobra was a real piece of crap with antique chassis that wasn't even American.

Then, for his ultimate act of defiance, Davey spent some of his race-winnings on a new Corvette Sting Ray, a flaming red one. And he continued driving it even after Ol' Shel promised him a free Cobra if he got rid of it. Not that he got to steer the Sting Ray that much. His driver's license usually was in the deep freeze, so Sherry, his loving spouse and soon-to-be widow, chauffeured him.

Those last months of Davey's life were full of still more sugar daddies squabbling over how his career must be divvied up. Lincoln-Mercury gifted him with one of its factory taxicabs for a Golden State 400 at Riverside, and after Davey took a close runner-up with his transmission locked up in third, L-M promised him a taxicab with a better gearbox for the Daytona 500. Then a marine sugar daddy made plans to have Davey race a jumpin' canoe—a big 406-inch cigarette boat—at the Salton Sea. And then the killer:

After doing Nassau Speedweeks that December for Ol' Shel, Davey got home and was overwhelmed by Mickey Thompson playing sugar daddy and telling Davey he really dug his driving, and that if he wanted it a brand-new Indy car was all ready for the 1964 500.

Finis.

RAJO AND THE ACE OF EIGHTS

In August 1965, total rebellion was raging in the ghetto of Watts, and the rioting ultimately would ravage 11 square miles, kill 34 people, maim 1,000, and cost insurance companies millions in property damage. It was also

Above and left: Prelude to a holocaust. Davey and Mickey Thompson together at Indianapolis, 1964. *Greg Sharp*

things cooled off, he explained. Just now, Whitey ain't welcome.

Willie was one of the hero athletes of Ascot Park's jousts on Sunday evenings, nights when promoter Harry Schooler pushed a ragged competition called figure-eight racing: dilapidated and ancient Buicks and Chryslers careening around an infield track shaped like an 8, everybody crisscrossing and threatening to collide with rending impact right in the middle of the intersection.

Such wild-west motoring required talent, just as Jalopy Derby did, and during its semiorganized beginnings, figure-eight's hottest proponents were a gang of obviously dirt-poor blacks, including Willie, who seemed totally fearless when it came to asserting right-of-way privileges across the intersection.

Yet their reflexes, eyesight, and judgment were stunning, because I can't really remember any of them ever having an accident. They hauled to Ascot with their old bangers chained to the backs of trucks with impossibly pitched ramps. Skinflint promoter Harry, as an economy measure, switched off all electricity the moment Ascot racing ended, and I used to marvel at the skill of Willie

the summer I'd made an appointment to visit Watts and finally interview Willie Kimbrough, L.A.'s most spectacular figure-eight driver.

Not particularly wishing to get taken down by a sniper's bullet, get lit up by a Molotov cocktail, hit with a brick, or doubled up by a cop's truncheon to the gut, I was relieved that every time I telephoned Willie, he warned me off. Come to Watts and interview him when and the others grappling their rattletraps back up their pitched ramps in total darkness for the haul back to Watts or whatever other end-of-the-earth slum they came from.

One of the questions I'd intended to ask Willie was if he'd ever heard of Rajo Jack.

Rajo Jack was the nomadic, all-but-forgotten black driver who was a pioneer to all his brothers, and was racing on dirt tracks before and after World War II. Watts, his residence, was then named Mud Town. And Rajo's true name, his first wife once told me, was Dewey Gatson. At first he called himself Jack DeSoto, but when Joe Jagersberger, the father of the Rajo cylinder head for Model T Ford, made him the L.A. distributor and salesman, he became Rajo Jack. This was in the early 1930s, before injuries and wear and tear set in, and he still was a muscular and handsome man with a narrow clipped moustache and a lean and trim Dalmatian dog mascot.

He loved talking and embellishing, variously telling people he was a Native American, a West Indian, and once claimed to be the renegade son of a state senator. Of course it's possible he wasn't embellishing at all but unsuccessfully trying to muddle his ancestry, because his color excluded him from getting to race at the place he most wanted to be—Indianapolis.

Los Angeles was almost equally racially backward yet at least permitted Rajo to compete as an outlaw driver. It was, however, a struggle. Frequently he scuffled for a living operating a steam-clean rack, hauling oranges, collecting scrap, running a hen ranch, and being a hustling showman. At Atlantic Speedway he would challenge spectators to come down from the grandstands and then race and beat them around the track with his clapped-out Miller in reverse or while wearing a blindfold.

He was a constant traveler, as restless as a gypsy. He raced in Idaho, Nevada, Arizona, and all over California—most notably at Silver Gate, where he was the track's best driver, and at Oakland, on whose bankings he once won a big meet and purchased a new truck with the prize money.

This may well have been the same race where his wife and his mechanic Herman Giles had taken turns driving the tow vehicle all night from L.A., while Rajo worked in back by flashlight repairing his race car, which had gotten wrecked just the previous day.

The holocaust's forgotten second victim, ex–big cucumber king, Eddie Sachs. A floral bouquet from Sherry MacDonald was displayed at his obsequies. *Bob Tronolone*

So many great L.A. race drivers, and so little space to document them all. This is belly tanker boy Leroy Neumeyer, who left the salt flats to have an astounding second existence as a dirt track racer, rim-riding Langhorne. Never in his career did he get to chauffeur a race car without its flaws, yet he always charged hard anyhow. *Greg Sharp*

He was a natural mechanic but was considered an unlucky and somewhat accident-prone driver. He was strong—Scotty Cain strong—and could single-handedly pick up the front of a 1,500-pound sprint car, could miss three nights of sleep and still race creditably, and was so indifferent to injury he used to cauterize his racing wounds with chewing tobacco.

Following the war, he took a bad spill at Kelly the Shiv's three-corner speedway in San Diego. He was no longer as fast as before, and his dying Miller began swallowing so much grit from running in the middle of dirt-track packs that only the hottest spark plugs in Jiggler Gemsa's toolbox could keep it from blowing up. And eventually it did blow up.

By then, all of Rajo Jack's racing hurts had cost him an eye and given him an arm as badly bent as Ol' Shel Shelby's—he could barely reach the steering wheel. Also, he had found religion and turned a little strange. Telling a friend he was going to the market, he might instead drive clear to New Jersey, immediately turning

around and heading home. Finally, and fatally, in the middle of the California desert in 1956, he suffered what was reported to be a cerebral hemorrhage. He'd been in the middle of another of his cross-country hauls at the time.

The riots roared and burned on for another five days. Every morning I woke up thinking the rebellion was over and I'd get my chance to interview Willie and ask about Rajo Jack. But the city skyline was still aflame and the sirens of fire trucks and police cars endless. Ultimately, the insurrection got stomped out by the National Guard and the crack skullbuster squad of the Los Angeles Police Department.

When the churning streets at last went quiet, I tried Willie Kimbrough's phone number many times. I only got a disconnect tone. And I never again saw him race the Ascot figure-eights. Watts had claimed 34 deaths, but I never worked up the nerve to check out the records to discover if Willie's was among them.

When Clay Smith and Bill Stroppe assembled wheelmen for their Lincoln town cars in the fantastic Mexican Road Race, Carrera Panamericana, they collected, left to right, Chuck Stevenson, Jack the Bear Faulkner, Jack McGrath, and Johnny Mantz, who once worked in a traveling circus. Amazing L.A. talents all. *Greg Sharp*

BUCKNUM

As great a racing milieu as Los Angeles offered, there were always ambitious dreamers out here who couldn't wait to split the scene and go become big shots at Indy, or at international long-distance sports car racing, or even at Formula 1. That many of these dreamers, including Ronnie Bucknum, ended up living their dreams was more proof of L.A.'s potency.

Ronnie died in 1992, just 18 days after his 56th birthday, and it wasn't an easy exit. Body burned out by years of relentless boozing, he was a victim of acute diabetes, which first knocked out his eyesight and then got the rest of him. Afterward, there was a Bucknum mystery: Why did somebody having a quarter-century's worth of fun racing sports cars, Formula 1s, Indy cars, and TransAm sedans feel the need to medicate with the sauce?

Nothing in the family tree suggested that Ronnie's destiny involved mashing throttles or throwing speedshifts. L.A.-born Ronnie came from a long strain of quiet, steady engineers and surveyors who could do anything from laying out a housing subdivision, to plumping and stringing a downtown freeway. And because it was a decent way to bankroll his early racing, Ronnie, too, got into the surveyor's dodge. He proved quite good at it. I recall driving with him on the Hollywood freeway and having him point out an overpass and saying modestly that he was the party who'd laid the sucker out.

At Pomona in the fall of 1956, the engine-division winner at the wheel of a Speedster Porsche was a Ronald

Something in the manner of Frank Lockhart, John Morton abandoned his birthplace in the nowhere precincts east of the Mississippi River to migrate west and hot-wire himself into L.A.'s soaring racing milieu. After risking his bones campaigning a Lotus Model 7, John and his talent bloomed and he spent a merry life in single-seaters, sports cars, and sedans; on roads and ovals, sprints, and marathons; with big scores at Daytona, Sebring, and Le Mans. *John Morton*

Bobby Drake was so ridiculously fast he could have won races anywhere in the world in any sort of race car. But he had the L.A. evil and couldn't bear leaving. *Bob Tronolone*

J. Bucknum. It was the first Sunday main event he ever participated in and where his extraordinary career began. For the next seven seasons, variously in an AC Bristol (later banned as a high-compression piston bamboozler), a dreamy blue Austin-Healey, a sensational B-model MG, and occasionally a celebrity start in a Max Balchowsky Ol' Yeller, the surveyor/driver proved so swift that Honda of Japan, the motorbike champion that was moving from crotch-rockets to four wheels, named Ronnie-san captain of their new Formula 1 team.

Well accustomed to celebrating the rites of passage of previous L.A. dreamers, *Motoracing* gave Ronnie the cover, and Editor Gus Vignolle was in fine, volcanic form: "We have been pumping for Ronnie Bucknum for a long, long time. He's out of the league of the honky-tonk

Constructing behemoth taxicabs and off-roading tanks wasn't enough for busy Bill Stroppe. He occasionally performed race-driving duty in this haulin'-tail flathead Merc Kurtis-Kraft. *Greg Sharp*

racing we see here. He's overdue for the Big Tent. Let's hope that this is the Open Sesame to the GP circuit for Ronnie . . . Salud!"

Three seasons, 10 starts, and only four championship points later, Ronnie was out of Formula 1 and Honda was farming out its team. Of course, losing the Honda ride could have landed him in serious trouble, except that this was the era of FoMoCo's ongoing attack on Ferrari. Ronnie simply moved over to the big day-and-night marathons at Sebring and Le Mans; employed by both Shelby American and Holman Moody, he was partnered with a solid L.A. dream block that included Dan Gurney, Phil Hill, Bobby Bondurant, Richie Ginther, and Ken Miles. And after Ford's money tap at last got turned off, Ronnie headed for Indianapolis and Michigan International Raceway, where in October of 1968 he joined 25 other nervous participants on the steeply pitched bankings. He wasn't even in a front-running car, yet won anyway.

His whole career might next have taken a different shape had he not fallen into the catastrophe of too much drink. He couldn't stay off the stuff, even though the L.A. dream continued bestowing to him its usual charms and good fortune: not only did Ronnie have the special opportunity to keep going and become a marque name in Indy cars, but Roger Penske was beginning to employ

continued on page 114

Ronnie Bucknum moved from heel-and-toeing AC Bristols around L.A. municipal airports and parking lots to captaining the first Honda Formula One team at Monte Carlo and Monza. His reputation grew as the L.A. invader who beat the Indy toughs at their own game, blowing everyone off in a supersonic battle across the walls of Michigan International Speedway. *Bob Tronolone*

Both Ronnie and his high-stepping AC Bristol caught the eye of Shelby. First Ol' Shel used the AC to create his Cobras; and then, among many hot dogs, he employed Ronnie to race them. *Bob Tronolone*

"L.A. race drivers are everywhere," lectured a skeptical racing chief mechanic. "They're like leaves on trees." Perhaps so, but there were many colorful buds in the L.A. garden. Cat-with-nine-lives Mike Mosley, timid and troubled, survived many wipe-outs such as this one, afterward briefly disappearing to reset his batteries before roaring back, fighting fit again. Mike, eerily introverted, won five career Indy car matches; plus, he possessed the natural skill to go fast whether a race car was right or not. Something was ticking along with Mike nonetheless. Those closest to him occasionally wondered if he was counterphobic—somebody who raced because he only felt good when all the fear and risk scared him stupid. That was a hard one. Under attack from personal demons, Mike perished in a brutal highway smash, his head full of Mexican laughing tobacco.
Bob Tronolone

1

2

3

4

5

6

7

8

9

10

Eastern European racing radio show host, Frank "Mr. A" Alten interviewed L.A.'s fastest. Here Knothead Allen Heath is made unconscious by Frank's strange Transylvanian tones.
Joe Scalzo collection

Continued from page 111
him and made Ronnie a member of the Penske team that won the 24-Hours of Daytona. But he blew it all off for the booze. It got so bad that during the months of his last Indy 500, mechanics had to bang on the motel door to rouse him from his morning stupor.

Incredibly, he still hadn't run out of steam, nor had the L.A. dream. Ronnie went to AA and put the long dance with alcohol behind him. He knew how good he was, and all that he'd accomplished, and where he'd been. Before cottoning to the grim fact that the physical damage he'd done to himself was going to kill him, he acquired yet another racing gig—perhaps his dozenth—this time with a Mustang team in a radial tire series. It was small bore compared to Formula 1 and Indianapolis, but Ronnie—ever the lucky L.A. dreamer—seemed certain that it was going to lead to something bigger. "Listen. Nobody ever got more breaks than I did," he bravely declared right at the end, dying like a man.

STEVE

Sal Scarpitta, the racing artist who used to reside in the Hollywood Hills right below the Hollywood sign, talked about a contradiction of living out here: "Hollywood is part of Los Angeles. But Hollywood is the culture of movies and land of make-believe. And our race drivers don't live within the make-believe, but with tremendous reality."

Certain local matinee idols, who portrayed race drivers in various Hollywood turkeys, later ditched the make-believe to attempt racing for real. To disastrous effect, mostly. Wally Reid, handsome devil and morphine freak from the roaring 1920s, made hundreds of silents, many about racing. Reid decided he was a race driver himself, had his studio barely block him from racing a Duesenberg at Indy, and, for an epilogue, got stuck in an asylum and died raving mad . . . Jimmy Dean and his Spyder Porsche hurtled north for a race meet in Salinas, but in the California 41 crossroads collided terminally with Donald Turnupseed . . . and Tom Pittman, budding stud of television, died in the wreckage of his overturned racing Glochner Porsche in the Hollywood Hills. Afterward, the totaled Glochner got taken up for restoration by Frank "Mr. A" Alten, Tom's father and the sage of L.A. racing radio broadcasting. Semicommunicating via a heavy Transylvanian accent, sometimes you'd listen to Frank for an hour without understanding a word. I thought it sick that a parent would make a shrine out of the automobile that destroyed his son. I hate race cars that kill people.

And finally Steve McQueen, wooden actor but cool bad-ass, overobsessed while making *Le Mans*, his big racing movie, and proceeded to flush his marriage, career, and health.

Steve in his big decades, the 1950s and 1960s, really was the ultimate refrigerated bad hombre of Los Angeles. Desert racing was alive and wide open. During any of those crazed motorcycle free-for-alls across the rolling Mojave to the smoke bomb, Steve, packing 400 pounds of desert sled between his legs, constantly was up front. Indeed, he was one of the very best, and a motorcycle scene purposely got written into *The Great Escape* to take advantage of his skills—even though a double, an L.A. stuntman named Bud Ekins, was imported to perform the movie's big jump. Bud, who was among Steve's best pals, also stunt-drove for the actor during *Bullitt*'s hyperactive, 6-minute-and-40-second car chase up and down San Francisco skip-ramp avenues. Making the movie an even better all-L.A. story yet, *Bullitt*'s dueling, bashing green 390 Mustang Ford GT and black Magnum Dodge Charger got prepped by Max Balchowsky himself.

Steve made a fast start in sports car racing. First in production slugs, but later in one of Chapman's ridiculously fast and fragile Lotus Model X1s, he made Jimmy Dean's earlier attempts look childish.

Sebring's 12 hours of 1970 became his great moment. Amongst the usual international field, which included a full factory team of Ferraris, Steve and a cosmetics heir were co-drivers of a somewhat elderly Porsche that was no great chariot of either beauty or speed. Increasing the odds in his disfavor, Steve had damaged a couple of bones on a dirt bike the week before, arriving in Florida with his left foot and ankle locked in plaster.

Cast and all, he still drove for 3 out of the 12 day-and-night hours, including double-clutching and braking in a storm. Out of 68 starters, he and the cosmetics heir finished second to three Ferrari drivers, one of them Mario Andretti. And had Mario not gone berserk at the certain humiliation of being beaten at Sebring by some phoney-baloney cinema ham, and not gone on a win-it-or-wear-it binge in the final hour, Steve surely would have won.

With an ego-pumping boost like that, he was hot to begin filming *Le Mans* when he hit France that June. Shooting began, and from the beginning, he was fanatical about not bringing anything fraudulent to the screen.

But he still lacked a librettist to hang together all the ever-accumulating thousands of feet of film on raw racing. His money men would fly in and ask how things were going. Steve, in response, would screen hours and hours of in-your-face-racing. Afterward the money men would enthusiastically chorus: "Great! But now what?"

The inevitable occurred. *Le Mans* was costing 100 Gs a week and insufficient progress was occurring. Following a series of tense meetings on the set, and amidst insider reports that he was being replaced by Robert Redford, Steve flew off to Morocco for a weekend breather.

Returning, he agreed to forfeit all creative control of *Le Mans*. New directors and producers were recruited, and from then on it was just a matter of everybody saying, let's hose down this dog and go home.

Le Mans at last opened in Indianapolis to tie in with the 500. It was the worst possible setting for a movie about sports car racing, but the choice wasn't Steve's—by then he had nothing to say about anything. He never made it to the premier at all.

So *Le Mans* bombed. But what a movie it could have been, had its subject been the *filming* of *Le Mans*. "We don't plan," Steve had declared at a press conference, "to make a film about some race driver sleeping with another race driver's wife." Which begs the question of how well *Le Mans* might have been received had it been about

actors sleeping with the wives of other actors, and vice versa . . . as actually occurred.

As revealed in the memoirs of the dancer Neile McQueen Toffel, the actor's ex-wife, the strain of *Le Mans* was so debilitating that Steve was battling stress with a pleasing but ruinous diet of loose doll faces and blow. So in the subsequent showdown between husband and wife that not even the ugliest Hollywood flicker would attempt, Neile—herself high strung and sexy—erupted with a confession of a hot dalliance of her own with some hunk of a foreign dream-boy.

It was the end. Steve flipped out. By Neile's account, he whipped out a revolver and demanded the name of her lover, in an unsuccessful attempt to add him to the cast of *Le Mans* so that Steve could involve him deliberately in a disfiguring wreck.

Steve was godfather to one of Ronnie Bucknum's sons. His early death to cancer was as pathetic as Bucknum's, yet he handled it bravely—one cool badass to the end. He left us way too young, just as Ronnie did, just as Davey did, and just as poor, poor Eddie Sachs did.

Son of a bitch.

You seldom find his name in any of the anthologies, but L.A.'s hardest-racing chauffeur, horsepower-for-horsepower, was volcanic Frank Monise. He road-raced nothing larger than 91 cubic inches, and was the unholy terror of the small-bore world, battling harder than all big-car chauffeurs combined. Flyin' Frank's licks and riffs could slay you. Lack of horsepower can be tricky, providing false security, but with his hot blood and cool brain, Frank always stayed on top of it—except once. He dropped his concentration just long enough to dump and have to be rescued from the wreckage by course marshalls wielding axes. *Frank Monise*

CHAPTER SIX

SUGAR DADDIES

There are more morons collected in Los Angeles than in any place on earth.

—H. L. Mencken, op. cit.

Its flyweight aluminum skin is one-of-a-kind coachwork hand-formed by Frank "Willie" Sutton. Its custom steering seat was occupied by the celebrity likes of Carroll Shelby, Dan Gurney (here), Tony Settember, and poor, over-his-head newspaper dealer and future corpse, Ron O'Dell. With a rap sheet like that, no wonder Frank Arciero grieves that he ever let this legend-streaked Ferrari 4.9 get away. *Bob Tronolone*

January, the cold winter of 1964: Outdoors, Los Angeles is storming and raining. Indoors, my road-racing Honda Super Hawk and I are domiciled together in a grubby grotto, whose props consisted of a telephone, a wind-up Victrola for listening to jazz, a stack of Dunlop Green Spot rubber, a case of Castrol R lubricant, an oil drip pan for the Honda, and an unmade bed to lay on top of as I recover from my the latest assault-and-battery job.

This lovely little bungalow, the Tarantula Arms (actually named the Bella Vista Terrace), is located due east of Pasadena at the mouth of a firetrap canyon on the lower flanks of the often-fiery San Gabriel Mountains. Once an Irving Gill classic, now it is in such total ruin

Opposite: Davey MacDonald hones his Corvette moves in No. 00, prior to graduation to the rugged Simpson Special of sugar daddy Jim Simpson. *Bob Tronolone*

that when I offer to pay money to live here, the guy who manages the Bella Vista Terrace is overcome with gratitude. He even meets my request to quarter the Super Hawk inside.

Various things consume me: becoming a motorbike champion as quickly as possible; remembering to change the dressing on my leaking elbow; smashing out of the plaster of Paris cast trapping my broken foot; and, crucially, locating a crazy sugar daddy to go to Yamaha International and buy me a model TD-1, one of the hot little two-strokes that have rendered my Honda obsolete.

Chettie Baker is coming out of the gramophone, his voice assuring me, "It could happen to you." I don't believe him.

Whereupon it does happen to me. The phone rings, and it is my old pal Neil "Peachtree" Keen, a prominent member of the two-wheel danger gang running the curves without brakes at Ascot Park. Peach's instructions

Willow Springs Raceway, the dream works where Tony Parravano made the wildest wishes of L.A.'s wannabe race drivers come true. *Joe Scalzo collection*

are that I make myself and my sore body parts presentable by drying out the elbow, taking a chainsaw to the cast, and in the morning gassing it across Antelope Valley to the Tehachapi crucible of Willow Springs, nine corners and 2.5 miles. Yamaha International is itself playing sugar daddy and holding auditions for players for the season's TD-1 blacktop squad.

I am ashamed of myself for forgetting that this is Los Angeles, where wonderful sugar daddies who commit seemingly irrational acts of largesse for the village's racers—whether two wheels or four—are always around.

In fact, during the prior decade, Willow was already serving as Tony Parravano's private auditioning grounds, back when Tony was playing L.A. sugar daddy, filling positions on his mysterious million-dollar scuderia. A shadowy building contractor and secretive businessman, Tony, before he abruptly disappeared, had the true Italian passion for racing: exotic red toys he passed around, included something like 13 Maserati sports cars and Formula 1s and 14 Ferraris—one of which bore the designation 4.9, the hottest Ferrari number going.

During the go-go-go Parravano days, you'd see everybody from Indy 500 winners to sports car champions trying out, hoping to claim a ride. Well, at Willow for the Yamaha International workouts, matters were standing-room-only also.

Frank Arciero cuts up with multi–Indy 500 winner Rick Mears. *Joe Scalzo collection*

Frank: "You work your ass off, and then you die." *Joe Scalzo collection*

All sorts of lively personalities were parachuting in. These guys weren't clowns. Eddie Wirth, a future sprint car champion of the California Racing Association, was bending his 6-foot frame around a TD-1; Dickybird Newall, later to draw slammer time, was lapping very fast; as was Prince Albert Gunter; and, of course, Peachtree.

Under the desert sun was a whole *fleet* of TD-1s, maybe two dozen of them, white streamlinings and blood-red gas tanks gleaming. I got aboard one, took it down Willow's hammerhead downhill, cruised in and out of tightening Turn 9, and was captivated. What an ax! Nobody at Yamaha International seemed to know or care what was happening to all its TD-1s, so I steered mine off the racetrack straight to my red panel truck, an old Chevrolet, where I ramped it into the back. And before anybody could begin shouting, I then boogied out of there with my new TD-1.

Nine months later, when I returned it to Yamaha International with thanks, the TD-1 and I had gotten the company ink at all the local L.A. meets, plus up north at Vacaville and Cotati, as well as in Florida, Ohio, Illinois, Iowa, Kansas, and even Tecate, Mexico. For eight glorious months I led the free-wheeling life of the itinerant motorcycle racer. The binge had fed the rat and now I was wrapping up my racing. Later, I felt terrible when I discovered that the sugar daddy executive responsible for the Yamaha auditions had gotten fired. But so it goes with sugar daddies. Tony Parravano wound up losing everything, too.

At first there'd been no stopping his sugar daddy ways. He neglected the construction business and everything. But in 1958, Scuderia Parravano tanked, and all of that fine Tony machinery got put up for auction. Tony went missing. Nobody ever heard from him again. Street talk had him being a criminal entrepreneur with juice from the Mafia.

High praise, but in reality the enemy that ruined him was the same one that took out Lance Reventlow: the Internal Revenue Service. On the run from the IRS, Tony plunged from uncommon sugar daddy to commonplace tax dodger.

MANTIENTI FORTE

"I was the last one to see Tony Parravano alive," Frank Arciero informed me in that harsh and scratchy Monte Cassino accent of his.

It was 1989. I was doing research for a magazine article about Frank, the L.A. building contractor and sugar daddy from Orange County who'd followed Tony. I was riding shotgun, Frank was at the wheel of a knockabout Jeep with 87,000-plus miles on its clock, and swirling along beneath us was California Five, the main north–south alley. We were on our way to the San Joaquin Valley and the $10 million winery Frank had built with construction company profits.

The author and his hijacked Yamaha TD-1. It turned into his flying carpet to races in six states, one foreign country, and for six lovely months turned him into a first-class tramp motorbike racer. *Joe Scalzo collection*

Left and below: Davey and Thongs Burrell brainstorm, stroke, and sort out the Simpson. *Nat Reeder*

"Tony and I were having dinner together at Dino's, Dean Martin's restaurant on the Sunset Strip," Frank went on, "the same place where Tony had introduced me to Sophia Lauren, who called me '*paesano, paesano,*' because we both come from Monte Cassino. So after dinner, we say good night, and the next morning police found his Cadillac abandoned. Then the FBI called me. Nobody has seen him since. I don't know, a while back somebody said Tony's in South Africa."

Frank maneuvered the jeep into the fast lane.

"I'm uncomfortable now," he explained. "My back's kicking up again. My regular chiropractor is out of town, and people are telling me I'm crazy driving an old Jeep to the winery when I could be flying. Or, people say, drive your Testarossa. I do drive it—I love Ferraris—but recently I got stopped for going 140 miles per hour, and the cop only wrote me up for doing 85, but I was sweating. With this Jeep I can relax."

The Jeep had climbed through some mountains and we were near the community of Gorman. "You hungry?" Frank asked. "I always stop here." He parked in the restaurant parking lot of a Caravan Inn, we went inside and ate quickly, and then got back into the jeep and drove off.

Now we were rolling across Turnupseed crossroads, Frank settled in the seat, and I was reminded of a midnight three decades earlier and my adventure with Bruce Burness, the late Jim Culleton, a Shelby American station wagon, an instant-whip trailer, and a King Cobra.

"This is where Jimmy Dean got killed," Frank remarked. "I knew him. Or, at least I met him once. That was again through Parravano.

"I first met Tony right after the war in Detroit, where I'd ended up while my family was emigrating to the U.S. My father was working on the Plymouth assembly line days and doing construction work nights. I never had any formal schooling and, in Detroit, went straight to work digging sewer lines. The deeper under the ground you went, the more money you got paid, so I dug pretty deep. One night the damn tunnel caved in and my brother and I got stuck. It's why I'm still bent. I took the compressor that ran the jack hammer and disconnected the hose to build up air. My brother and I were saying Hail Marys through all four of the hours it took to get us out.

"Anyway, Tony already had his construction business and asked me to join him in Los Angeles, where he put me to work building homes for aircraft workers out by LAX. Pretty soon I had my own general contractor's license and was starting my own company.

"Tony was crazy about racing. He made *me* crazy about racing. This one day he came by my house and said he was taking me to the sports car races at Palm Springs, and that's where I saw and heard my first Ferrari. I had to have one, and soon did—a little two-liter Mondial. But my business was starting to take off, and the bonding company wouldn't let me race it.

"By then Tony himself was really starting to collect the Ferraris and Maseratis. My favorite was his 4.9, a 1954 Ferrari Monza. It had been supposed to go to the Mexican Road Race, and then Tony had gotten hold of it. Lots of different drivers were in and out of it. And when all of Tony's stuff went up for auction, I bought it. It was how I got into racing."

I told Frank I well remembered this particular 4.9. And how accident-prone it had been.

At Palm Springs, it was in the middle of the celebrated starting line contretemps that delivered a battering to its big-ticket chauffeur, Ol' Shel. Afterward, Jack "Willie" Sutton had had to be brought in to create a whole new aluminum body. Later, at Riverside, it took straight up its exhaust pipe a hurtling Pontiac-powered Aston Martin, raced by a nearsighted plumber from San Jose; this time the 4.9's big-ticket driver getting clobbered was Dan Gurney. Following that farce, an unlucky beggar named Ron O'Dell was assassinated on account of the 4.9. By then, Frank had long since parted with it, but still was kicking himself for allowing it to get away from him. Circa 1989 it was supposed to be part of a private Japanese collection.

During the 1960s and 1970s, Frank overspent while remaining among L.A.'s last sugar daddies and taking care of race drivers he liked, not all of them L.A. issue. Owner of dozens and dozens of fast chugs, his most successful was a Colin Chapman Model 19 sports car, a vehicle so coveted that every discipline of racer from world titlists of Formula 1, to champions of back-it-in sprint car racing, were fighting to occupy its wheelhouse.

For the 1980s, Frank had decided to expand and become sugar daddy of Indianapolis. Now he was losing interest in that. Unfair Advantage Penske had succeeded in changing the Indy 500 from an art into a business—an insanely expensive, terminally greedy business. A race driver required a corporation now, not a sugar daddy.

"I still love racing," Frank was saying, "but I could never get in as deep as Parravano did and lose my business." By then we were pulling into the Arciero winery and confronting lush vineyards and verdant rolling hillsides.

"*Mantienti forte*—be strong," Frank concluded. "You work your ass off and then you die."

"Which one of your old race cars do you miss the most?" I asked.

Being a Max Balchowsky invention, the Simpson was alchemy itself, blending bric-a-brac borrowed from Studebaker, Jaguar, Morris Minor, Pontiac, and Buick (naturally). Risking heresy with this Chevy-based product, Max also tweaked the Simpson with a hood scoop off a T-Bird. *Joe Scalzo collection*

He shot me a don't-be-stupid glare. "What the hell do you think? That Parravano 4.9."

FON AND LUIGI

He never should have stopped to romance the doll face!

The sexual gymnast and rascal Fon de Portago, the Marquis de Portago, was famous for racing factory Ferraris all day, fucking all night, and finally—and most famously of all—for his violent apocalypse during the Mille Miglia of 1957, Italy's final Mille Miglia.

He burst out of Brescia at dawn, 12 wicked Ferrari cylinders firing banshee bolts of bang off graffiti-smeared stone walls. Rocketing along the Adriatic shore, everything was still going to plan until the crossover at Rome, where Fon noticed a member of his floating harem of doll faces, a burnt-out blond movie actress, waving at him from the crowd. The fool's brain truly was hard-wired to his dick, so Fon could not resist coming to a smoking halt in the streets of the eternal city to hungrily toss a lip-lock on her.

Was the tongue-job worth it? Hopefully yes, because it ended up killing him. While hauling the mail across the Po Valley—driving the Ferrari like an utter madman to make up the lost time—a wheel separated from the axle and he was off the road and into the spectators. Immediately wiped out were 11 spectators, Fon's ride-along passenger, Fon himself, and the Mille Miglia.

His Ferrari too was largely destroyed, but its heart, the big screaming V-12, survived. Accordingly, and not so long afterward—when L.A.'s big cucumber roadster boys with their intimidating moves invaded Monza for the Race of Two Worlds—Italian honor was mostly to be upheld by an intimidating Ferrari single-seater superpropelled by Fon's old mill. The vehicle's chauffeur, law school-trained Luigi Muss, proceeded to boldly rim the topmost line of the bankings at almost 3 miles a minute, 12 pulsating cylinders talking and ginning; afterward, the appreciative L.A. boys rewarded Luigi with the sobriquet, "bravest man in two shoes." Next, Luigi took Monza pole position, soundly blowing off all Meyer-Drakes. And he and Fon's former engine were further destroying them in the Race of Two Worlds until heat chocked the Ferrari to silence.

The immortal engine got its last, best hoorah in Los Angeles later that same winter. Needing heavy troops to crush the Reventlow Scarabs, and taking no chances that his existing stable of caterwauling flying V-12s would lay down to some pushrod L.A. hot rod, the town's Ferrari distributor and sugar daddy, Johnny von Neumann, imported the Fon/Luigi motor for the inaugural *Los Angeles Times* Grand Prix at Riverside. Naming its chauffeur Phil Hill, the future world champion, Johnny awaited the inevitable defeat of the Scarabs.

It never happened, largely because Riverside's temps were even worse than Monza's, and the fast but unhappy engine strangled and again died in the heat. But before that happened, something magical occurred. Sugar daddy Johnny's man Phil was already the most operatic of L.A. pedalers—all flailing arms, gesticulating hands, emotion-wracked facial expressions—and additionally owner of the most jittery throttle foot since Kelly the Shiv, loud-screaming rpms flying wild.

It so happened that I was seated in Turn 8 on the first lap of the Grand Prix, when everything with Phil's Ferrari was still healthy. So when Phil proceeded to fiercely stab that big beautiful engine for its very first reverberating back-straight trip, the resultant gorgeous scream of rage and anger burst all over Riverside. And in it you could almost hear the voices of Fon and Luigi—the latter a casualty of the French Grand Prix only the week after Monza, the shock experience of battling the big cucumbers of L.A. having possibly deranged him—as if they were still both riding in the car with Phil. Bravo!

The list of benevolent sugar daddies from the twentieth century to whom I never got to say thank you is long. The late Johnny von Neumann is among them. Salud, Johnny.

The Simpson's and Davey's greatest grapple occurred in the spring of 1962 at ever-loving Riverside. It was against Bobby Harris, a Hollywood stuntman highly rated for smashing up speeding cars and motorcycles, and somebody as stone brave as Davey himself. Bobby also was one of Davey's best race-driver buds. Bobby's weapon of choice was a curiosity called the Campbell Special, which had started life as a rear-engine pocket rocket containing a chain-drive motorbike mill. Then somebody had gone crazy and replaced it with a gargantuan V-8 of nearly 400 cubes, giving it an even greater power-to-weight ratio than Davey's Simpson. Davey and Bobby went at it like mad animals over hill and dale, the outcome in doubt until Davey ran the Campbell out of brakes. *Joe Scalzo collection*

THANKS A MILLION

Seven, come eleven. One of the creepiest things about being a Los Angeles sugar daddy was having your good intentions boomerang and become disasters.

Certainly it was disastrous to give Danny Ongais and his Hawaiian war-god face custody of a fast car for Indianapolis, particularly when what Danny did best was divine crash walls. And, sure enough, Danny tried knocking down Brickyard walls in the 500s of l979, 1981, 1985, and 1987.

The 1980s was an especially sick decade, because even though the little redcoat ground-suckers were piled high with scientific gewgaws and various space-age gizmos, somebody back in the United Kingdom had neglected to arm the noses with foot-box protection, for when a driver went telescoping head-on into the wall. Small wonder the Hoosier osteopaths were tooling around in Ferrari 308s, or that during some months of May the entire seventh-floor bone ward of Indianapolis Methodist Hospital was domiciled by race drivers nursing broken knees, fixators, or critically fractured lower extremities. Symbolic of the whole sadistic decade, for the rest of their lives, the likes of Danny-'n'-the-gas would lack a complete compliment of toes, as well as walk the "Indy Shuffle" while packing enough steel in his feet to light up every airport metal-detection alarm from Newark to L.A.

But all that wasn't supposed to happen! Danny's candy poppa, Ted Field of Marshall Fields newspaper and department store riches, had wanted only the best for his friend Danny, by keeping him in race cars to help him overcome the blackballing he experienced at Indy as an ex-AA Top Fuel digger merchant trying to be assimilated into the 500.

And at Indy in 1948, certainly it was the equivalent of first-degree murder—Walter Winchell said so on the radio—for a sugar daddy team to bring out of retirement pale and infirm Hep Hepburn, and to strap Hep inside the aircraft carrier-sized V-8 Novi. Hep by then was an exhausted old galoot with blinking eyes, a deathly pale face, and a heavy limp—a medical basket case from all the near-fatal wipeouts he'd known as a starter in 15 Indy 500s (needing driving relief help in five). Asking him to get his obsolete charisma cooking, and expecting him to twist the tail of the Novi, and force it to sing its supercharged shriek one last time was a sure recipe for pulling the plug on poor Hep and his 52-year-old reflexes. And so it was.

Yet again, the motives were honorable: Bud Winfield and the syndicate that ran the Novi saw it as a way to put Hep—still Indy track speed record holder—back to work and rescue him from the banality of his post-racing L.A. life as Tucker Torpedo salesman and servant at Bruce Randall Tuxedo Rentals.

Somewhat similar was the fate of the late Ernie McAfee, who cracked up at Pebble Beach in a deadly forest. A veteran of hot rod racing on the lakes, plus sports car racing on harmless airports and parking lots, Ernie never, ever, should have gotten strapped into the oversized powder-blue Ferrari that had led the Mille Miglia and Le Mans. And he also never should have followed instructions, on a wet and fatal l956 Sunday afternoon, to take the brute flat-out down a narrow corridor edged on both sides by stands of tough-looking pines with no escape routes. It was the equivalent of playing Russian roulette with all chambers loaded.

But Ernie had had for an L.A. sugar daddy the notorious Doheny clan—paterfamilias Eddie Doheny was the bandit who made the robber baron varsity by slicking Warren Harding at Teapot Dome. And the Dohenys had only wanted to give Ernie the fabulous opportunity to race the mighty Ferrari they'd obtained for him to pilot in the Mexican Road Race, which had gotten cancelled first.

Surely, however, the most flagrant of all good-intentions-gone-wrong stories, with all the lives it wrecked, occurred at the l964 Indy 500. Davey Mac-Donald, who'd just wrapped up several breathless campaigns as the sideways front-engine man of L.A. road courses—circuits with plenty of wide-open spaces where there'd been nothing to hit—now was forced to suck it up to grapple a maverick rear-engine rig (front-engines were Davey's things) around 2-1/2-mile Indy, where bordering cement walls on both sides loomed up to be hit. Furthermore, even in comparison to all the other outlandish L.A. equipment of that era, Davey's Mickey Thompson rig was strange: a real cutie-pie. It rode on what appeared to be go-kart tires, and came booby-trapped with a pair of oversized sidesaddle gasoline tanks brimming with volatile high-test.

Somehow, though, Davey had managed to time trial the contraption among the first quarter of the field. His only comment afterward was sober: "If you get in trouble here, there's no place to go. All those walls, you know." Upon hearing this, A. J. Foyt immediately informed Eddie Sachs, "That's the guy who's starting in front of you, Eddie!"

In other words, a made-to-order, imminent disaster-in-the-making.

Yet little Davey was far from a crash hound. He'd yet to experience even his first accident. And as strange as Mickey's rig surely was, Mick had previously done solid work, like inventing the original slingshot dragster. What's more, his Indy plaything had successfully passed all of its safety inspections. And Mickey had made Davey captain

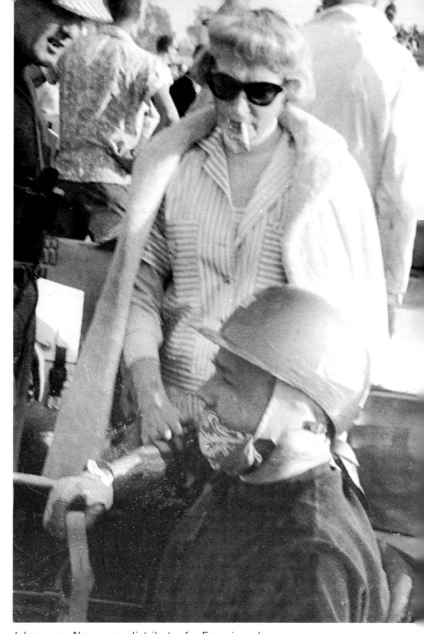

Johnny von Neumann, distributor for Ferrari, and spouse Eleanor von Neumann, ex-Zeigfield hoofer, were L.A.'s sports car racing power couple. *Joe Scalzo collection*

of his team because, just like Thanks a Million Simpson with the Simpson Special, he regarded Davey as L.A.'s next Frank Lockhart, and no finer compliment could flow from Mickey. Finally, A. J.'s quip to Eddie was not intended to be a warning but an example of the gallows humor favored by Indy 500 drivers of that age.

Nobody, then, was expecting a second-lap holocaust—unless it was soon-to-be-widowed Sherry Mac-Donald, who'd had a premonition. Also what nobody was expecting was for Davey to revert to racing Mickey's car as sideways as he had his old Simpson Special.

Thanks a Million Simpson wasn't filthy rich with a million or so in his poke, yet among Los Angeles sugar daddies he had perhaps the strongest résumé of them all

Davey and the Simpson win again, this time at Reno, Nevada. *Joe Scalzo collection*

(i.e., decorated military hero, reckless dreamer, burn-the-candle-at-both-ends reveler, and more).

His life's supercharged rhythms started early. World War II flared up, and within months, Thanks a Million was a 20-year-old infantry grunt aboard a South Pacific-bound troop transport with lots of other infantry grunts. Enemy flame throwers, hand grenades, torpedoes, mortars, and mines awaited them. Following the war was generous battle commendations; all of them had taken wasting fire.

Returning to mundane 8-to-5 civilian life proved difficult. First, Thanks a Million got into selling, but the real estate market lacked pop. So friends reoriented him and pointed his million-watt personality toward the cutthroat universe of car lots and sales commissions. Deftly blossoming from plain old Jim Simpson into Thanks a Million Simpson, he became seller king everywhere, from $75 iron lots to the shiny showrooms of L.A.'s major dealerships.

Around this time in the late 1950s, General Motors' newest Corvette, with all its Eddie Cole go, struck L.A. like a bomb detonating. And when GM was thinking of the Corvette, it must have been thinking of Thanks a

Million. Among salesmen he became perhaps the Corvette's most ardent advocate.

Soon he was hustling them out of showrooms and onto highways, where they belonged. And he was automatically drawn to L.A.'s boomer Corvette road-racers, with all their sideways veers and dive-bombings.

So one riotous Memorial Day weekend, he was up in Santa Barbara at the sports car matches, where one of the top Corvettes took ill. All the Corvette cats were expert mechanics in their own right, but by late Saturday night with all remedies having failed, time was running out. "Better call Davey," Thanks a Million heard someone suggest, realizing that whomever this Davey they were telephoning was, he must be Corvette guru of them all.

A call was placed. And after he'd been told in painful detail about all the solutions that had been tried and failed, then weighing them, Davey's soft voice at last came out of the telephone, inquiring, "Is the tachometer cable screwed on tight?"

Low and behold it wasn't. Sunday, the sick Corvette ran like hell.

"Who *is* Davey?" Thanks a Million demanded.

"Davey MacDonald."

After his Indianapolis death trip of 1964, when it was time to reconnoiter Davey's last miserable effects, searchers found in his wallet a snapshot of a green Corvette with white upholstering, the very first of the dozen odd 'Vettes Davey had owned. He always had Corvette fever.

Becoming fast friends, Davey and Thanks a Million started traveling to races together—L.A.'s hottest Corvette salesman mingling with L.A.'s hottest Corvette racer. By and by, Davey let Thanks a Million in on his secret ambition. Just beating up on the other stock Corvettes was becoming a yawn. He had the hots to get into main events and hunt down the big stuff, the pedigreed Ferraris and Maseratis. But with the meager grease-monkey salary he was dragging down, how was he ever going to collect the serious change to buy something that hot?

By now, in the manner of all L.A. sugar daddies, Thanks a Million Simpson was captivated by automobile racing. Exactly like Davey, Thanks a Million was beginning to find life a yawner. Getting his kicks moving Corvettes was too tame; so was running with the dogs at old soldier reunions.

So Thanks a Million dramatically acted. For years he'd been squirreling away $500 here, $500 there, imagining he would one day purchase his own digs. Taking the all-or-nothing plunge, and feeling guilty about his bourgeois house money, Thanks a Million turned sweet daddy and vowed to spend it on a race car for Davey.

Late one midnight, Thanks motored to the most trick hop-up parlor he could think of, Hollywood Motors. He pounded on the door of the tumbledown garage. The door was opened and Ina Balchowsky escorted him inside for an audience with her old man Max—great and frugal hero of all blue-collar racers, with his stable of Ol' Yellers the ruling warlord of the front-engine backyard bomb. Thanks a Million paid Max a commission to create for him what became the Simpson Special.

They went back and forth at first. Ever hot to spread the legend of Ol' Yeller, Max wanted the future Simpson painted Balchowsky yellow with power-by-Buick; Thanks a Million held out for jumpin' pumpkin orange and V-8 Corvette blast. Most of all, he mandated that the Simpson Special look like a Corvette, but a one-of-a-kinder—with dropped, narrowed, and thinner coachwork, everything looking badass.

A pair of insomniacs, the husband-and-wife Balchowskys worked from dusk to dawn instead of the other way around. This perfectly suited Thanks a Million, who regularly visited them after a day's selling. Sometimes he even tried working alongside them until having to bail and freshen up for the morning's sales fleecings. Thanks knew how to move the fiberglass.

Davey's contribution to the project was one very choice and diabolical mill. It was Chevrolet's new ripper of a 327, made really fast by Davey's polishing the cylinder heads, installing Isky roller camshaft, then balancing and opening everything up with a 4-inch bore and 1/2-inch stroked crank.

In its very first test, as the Simpson burst the length of Riverside's mile straightaway, Davey clipped 180 miles per hour. There goes my house, Thanks a Million smiled, digging his namesake orange missile.

Max had for once gotten something wrong with his suspension specs, and the Simpson's problem was that the one way—the only way—it would submit to going round hairpins and sweeper corners was courtesy of epic lock-to-lock steering wheel work, mixed with withering bursts of ragged broad-sliding as Davey—in his familiar rearing head, jutting chin, and flailing pipe-stem-arms mode—gives it the works. Never having made a fetish of keeping his own No. 00 in a straight line, all this stirring sideways behavior felt perfectly natural to him.

He oversteered and overdrove all corners. Then, following rigorous snaps of the steering wheel, he whammed the gas to provoke a reverberating, skull-bending, trademark burst of orange rubble. Next, he disappeared from sight still all sideways, preparing to hurl himself and the Simpson at the next turn.

Thanks a Million got a good run off the Simpson. He got to name it after himself. He also got vamped and taken to bed by a good ol' doll-face racer, who had ideas of racing the Simpson herself, not understanding its cockpit was reserved for Davey alone. And throughout 1962, Thanks also got to observe with pleasure Davey sliding all over the place and winning from Riverside to Cotati.

Sure enough, after just one season's worth of manhandling the Simpson, Davey's race-driving career was up and running, exactly as he and Thanks a Million had planned. Ol' Shel had Davey ticketed for his Cobras, Lincoln-Mercury was hot to have him inhabit its taxicabs, and, fatefully, Mickey Thomspon was booking passage for him to the Indy 500.

Now that his Simpson Special had done its work, it was time to sell it, so Thanks a Million located a Corvette enthusiast buyer in Honolulu. However, as Thanks a Million later told it, when he and Davey trailered the Simpson to its cargo plane at LAX, they were confronted by a customs bureaucrat who argued that before being shipped the Simpson must he drained of all its premium fuel. Thanks and Davey argued in return

If only photographs came with sound. The caterwauling of Phil Hill's No. 2 Ferrari during Riverside's Grand Prix evoked Fon Portago, Luigi Musso, and the entire Ferrari mystique. *Bob Tronolone*

that they lacked the equipment to do that. The bureaucrat stonewalled and Davey grew restless. So, throwing up those pipe-stem arms in frustration, he climbed aboard the Simpson and lit off the huge engine. And for the following 10 minutes the whine of jets was overcome by the runaway roar of the Simpson echoing off hangars as Davey burned rubber up and down the runways, voiding the Simpson's surplus fuel in the most characteristic manner he could imagine.

Thanks a Million later said that that was his most evocative image of Davey.

My own strongest memory of Davey and the Simpson is more unsettling. It was the Riverside Grand Prix of 1963, won by Davey in a rout, and it was also the race that for the first time exposed him to the peculiarities of a rear-engine chug, the Shelby King Cobra. Rear-engine notwithstanding, lap after lap he continuing flinging everything just as eye-poppingly sideways as he'd done with the Simpson. I loved watching him do it. Only much later did it dawn on me that the Simpson had terminally locked him into that shivering sideways technique; and that for the rest of his career, whatever he raced, wherever he raced, Davey would be traveling sideways, even when

it was wildly unwise to do so. Such as between the walls of Indianapolis.

Damnable May 30, 1964: In the company of Davey's father and younger brother, Thanks a Million goes to the L.A. Sports Arena to see the closed-circuit broadcast of the Indy 500. They arrive late; the 500 has already started; and just as they're taking their seats, Eddie Sachs, 3,000 miles away, is realizing he's in a hell of a situation. Suddenly, the screen swells with a 15-foot-high image of Davey. His Mickey car is all sideways, as if he were back in the Simpson Special sideways at Santa Barbara. But the Speedway isn't Santa Barbara. Firebombing into the wall backward, a sidesaddle gas tank goes up. The Mickey car bounces free and slides back across Indy burning, with Davey in the cockpit burning, too.

Thanks a Million and the MacDonalds fiercely argue amongst themselves that it must have been somebody else, not Davey. But realization sets in, their voices panic, and somebody overhears them and sends for a security guard. The guard motions for help, and four cops on motorbikes lead a convoy out to the MacDonald household, where women are weeping and all the phones are ringing at once.

CHAPTER SEVEN

SALT SHAKERS

The abuse of Los Angeles has become a national pastime.

– Carey McWilliams, author and visionary

Smokin' Joe Petrali—remember him? Sure you do. The Sicilian-American and Los Angeles–based Harley Hog bullet that used to dress for board-track work in a cloth skullcap? The brainy race car mechanic who, with the incredible Chickie Hirashima, won an Indy 500? The best boy and flight engineer to Howard Hughes who was riding in the cockpit the day goofy Howard got his *Spruce Goose* up in the air, then actually flew it across Long Beach Harbor?

Following this last accomplishment, Howard locked up *Spruce Goose* in a hangar and never took it out to play with again. Aviation remained his obsession and piloting his passion, but he satisfied both with his stable of small aircraft.

Throughout the 1940s, he seemed to spend more hours up in the sky than on the ground. So did Smokin' Joe, still the faithful flight engineer. Together they flew all over the Western Hemisphere, and once clear to Shreveport, Louisiana, whose bulls mistook Howard for a hobo and arrested him. Smokin' had to bail him out. Smokin' observed way more Howard dementia than anybody else.

The cabaret ended abruptly. One day Howard handed Smokin' a sealed envelope containing fresh marching orders. First he ordered Joe to lather his hands with soap and water before unsealing the envelope. Then he told him to read aloud the contents. Following instructions as ever, Smokin' read Howard's wavery handwriting thusly:

"Do not convey communicate, telephone, or telegraph any message from me to anyone unless I repeat it to you word for word ten consecutive times. And when I do tell you to call someone I want you to put your hands behind you and count on your fingers. If I only tell you nine times, don't do it. When I have told you ten consecutive times, then do it. . . . These instructions shall remain in force for so long as you shall live!"

Disappointed that Howard had at last suffered the short-circuit that skated reason completely out of his mind, Smokin' Joe gave notice. But finding company as stimulating as Howard's wasn't going to be a snap. He thought he'd found it by joining a bunch of exciting chaps who were converting big PBY seaplanes for sale to various banana republic dictators who turned them into luxury bordellos.

Opposite: All in a day's work for Craig Baby. Jet cowboy Craig Breedlove, fastest man in the world, surveys the rescue of *Spirit of America*, which he'd just belly-flopped into a Bonneville moat. *Greg Sharp collection*

But this stimulating activity, too, paled in comparison. So, at the beginning of the l960s, Joe headed off to the Bonneville Salt Flats and, for the following 11 years, was official keeper of the Land Speed Record, living with all the fabulous LSR rats, the best ones out of L.A.

FRANK AND MICKEY

The 1960s were a terrific time at Bonneville; the LSR was in a period of growth and percolating. Craig Breedlove, L.A. cowboy rocket jockey supreme, was in a mad quest to obliterate 600 miles per hour. But the LSR isn't a mainstream activity because it's so dangerous that odds are excellent it will inflict serious pain or even annihilation. Craig's quest scared certain people who were old enough to remember what being a salt shaker had done to Frank Lockhart.

Among L.A. race drivers, Frank was the Parnelli Jones of his decade, the jazzy 1920s; not only was Frankie L.A.'s fastest, but he was also, along with Father Miller and fragile Leo, reputed to be the village's major internal-combustion brain. And his ambition was boundless. So, in the 1920s, he and his pygmy Miller of barely 91 supercharged inches took off on their spectacular speed binge.

Tournaments that hot decade were conducted on a wicked menu of brick, board, and sand surfaces. Frank possessed a special technique for each. He famously won the Indy 500 as a freshman, later managing the Brickyard's first 120-mile-per-hour lap. On a timber track he lapped at an insane 147 miles per hour, a record lasting 33 years. And out on the sandy open spaces of Muroc Dry Lake, he and the same blown little hot rod had an adventure in a windstorm and created international speed records of 171.02 miles per hour one way, 164.85 miles per hour round-trip.

Get hooked on speed and, ultimately, you start seriously thinking about big casino, the LSR. In 1928 Frank did, not least because his prior record-settings had exhausted much of his prize-money savings, and the LSR was supposed to be worth dough—big dough—in advertising and product endorsements. But up till now, the LSR had been the property of a pack of mad-dog, moneyed Englishmen, one of whom at Daytona Beach had recently topped 206 miles per hour, the standing LSR.

In comparison to the English monoliths, Frankie's own LSR contender, the tiny Stutz Blackhawk, weighed less than 3,000 pounds and was able to fit within the wheelbase of the redcoat rigs. It was his own concoction, a set of blown Millers in a V, with 16 cylinders[four engines?] of throbbing horsepower. Its construction process was complex. Being a typical penny-pinching

continued on page 132

Above and opposite page: Mickey Thompson, obsessed with setting the piston-engined LSR, was his own designer, constructor, mechanic, and intrepid driver. He nearly made it to 400 before Breedlove did. *Greg Sharp collection*

Continued from page 129
race driver, Frank abhorred the idea of spending his own funds in the pursuit of greater glory. So the miser began shopping around for a sugar daddy, as everybody does in L.A. eventually.

Silver-tongued personality notwithstanding, Frank got turned down a lot. In an odd twist, even Father Miller refused to endorse Frank's LSR attempt, payback for Frank's deep heresy of jacking around with existing Miller blower mills.

He hit Indianapolis. He visited Duesenberg, previously his and Father's bitter enemy. The brothers wouldn't help, either. But Frank shared Father Miller's gift of bonding with people and, in retaliation, carried off some of Duesenberg's best help. He additionally paid a call on the financially strained Stutz Motor Company, which fell in love with him and his pitch. Ultimately, Frank got Stutz sponsorship greenies, as well as the run of its plant, where construction began on his curiosity of a double-engine Miller, put together by Duesenberg workmen and bankrolled by Stutz.

The Brits tut-tutted the Blackhawk as too small and likely to fly and, on two occasions, both in April of 1928, fly it did. The penultimate one left Frank relatively unharmed. The second and fatal one happened right as he was exceeding 210 miles per hour along Daytona's surf.

It took L.A. culture four decades, until the 1950s and 1960s, to catch up to the potent mythology of Frank Lockhart. By then, one of the Brits had kicked the LSR up to 397 miles per hour. And in that time, the ocean salt of Daytona had been replaced by the desert salt of Bonneville, Utah, where in winter, the surface was prime and suicidally fast.

The L.A. figure that put L.A. back in the speed record business was Mickey Thompson, and how appropriate it was. Born in 1928—the season of Lockhart's passing—Mickey later would write in his autobiography that he saw himself as Frank incarnate. He may have been not so far wrong. Though hardly the race driver Frank was, he was fellow crash merchant, renegade hot rodder, and harem scarem fun hog. Exactly like Frank, he possessed mechanical ingenuity, wild ambition, utter fearlessness, and not nearly enough money to back up such hyperkinetic traits with hardware.

Frank had personally designed the Stutz Blackhawk, and so Mickey had also designed his own LSR streamliner, *Challenger*. Fortuitously, Mickey was better accomplished than Lockhart at discovering sugar daddies to finance his fun, in this case getting General Motors itself to slip him four oversized Pontiac V-8s for kicks. Hello, 400 miles per hour, Mickey reasoned.

It nearly happened. In the Bonneville season of 1960, Mickey's quad blew past 400 by some 6 miles per

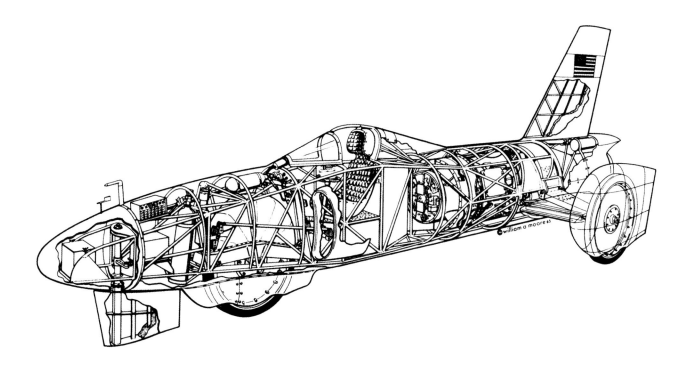

Shortly to become the planet's quickest tricycle, *Spirit of America* and its well-conceived design drew raves. *Greg Sharp collection*

hour. But the sadistic rules of the LSR mandate that the one record-setting run isn't sufficient—you have to make the return trip to be official. The effort of reaching 406 had badly wounded *Challenger*, and Mickey could not carry out repairs within the one-hour deadline.

Afterward, the Thompson attention span, always notoriously short, no longer fixated on the LSR, and Mickey subsequently set off for Indianapolis with Davey MacDonald, a bad career move for both them and Eddie Sachs.

As Mickey was exiting stage right, Craig Breedlove was entering stage left.

I'LL SET MYSELF ON FIRE!

Much like Mickey, Craig was of unrepentant L.A. hot rodder stock. But where Mickey was so thoroughly hung up on camshafts and connecting rods, and in the indisputable values of the piston or internal combustion engine, Craig was seriously steeped in a far more modern variety of candlepower: jet propulsion. And L.A. cowboy jet science, to hear Craig tell it, held the keys to 400 and beyond across Bonneville.

Around this time, something else important occurred: Craig heard President Kennedy deliver his inspirational "ask not what your country can do for you; ask what you can do for your country" speech and decided that the prez was addressing him, Craig Breedlove,

personally. It was all a matter of meshing JFK's wishes with his own. Craig was already a matriculate of the School of Helping People, and when not obsessing over the LSR and liquid-fuel propellants, he was a savant fireman for the community of Los Angeles. Therefore, it wasn't much of a stretch to imagine himself patriotically helping out the entire country by re-conquering the LSR for America. To a bored-out-of-his-skull hose roller with a broken marriage, heavy child-support payments, and a quivering impatience to play space man with the world Land Speed Record, that was a motivated responsibility.

Craig was just as handsome and heroic-looking as John Kennedy himself, and shared the earnestness and deadly charm of Frank and Mickey. These traits meant Craig could speak of his absolute need to careen across a bed of wet salt at 400 miles per hour and not sound demented. In fact, he presented himself and his mission so well while speaking his piece in front of Shell Oil, that Shell gave him more money than he had asked for. At Goodyear Tire and Rubber, world's largest vendor, it was much the same. A rubber war with Firestone was looming; Goodyear getting to advertise that it produced the fastest tires in the world was a terrific incentive. So, upon Craig's promising Goodyear that if it ran up the LSR doughnuts for him he'd work like a guinea pig testing them, he ended up receiving not only hot and free products, but bonus financial assistance in the six-figure range.

Craig checks out the Goodyear doughnuts on which his posterior will ride. To his left is famed big cucumber constructor Quin Epperly, who chose to kiss off the Indy 500 so he could create *Spirit*'s radical chrome molybdenum steel chassis and shapely aluminum and fiberglass panels and scoops.
Greg Sharp collection

Craig was no fly-by-night. Somehow the parable has filtered down that he was nothing but a scam artist whose primary aim was to rip off giant corporations with the fantastic attraction of the LSR. The reality was quite the contrary: Shell and Goodyear were impressed by Craig's knowledge of jet propulsion. A scale model of *Spirit of America*, Craig's three-wheel LSR chariot, reportedly got tested in the wind tunnel at Lockheed, drawing raves.

The first time *Spirit of America* demonstrated all its lethal authority at Bonneville was in August 1963. *Spirit*'s LSR virgin pass was an anemic 388 miles per hour. No alternative but for Craig to rush the channel and flood the nerve cells. While demonstrating his own considerable fortitude and the muscle of jet power, he opened up *Spirit* to 428 for a two-way mark of 407.45.

Back in L.A., the *Examiner* banner headlined: "407.45 mph. Some Freeway Nut?"

Smokin' Joe certified it as the new LSR standard.

Elation mixed with wild bolts of panic now afflicted Craig. The LSR was his, all right, but what now? The LSR is an activity best done in pairs. With the record already theirs, Shell and especially Goodyear were guaranteed to turn off the *Spirit of America* sponsorship tap unless enemy jet car forces suddenly threatened.

And fortunately for Breedlove, not one but two bitter jet-powered antagonists, each hoping to blow him off and seize the LSR for themselves, proceeded to appear on cue. And the pair of them, not—for once—from fertile L.A., but both out of backwater Ohio. Mobilizing for attack during 1964's hot Bonneville season were the volatile, not-on-speaking-terms Arfons siblings, Art and Walt. Walt would soon fade, but Art, the crazier brother, with his alarming *Green Monster*, went right on attacking and pushing Craig to the edge of 500 miles per hour and well beyond.

Art was a junkman alchemist, the Max Balchowsky of jets. His back 40 was one giant field of unfulfilled dreams, littered with the remains of prior unsuccessful *Green Monster*s. But this time, to properly come at Craig and *Spirit of America*, he'd paid a visit to a space-age flea market and returned home with the special prize he'd long coveted: an F-104 warhead similar to those the Blue Angels exercised at their jet air shows. Supposed to be worth $175,000, Arturo had characteristically swung the whole transaction for a fast five grand. One of the first things he had to do was make amends with his irate neighbors for defoliating their forest while checking out the afterburner.

Firestone Tire and Rubber was betting the farm on *Green Monster* traveling 500 miles per hour, so Art, like

Going after the LSR takes a whole bunch of people—driver, crew, sponsors, stewards, and timers. In there somewhere is Smokin' Joe Petrali. *Goodyear Tire & Rubber*

Craig and Goodyear, got lavish financing. Stubbornly, however, Art the junk merchant refused to put on the Ritz. After taking the appropriate soundings, he determined that *Green Monster* required a front axle out of a 1937 Lincoln, a steering system borrowed from a 1955 Packard, various elements of this and that swiped off a couple 1947 Fords, 1951 Dodge kingpins, windshield off a 1953 Buick, and instrumentation pried out of an ancient salvaged airplane.

Green Monster's opening run in October 1964 was only 396 miles per hour, disappointing pocket change. All it meant was that Art was going to really get the hammer down and earn his Firestone pay on the return. So he did. Hitting the afterburner on three separate occasions, he brought *Green Monster* lashing and shaking across the measured mile at a disquieting 479 miles per hour. The two-way average was another new record, 434.

Only eight days later Craig took the record back. *Spirit of America* achieved an opening pass of 442, and because Craig now well knew how truly dangerous *Green Monster* and Art were, he wore out *Spirit's* afterburners lashing to 498 on the trip back.

The new LSR was an intimidating 468.72 miles per hour. Might as well put *Spirit of America* back in its barn and go for 500 the coming year.

But on second thought, why? Bonneville soon would be water-soaked for winter. Just to be sure, why not go for the big five-oh-oh right now? Two days later, Craig did just that. Word spread, and crowds of disaster-seeking spectators drove the 130 miles from Salt Lake City to watch.

Their reward was getting to see Craig, on his first pass, become the first man on the ground to visit the far side of 500 miles per hour. Refurbishing *Spirit* for the second half of its journey—with everybody trying doggedly not to look at the coachwork and the dents that 500 miles per hour had put there—Craig calculated that an average speed of 500-plus could not be maintained if *Spirit's* throttle was left in its usual 95 percent of power setting.

Craig was taking no prisoners. *Spirit* had yet another setting—one never used before—named, appropriately, banzai!

Banzai! was precisely where Craig now set the dial; as he accelerated away, the flying salt and obliterating jet blast

The exotic Breedloves, Craig and wife Lee, the world's fastest woman. Lee later took up housekeeping with *Spirit of America*'s chief mechanic. *Goodyear Tire & Rubber*

in *Spirit*'s wake combined to somersault a photographer shooting images.

And then, 3 miles and roughly half a minute later, Craig arrived, corkscrewing past the timing traps.

All the extra banzai! speed burned out the brakes. And then both the safety parachute and its spare got ripped out by the roots. Having now exhausted *Spirit*'s triple redundancy of stopping power, Craig found himself rapidly running out of Bonneville's 13 miles. Awaiting him dead ahead were a telephone pole, a 20-foot ditch, and a 30-foot moat of salt water several hundred feet across.

Spirit sheared the pole in half, hurtled the ditch, and then crash-landed to a stop in the moat. Craig literally dog-paddled to shore. Ever on the case, Smokin' Joe, first to greet Craig, delivered news of *Spirit*'s two-way average: 526.28 miles per hour. Living off his endorphins and overflowing with bravado, Craig—upon review of his dealings with the telephone pole, the ditch, and the moat—promised, "For my next act, I'll set myself on fire!"

But when Craig added "Art Arfons will never break this record because *Green Monster* is about as streamlined as the side of a barn!" he offended Art.

Taking the remark personally, Art responded immediately with a new LSR record run of his own: 536.71

miles per hour. Though more prosaic than Craig's, Art's returning salvo provided high drama nonetheless. A tire cut, a parachute failed, and for a long time *Green Monster* was rollercoasting along out of control, with Art a mere passenger as helpless as Craig.

Fall, spring, and most of the 1965 summer passed. Craig had by now replenished *Spirit of America* with a four-wheel and even more thrust, while Art had fed *Green Monster* fresh pep pills of its own.

That November, Breedlove upped the stakes to 555.127. Just five days later, despite the handicap of all the twisting torque from the afterburner blowing out Firestones, Art registered 576.553.

In the meantime, while Craig and Art co-existed in either bliss or denial, the deadly realities of their unprecedented duel for the LSR were affecting their entourages in a predictable way: people were becoming stone-frightened. Mechanics for both men were having nightmares; wives and family members were awakening in cold sweats and tears; everybody, including Smokin' Joe, looked like they were ready to start screaming; and once they started, they might not be able to stop.

Prior to his next run, which made him famous, Craig took the precaution of mailing farewell postcards to his children. Then he went one way at 593.178. On the return he got *Spirit of America* moving to 608.21, a classic average of 600.60.

Wet weather, now as ever, flooded the salt and closed down the flats. Everybody could go home until Craig and Art started up their furious dance all over again in 1966.

Craig was L.A. hip, charismatically good looking, appeared deadly earnest, and knew how to get quoted and recite clichés like a well-oiled machine. Goodyear's public relations department treasured all this. Craig and the rest of family Breedlove, it seemed, would do anything to please. At one point it had become the wish of somebody at Goodyear that the world's fastest man should be married to the world's fastest woman. So Craig's smashing new wife, Lee, had jumped inside *Spirit of America*, fired it up, and, after a ride of 307 miles per hour, made herself just that.

But for Firestone's sad-sack PR guys, Art Arfons was a different story. There was little whiz-bang to Art, the junkman from the Ohio cabbage patches with his scrap yard and hypnotically horrible-looking *Green Monster*. Yet what the LSR vocation really comes down to is having an operator willing to push the button, and in that regard Firestone was blessed, because Art truly was the best in the world.

Back at Bonneville in November 1966, Art hammered *Green Monster* to a 585-mile-per-hour-opening pass. But he was well aware that to torpedo Craig's 600.60 he'd have to open it up like never before on his return. This was what he was undeniably doing, Art remarked later, when he realized that the blue sky's horizon suddenly was *underneath* him.

Green Monster tumbled through the air for a long time without hitting anything, but its ultimate crash-landing was predictably unkind. Upon striking the salt it caught fire, leaving behind a trail of burning debris almost 2 miles long.

Art was trapped in the rubble; rescuers with axes freed him. He'd briefly been knocked unconscious, there were gallons of salt in his eyes, but otherwise the worst thing for him was knowing *Green Monster* was totaled and now he was forced to find the junk to construct another one.

"What are we going to do," Art, giggling, demanded of Craig, in joking recognition of all the chemistry and LSR fever flickering back and forth between them, "just keep trying to beat each other until we kill ourselves?"

Craig giggled back: "I guess so."

In that, Craig was dead wrong.

Unbeknownst to him and Art, forces outside the LSR were combining to unplug everything. Art felt the new reality first. Following the destruction of the old *Green Monster*, Art got busy creating a replacement—a new *Green Monster* that was a ton lighter and morbidly more powerful. So he got his feelings bruised when his friends and benefactors at Firestone refused to outfit this son of *Green Monster* with a set of rubber. In regard to the LSR, a less than adventuresome mood had descended over the corporation. Cautious new Firestone policy boiled down to: "The Corporation does not want to be party to someone getting killed."

EXIT ART

Craig's forced exodus from the LSR was more protracted. Upon exceeding 600, he had planned to keep right on trucking until he was punching through the sound barrier—somewhere in the neighborhood of 765 miles per hour. *Spirit of America* had reached its endurance limit, though; something stronger—perhaps a stressed-skin jet-powered cigar—was going to have to be the new ticket. But Craig's pitching it to Goodyear drew an unhelpful response: We've already got the LSR, and Firestone. Arfons, and *Green Monster* are dead meat. Forget it.

LSR income and endorsements subsequently landed Craig in business management, making Lee and him co-sovereigns of a palace on the heights behind the Palisades fronting the western sea, and plunged the world's fastest man into an existence of numbing boredom.

Above and below: Craig patching things up. Except for one fast and spectacular trip into the drink, he always brought *Spirit of America* back alive. After a 400-mile-per-hour run there might be bodywork dents and parts missing, yet *Spirit* was otherwise intact. *Greg Sharp collection*

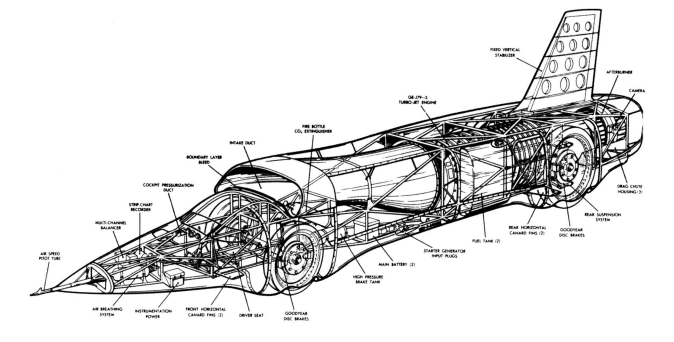

FIXED VERTICAL STABILIZER
AFTERBURNER
CAMERA
GE-J79-3 TURBO-JET ENGINE
FIRE BOTTLE CO₂ EXTINGUISHER
INTAKE DUCT
BOUNDARY LAYER BLEED
COCKPIT PRESSURIZATION DUCT
STRIP-CHART RECORDER
MULTI-CHANNEL BALANCER
AIR SPEED PITOT TUBE
DRAG CHUTE HOUSING (2)
REAR SUSPENSION SYSTEM
REAR HORIZONTAL CANARD FINS (2)
GOODYEAR DISC BRAKES
FUEL TANK (2)
STARTER GENERATOR INPUT PLUGS
MAIN BATTERY (2)
HIGH PRESSURE BRAKE TANK
GOODYEAR DISC BRAKES
DRIVER SEAT
FRONT HORIZONTAL CANARD FINS (2)
INSTRUMENTATION POWER
AIR BREATHING SYSTEM

Above, top, and left: Son of *Spirit of America*: *Spirit of America II*, a conventional four-wheeler. It devoured all of *Spirit of America*'s three-tire records. *Goodyear Tire & Rubber*

To remain semi-active, Craig loaded *Spirit of America* onto a trailer bed and struck out on the show-car circuit. He also indulged in absurd promotions, including "the world's record for 24 hours on a snowmobile." He even attempted to race an outboard boat, one that promptly heaved him into the drink after flipping over.

Craig's life began turning to junk. Certain financial miseries also began bearing down. A Goodyear tire dealership failed, and Craig blew an additional $200,000 in investments. Lee was divorcing and evicting him from their palace on the heights. Toiling away inside a little garage, he worked hideous hours fulfilling his last, lowest assignment, preening a streamliner with supercharged Javelin power to smash the global speed record for piston-engine cars. It was a task Craig undertook for the pleasure of American Motors, formerly the makers of such thrilling iron as the bathtub Nash Rambler.

L.A.'s winter of 1968 unexpectedly kicked in raw and rainy, as an epic tropical storm denuded mountains, flooded streets, and trashed homes. Straight through the front door of Craig's garage rode a 4-foot-high wall of water and mud that wiped out lathes, milling machines, and the Javelin project.

I happened to visit Craig during this time, when he was living on the second story of his destroyed garage and was prepared to demonstrate hearty gratitude to anybody who could slip him a fast million to put his life back together. Long hair and the psychedelic age were in, so Craig, in his latest remake, chose to affect the look of a hippie. He was sleeping on a mattress thrown on the floor of a bare and cobwebby room. It made me nostalgic for the Bella Vista Terrace.

He couldn't even make coffee, having none, so the least I could do was buy the poor guy some breakfast.

We tooled to a local Denny's, with Craig steering his sole remaining piece of transportation, a hiccupping old Buick with no reverse gear and acid colors pasted all over the doors. Even with the ignition off, it went right on hiccupping and dieseling from compression, so we left it in the parking lot doing that; when we came back from coffee, the miserable thing still was violently shaking and doing the dry heaves. Where were Max and Ina when we needed them?

Returning to the garage, Craig took the Pacific Coast Highway route so we could get a look at his former palace in the Palisades, now occupied by the world's fastest woman and her new significant other, Craig's old *Spirit of America* chief mechanic.

Seldom have I felt so sad. We'd surely hit the end of an era. JFK was dead, America was mired in Vietnam, and Craig Breedlove had become a flower child.

There's no keeping this Breedlove down! Twenty years after Craig's original LSR, in the mid-1990s, he unsuccessfully hit Bonneville anew with *Spirit of America III. Neil Nissing*

Bonneville's LSR years of the 1970s, after Craig and Art Arfons, were far from barren. Smokin' Joe got to play with L.A.'s Gary Gabelich, a Chicano/Yugoslav mystic and friend of Craig's, whose *Blue Flame* nailed 630-plus miles per hour; and Kitty O'Neil, a beautiful and deaf Native American, smashed the record of the erstwhile Lee Breedlove as a femme LSR plot.

Attrition got the pair of them: as motivation for doing what he did, Gary once explained that the cooldown period from 630-plus was better than sex, which was something to think about. Fast as he was on salt, Gary took to motorcycle racing, where he lacked the skills to make a decent cafe racer and was killed on the street. And Kitty lost her funding.

In those exhilarating LSR years, I was one of many scribblers who regularly used to bump into Smokin' Joe, imploring Smokin' to let me help him ghost-write his memoirs. Not the Land Speed Record memoirs, the Howard Hughes memoirs. We'd make a killing!

Because of all that Sicilian blood, however, Joe was seriously locked up in the concept of honor and silence—all that *omerta* jive. Or maybe he even still took seriously Howard's "These orders shall remain in force for so long as you live!"

Howard did at last die, aboard a charter plane ferrying him from Las Vegas to Houston. That was in 1976, after Smokin' Joe's own passing. By then, some small fragment of Joe's Howard memoirs had at long last surfaced in a now-defunct magazine, but none of the good stuff—meaning that, whether or not Howard ever knew or appreciated it, Joe was the most loyal employee he ever had.

ARTSY-CRAFTSY

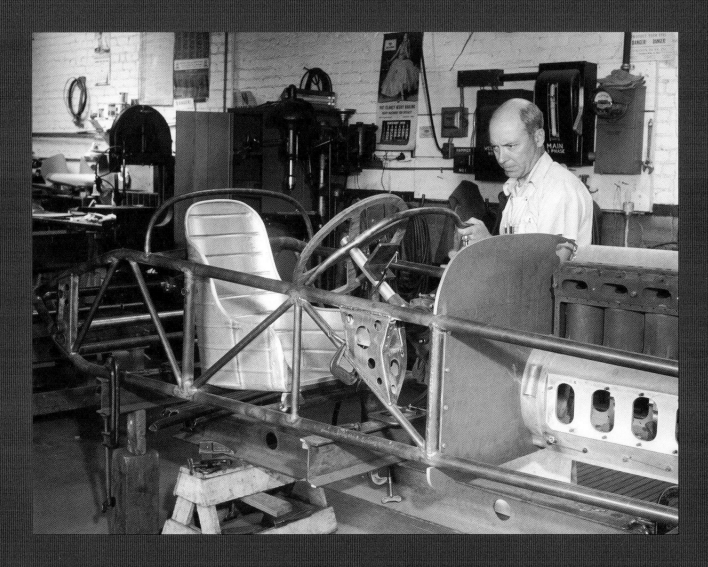

Los Angeles, give me some of you!

—John Fante, Bunker Hill sage

It was a sweeping and magical art show of breathtaking dimension unlikely ever to be duplicated again. Millermania at Laguna Seca Raceway, 1995. *Neil Nissing*

In the 1950s, the vagabond Los Angeles artist Sal Scarpitta isn't living and working out of L.A., or Europe, but in New York City, where he is happily painting, sculpting, and hanging at Cedar Inn. In these years he is a triple threat: artist, volcanic drinker, and dangerous talker.

This one night at the Cedar, he's in a party of Abstract Expressionists, those monster egomaniacs who are art's equivalent of L.A.'s Corvette-racing corps. Everybody is having a hell of an evening. Gallons of whiskey are being served, right at the table before dinner. And Sal is *loud* this night.

So all of a sudden, just as he is in the middle of telling some outlandishly screwed-up story, a tumbler of whiskey catches him square in the chops. Willem de Kooning,

Opposite: Lujie Lesovsky was a natural craftsman and brilliant L.A. primitive whose strong suits—all self-taught — included shaping aluminum, working with sheet metal, and fabricating race car noses, hoods, seats, and fuel and oil tanks. Everything churned out from scratch, of course. *Greg Sharp collection*

seated across the table from him, has had enough of Sal's mouth.

"And," Sal recalled recently, all sparkling eyes and animated face, "according to people who were at the table, I continued right on talking without breaking a sentence. The whiskey in the face did nothing but sharpen my intellect!"

Sal's still every bit the impassioned and uninterruptible conservationist.

"WE WON THE RACE!"

"I've never been interested in the *reconstruction* of race cars," Sal once explained. "You know, making a race car so beautiful it looks like something you put over your fireplace. In other words, sterilizing the race car into being nothing but an object. That's being a curator. It's taking custodianship of a thing. And that belongs to another world.

"I'm in the participatory world, the world of memory from when I was a child at Legion Ascot. Memory is more than visual. Capturing the essence of a race car means capturing the essence of its people. The very first

The aluminum bodywork of the 1930s Legion Ascot fliers frequently came from the houses of Clyde Adams, Emil Deidt, and Myron Stevens, whose only shaping tools were hammers, sandbags, and sand paper. All three masters practiced the art of doing something difficult with the appearance of no effort. With their always-shimmering coats of paint and chrome and nickel plating, these dazzlers as a group were perhaps the most spiffy race cars ever to compete anywhere. *Neil Nissing*

car I ever restored was called *Rajo Jack*, and I had to make it look like my recollection.

"Except for its Dayton wheels, the car called *Rajo Jack* is an optical illusion made from wood. Even the steering wheel is an old motion-picture reel taped up. But *Rajo Jack* is purposely all gunked up with oil and with powdered rubber rubbed into it. A smell of castor oil emanates from it. Because memory is not just visual. It has to do with hearing. It has to do with touch. It has to do with smell."

Next, he talked about being in Venice, Italy, and experiencing the sensation of having two of his facsimile race cars—one of them the *Ernie Triplett No. 12*—being the co-shocks of the 1972 Biennale di Venezia, proudly parked out among the pigeons of the Piazzo San Marco.

"Even getting them in wasn't easy. First, there were guidelines. The city fathers were extremely wary of having *any* kind of race car, and under no conditions could the engines be started. Hell, the reverberations of a l934 Miller might have brought down that whole tenth-century basilica at St. Mark's!

"The two cars got sent from the U.S. by container ship. One was the *Ernie Triplett No. 12*, the other a l935 McDowell called *Rail Duster*. We got them out of storage, spruced them up, put them in big haulers, and when they arrived at Venice they were put onto a huge barge. And when I saw those two cars go out on that barge in that huge city of waterways, I flipped out. I said, 'Hey, I'm jumping in with the cars!'

"The barge was being pushed by a small tug, and I was so thrilled that if they'd torpedoed the barge with me and the two cars on it, I would have gladly gone to the bottom. With big 12-foot planks, we wheeled those

things down to Saint Mark's Square, where no racing car of any country had ever stood.

"Elegance in Europe is a given. Elegance in the U.S. is not a primary consideration. In comparison to Alfa Romeo, Talbot, Mercedes, and Jaguar, our two Los Angeles race cars looked like cans of baked beans. But we got there first! We won the race. It was one of the great joys of my life, and thousands, perhaps millions of people, have since seen those two cars. At one point there was even an American battle wagon offshore. And when the commander found out there were two Los Angeles race cars there, he delegated seamen to stand guard. So we had shore patrol!

"Within six hours the *Ernie Triplett* and *Rail Duster* belonged to other people—my agent Leo Castilli came down from Paris and concluded the deal. So the Europeans didn't know about Los Angeles racing, but they knew that these race cars were animals they'd never seen in Europe and decided to capture two of them. And it was very smart because they've still got them now. I almost wept because they sold for so little. Yes, it bothers me now. It was the culmination of an incredible epic in my life."

Complexities of his Italian and Russian bloods notwithstanding, Sal is Los Angeles to the heart. He is Los Angeles racing to the heart. Getting a taste of Legion Ascot—Valley Boulevard and Soto Street, in Boyle Heights—did that to you. The sensation of visiting his first-ever Legion Ascot Wednesday as a 13-year-old knocked him out:

"First the sounds of the Millers getting louder and louder as you approached Ascot up a dirt road . . . then this strange wonderful smell that turned out to be castor

The best Indy car bodymen were touchy about their high-art handiwork and objected to it being covered up by bumpers or any protection at all. As a result, beautiful but naked noses and tails—like those of ill-fated Jack McGrath's Hinkle Special Kurtis-Kraft—were the first items to get wadded in the inevitable wrecks. *Joe Scalzo collection*

oil, which interested me a lot because it had nothing to do with automobiles as I knew them . . . and then the sight of the racetrack and of Ernie Triplett, Al Gordon, and the others who were wonderful people, the humanity in their faces so obvious. . . ."

He went on to lead a life of so many twists and turns, risks and thrills, as to render racing tame. During World War II, he was in Italy working with the underground, and his name turned up on a death list drawn up by the fascists. Whatever he did, wherever he went, he was always equipped with limitless energy and those bottomless reservoirs of Scarpitta emotion. After the war, he got to pull on a toga and carry a lance while appearing in a big Hollywood epic about ancient Rome. The one line he got to mouth was: "The whorehouses are burning."

Talking about and describing art without becoming incoherent is almost impossible. Sal manages it:

"Friends of mine wondered where I was coming from. I was coming from Ernie Triplett, Al Gordon, and those guys. When little kids watch, they learn. Ernie Triplett taught me that a race driver does not scare. The only thing that scares a race driver is something that happens while he's racing. A race driver is someone who believes in the actual experience. He's not preconditioned.

"And just what in the hell is art, anyway? Where does it come from? What is it for? Sometimes I question myself: Am I an addict of thrills? Am I an addict of this thing, racing, which risks lives, including my own? I felt in racing, and especially Legion Ascot, a metaphysical destiny. If I was to know good, if goodness was to be part of my life, there was a lot to be learned there. It determined my understanding, as a boy, of what I thought a man was. A man was somebody who played for keeps.

"Now some people discount that. They say that race car drivers know what they're doing—they know they'll get killed. A response like that is sacrilege to me. It's arcane crap! And people who use cynicism to help their staying power are wrong. It's not a matter of saying, 'I don't care what happens.' Of course you care. I missed and grieved for Ernie Triplett when he was killed. And I celebrated him by going immediately back to Legion Ascot the next week. He was missing, but, hey, that race was still running! And the race always wins."

All Sal's views are like that—fascinating and positive. And the fact that an artist who has led such a wild and fascinating life finds racing reassuring is reassuring itself. Racing is far more than sport and dollars. It is brotherhood, even salvation. "Whenever the humanity exists that corresponds to my way of investigating life itself," Sal concluded, still speaking of racing, "that's where you'll find me."

"ALL RIGHT YOU SOTS, DRINK!"

Upon learning that the organizers of the Monterey Historic Automobile Races were turning their entire 1995 edition into a huge celebration of Millermania, attended by all the planet's known Miller restorations and replicas, I sensed serious danger. A few years earlier, I had taken part in a similar celebration involving a bunch of Bugattis and it had ended badly. I was living in Europe (trading in L.A.'s sunny hues for the continent's damp, battleship grays was a disaster; a cruel gig that almost croaked me) and Molsheim, the famous Bugatti lair in France's extreme north, had the six existing Royale limousines under exhibit. Simply laying eyes on those half-dozen rare and unspeakably valuable bull elephants under one roof turned into an experience so devastating for one Bugattiphile that he became physically ill and then emotionally unhinged. Ultimately he was hospitalized and had to be locked away in severe solitary confinement.

A Millerphile is, at minimum, as obsessed and twisted as any Bugattiphile. This led me to wonder how many of them, myself included, might go berserk and have to be institutionalized up at Monterey.

The Pacific countryside looked stunning, as did the 20 Millers. The Smithsonian had sent one, the Hall of Fame Museum of Indianapolis topped that with two, and the remaining 17 were the choicest jewels from the private collections of Davis, Rubin, Uihlein, and Boudeman. Fat-wallet Millerphiles all.

Artifacts sustaining the greed-rat soul of 1920s society and racing, they were on view for four days. And during all four of those freak-out days it was as if someone had flung open the doors of a saloon to a bunch of desperately thirsty alchoholics and declared, "All right you sots, drink!"

I was mesmerized, in particular, by the 1928 Leon Duray No. 4—holder of the Indy 500 lap record for nine years and the world's closed-course mark for

David Kimble illustration

six—illustrated here in perfect, obsessive detail by the peerless David Kimble, himself a brilliant Millerphile. Running all over the joint with pen and paper, eyeballing everything, and risking giddiness, vertigo,

and apoplexy, I took crazed notes that afterward could barely be read. "Unbelievably complicated steering system!" "Gorgeous, finned, and godly front-drive!" "Fantastically beautiful tapered springs, tail, and firewall!" "Lightweight hubs of hand-formed aluminum!" "Simmering coats of lacquer!" "Trademark Miller polished nickel!"

Institutionalized indeed.

The Father Miller hothouse of the fertile 1920s, with Father's best artisans on display. *Greg Sharp collection*

METAL BEATERS

So early one a.m. in 2006, out by Malibu, this Swede scofflaw gets cockeyed on the Pacific Coast Highway and his million-dollar Ferrari Enzo strikes a power pole that rips it completely in half. He gets off unmolested, but afterward, laments go up about the destruction of the million-dollar Enzo, one of about 400 in the world.

Well, children, 400 is a goodly number compared to the bare 50—at best 60—race cars produced by Father Miller during his fantastically fertile period of 1921 through 1927. Those Millers were the world's most painstakingly hand-wrought race cars, and they and their *objet d'art* coachwork came with blinding speed built in, meaning that all crack-ups, collisions, and clobberings occurred at peak velocity: hauling-ass Millers got piled up all over the fast lane, dying variously of mutilation, dismemberment, and fire.

In retrospect, the artists hired by Father to construct his Millers were doubly dumb. Theirs was the most fruitless kind of labor. Beauty counted first with Father, and his artists were instructed to use only the finest and most delicate materials while creating a succulent body out of the lightest-gauge aluminum going. Of course, any crash would annihilate it in an instant. Their best beauties, in other words, were bound to get wrecked. Second, they entrusted their gorgeous but frail product to race drivers, the destroyers of race cars. Accordingly, fabrication-artists most in demand were on crisis-call around the clock.

They were self-taught, hard-working, creative primitives, under-financed as well as under-recognized, doing everything by hand except for hammers, sandpaper, and perhaps a disc grinder and tubing torch. A goodly portion of them descended from Eastern European and UK

Above and right: Eddie "Kazoom" Kuzma hit L.A. from out of the Northwest after World War II, staying around setting fresh standards for aluminum sculpting. *Greg Sharp collection*

coach-makers. Lujie Lesovsky, the stooped Czech, insisted on creating in absolute silence and solitude. Meanwhile Jack "Willie" Sutton, a transplant and diminutive Brit, never quite understood why all his choice projects were snakebit. He sank hundreds of hours of exquisite tin-bending into the Novi, which was always getting trashed, and the Parravano 4.9 Ferrari, which got badly mauled on the starting lines of Palm Springs and Riverside. Most uselessly of all, Willie did *Bluebird III*, Donald Campbell's unsuccessful all-aluminum Land Speed Record streamliner, which Campbell fecklessly proceeded to roll and wad at 300 miles per hour.

A fond tradition held that a lot of them were temperamental and even half batty—all that hammering, all that working by night instead of day in the mode of Don "Prince of Darkness" Brown. You also might imagine that a sensitive artist would work to sensitive music, but Eddie "Kazoom" Kuzma labored with the radio blasting away at peak decibel. Talking of temperament, Kelly the Shiv's pet body-man, Harry Lewis, had two sets of hammers, one to work with, and the other to throw out the window.

Yet by all odds, the most notorious of all was Wayne "Fat Boy" Ewing. Fat Boy was, by all Babbitt standards, a disgrace to the human race. He was a total flake who depended on random breeding for his welfare checks, and was so unreliable that to make him finish a job, he sometimes had to be locked inside the garage. But Fat

Boy's high position as one of the master tin men of the colony never was in doubt after he crafted the classic shark nose of the Watson Meyer-Drake big cucumber. A social dropout to the bitter end, he took up squatters rights on the back parking lot of Neil Nissing's photography studio in Burbank, near Autobooks, living out his last days in a seedy Econoline van.

NAT THE GLASS MAN

Los Angles is a healthy place to live; so many flowers bloom out here, but the tin guys died out. They didn't die because race drivers quit crashing—they'll always do that—but because fiberglass supplanted aluminum. And that, in turn, created a whole new subculture and life for Sunset Boulevard racing folk hero Nat "The Glass Man" Reeder, a virtuoso of fiberglassing. He did the coach work of the *Jim Simpson Special* and, for years, was Indy 500 detail man to hard-to-please George Bignotti and A. J. Foyt—a really high compliment to his workmanship—as well as the Granatelli brothers and their flagrant STP turbines.

Glass Man hung with Dean Jeffries, the painter, and Ed "Big Daddy" Roth, and with the star of Daddy's Body Shop a couple of blocks up Sunset, Jim "Thongs" Burrell. Burrell was yet another primitive, one who always wore thong sandals while working, wholly oblivious to the red-hot metal striking his bare feet as he raised arc welding to an art.

Always a loner working outside the system, Glass Man was also a comic who, on the strength of two chance racing events in the middle 1960s, earned a special reputation as a wild hair. We were in the middle of an old-fashioned beer klatch when he told me all about them.

His fun had started when into his possession had come one fine competition chariot, a cruncher 409-inch Impala Chevrolet taxicab. George Follmer, a dangerous character who always raced with a mad gleam in his eyes, got the assignment to race it in bullring stock car competition.

Alarmed when he noticed that the track they were visiting at Vallejo up north came equipped with an unmovable dirt embankment and outside steel railing as tall as the Impala's door handles, Glass Man requested that George not be a bad boy.

"I said, 'George, I'd like you to keep it clean.' George answered, 'Then you better go sit up in the grandstands and not watch. You're going to need metal work. It's going to get crashed.'

"Well, I said to myself, good luck. George took off like a big bird. One fender went away, then another, then

the grille, and finally the deck lid. My Impala ended up on the crash wall with its outside wheels pointing north and its inside wheels south."

"Did you get a new driver?" I asked.

"I couldn't wait to have George drive for me again. This other time we were back in L.A. at Ascot, 200 nighttime laps on dirt. George was working his way to the front—crash, scratch, and push. He came up behind Johnny Steele, who was a quiet stroker kind of guy, and hit Steele so hard that his axle lifted off the ground. And of course George never stopped. He just kept on truckin', lapping faster than anybody."

"Then what happened?"

"Somebody else flipped and got on fire. They had to stop the race, and the delay was lengthy, and when it got to be midnight, George told me, 'Listen, I've got to leave to catch a plane for a Firestone test back east. You'll have to race it yourself.' I went, 'Oh, really?'"

"So what did you do?"

"I was sitting in the car wearing George's helmet when Johnny Steele came walking by. He'd had so much damage from George's hitting him he couldn't continue. So I called, 'Johnny, come drive this thing!' He said,

'Fuck you, Follmer.' I said, 'No, no, this ain't Follmer. I fired Follmer. Get your ass in here.' "

"And?"

"Johnny got in and finished the race for me. Did a good job."

Hang out with L.A. racers, and you run the risk of wanting to become a race driver yourself. I already knew that from motorcycles. Glass Man eventually made the decision to go that route with another Impala, a 409 Super Sport bubbletop with rare six-lug wheels once belonging to Thanks a Million Simpson, who had purchased it from Frank Arciero and briefly turned it over to Davey M.

For his debut match Glass Man chose Ascot, a ballsy move in itself. Starting in the extreme rear, he spun out five times, got into a loser's pileup that set him back another five laps, and he finished 11th and miserably last. But during a second Ascot outing, Glass Man spun out less and only caved in one door, his own. Encouraged, he decided to go after bigger game and join the NASCAR boys participating in Riverside Raceway's big taxicab 500.

For all three warm-up days prior to the 500, stewards wouldn't allow Glass Man and the Impala to go through tech inspection or take practice. Finally, at 4:45 p.m. Saturday afternoon, with the track closing in 15 minutes, Glass Man was permitted to terrorize the steering wheel for a single lap. Doing zero damage, he managed to waltz the Impala off the Turn 8 kink.

Stewarts assured him he'd done well, then told him he could start 43rd and last.

Glass Man constructed a raggedy-assed pit crew that included a retired race driver and a good ole boy. Thanks a Million Simpson was still around and also got selected. Everybody was in unanimous agreement that Glass Man send up an early mayday and get off the track before any of the 500's brand names got a chance to lap him and reduce him to cannon fodder. But on Sunday morning, having borrowed a driving uniform from his sometime-employer, A. J. Foyt, Glass Man experienced second thoughts and vowed to remain in the hot seat for as long as he could. What would Super Tex think of him if he folded early? Complicating matters was that Glass Man's skeleton crew lacked a signaling blackboard, as two-way radios had not yet been invented. Finally it was agreed that Thanks a Million would stand up on the pit wall whenever it was time for the Impala to be refueled. Glass Man couldn't help noticing that trademark Simpson orange shirt.

Taking his position three abreast of the rear row and expecting to be handed his lunch by even the worst stragglers, Glass Man gratefully discovered that he and the Impala could smoke off at least a couple of enemy taxicabs, and did.

Parnelli Jones was the first of the brand names to lap him. And when his uniform-lending pal A. J. did the same, Glass Man decided to throw caution to the winds and give chase.

Dropping too low in wonderful Turn 1, he veered up on two wheels, took a long lazy spin, and for his finale went pirouetting up the switchbacks traveling backward. Congratulating himself for remembering to pop the

Lujie Lesovsky's house. Over time he extended his tool manifest to include press bucks, arc welders, punchers, notches, mills, and lathes. *Ron Lesovsky*

clutch and not stall, and to avoid running over a track steward pedaling to his rescue on a bicycle, Glass Man, adrenaline abroil, resumed the fight.

The orange shirt was on the wall, signaling that the Impala had burned off its fuel load and it was time to pit. But when Glass Man did, the track steward on the bicycle was there waiting for him, screaming that as a result of the spin Glass Man's front wheels were all out of alignment and that the Impala required inspection. Glass Man's good ole boy pit crew member counseled Glass Man that if he obeyed the steward he'd fall way behind, so why not ignore him? Infuriated, the steward responded by ordering Glass Man behind the pit wall for six laps.

The miles accumulated; a pattern developed. The leaders were lapping Glass Man once every 10 laps. So Glass Man set his pace accordingly. He was having a good time. Every pit stop got better. By the next-to-last refueling, with barely 100 miles left, attrition had done its usual savage number on the 500's other 42 starters, and Glass Man's pit crew announced that he was running 10th! . . . then lit him up a big cigar as a reward.

Suddenly, things became ominous. Right where the back-straight ended the winds rose, and across Turn 9 boiled a dark cloud of dust. Plunging straight into the cloud, Glass Man took a brake scoop through a port window, then ran over a windshield lying in the groove.

The owner of his uniform, A. J., had lost it and gone bailing to the bottom of 9's inside canyon. Ugly bolts of reality spoiled Glass Man's reverie: Jeez, a guy could really bust his ass doing this.

Meanwhile, the orange shirt hadn't been visible for a long time, and Glass Man felt the Impala burble and begin to die. Sure enough, the pit crew had committed its one and only mistake of the 500 and allowed him to run dry. Momentum, however, carried the Impala clear to the top of the switchbacks and Turn 6.

He'd been out there almost six hours. Unstrapping himself and climbing out the window, Glass Man discovered that, gasless or not, he'd still placed 13th out of 16 finishers. And that A. J. was badly busted up but was going to recover. The cigar still cinched between his teeth, a groggy ear-to-ear grin plastered across his mug, Glass Man noticed yet another buddy cracking open a can of ice-cold Budweiser and passing it to him in tribute.

Nirvana!

FOOLS, IDIOTS, BASTARDS

The music of Los Angeles sports car racing used to be West Coast jazz—mad Saturday eves at Shelly's Manne-Hole, followed by bright Sunday afternoons in The Lighthouse at the beach, with Lou Levy, Shorty Rogers, Jack Sheldon, Bud Shank, and all those cats blowing,

Above and left: If not-of-this-planet Von Dutch was L.A.'s Jackson Pollack and had the franchise on pin-striping, and if Dean Jeffries was the Rembrandt of painting, then Nat "Glass Man" Reeder was the Rodin of fiberglass structure. Glass Man's credits encompassed Corvettes everywhere, including the Thanks a Million Simpson Special; many of George Bignotti's brightest innovations; and molding together the nine-piece coachwork of the freaky STP turbine in just eight hours. *Nat Reeder*

Classic pianist Don Hulette was devoted to the sweet music of Bach and Beethoven, yet on weekends hit the sports car smoke paths to chase the likes of Ol' Yeller with his crude and short-fused No. 204—fast but totally unreliable. *Bob Tronolone*

along with June Christie, that sultry canary, softly warbling "Something Cool." Curiously, the one race driver I knew with a musician's passionate and punishing temperament was Don Hulette (silent "e")—not jazz but Bach was his master. When things went bad with his racing, he'd pound the tar out of the piano as catharsis.

Los Angeles memory addicts surely still remember the young man with the rough mouth, the rag-tag and underaged pit crew, and the horribly dilapidated race car that was a heroic underdog everywhere from Paramount Ranch to Pomona. That was Don. Besides being an amateur classical pianist, he operated his own hellhole automotive garage behind a gas station out in the wrong end of L.A., the far San Fernando Valley.

He lusted to be the next Ronnie Bucknum, make the cover of *Car and Driver*, and to win the big races like Sebring right away.

So at bargain-basement rates, he'd acquired the blasted remains of a vehicle called the *Pickford Special* and, as usual in L.A., dropped in a huge V-8 Chev. Once the *Pickford* had been a choice amalgamation of clamshell fenders, Borani wire wheels, and finely tuned torsion bars. But when Don purchased it, it had been raced well beyond the age of senility; race stewards regarded it as a unanimous candidate for the black disqualification flag.

The routine was always the same. Don would circle a track trailing a haze of lubricant smoke, while inside the

wheelhouse he was busy rummaging through the contents of a box of Kotex, such filters being perfect for dealing with cockpit oil leaks. Making impossible pass after impossible pass, almost always gaining the lead before worn-out pieces began collapsing or falling off, Don either pitched backward or caught the black flag.

Racing, he couldn't restrain his musician's bearing. He was looking for a sugar daddy, but couldn't control the Hulette mouth. He was like a tyrannical conductor trying to bring off a smashing performance, but who manages to offend everyone in the orchestra with his wonderful platitudes. "Fools, idiots, bastards," he cooed at his crew of slave-labor mechanics, all teenagers, all volunteers—the only help Don could afford—of which I was one. Hulette had one of the sharpest tongues in racing and enjoyed using it to lash us. Yet even when he was being an asshole, we were prepared to die for him. Honestly, we weren't that bad. The only other backyard team that could cut us was *Ol' Yeller* and Max and Ina.

Understandably, Don was growing impatient: at this rate, his antique banger, his ridiculous pit crew, and his hellhole garage weren't going to carry him to Sebring or Nassau. So, in an attempt to win more races, we towed to the far north of California where competition wasn't L.A.-warm. At Cotati, our sole competition on Saturday appeared to be a bulbous Costin-Jaguar with all its streamlining removed to save weight. This thing we

Don and his roaring Lister-Corvette, the No. 204 Fike Plumbing Special at Riverside Raceway. One lap before the big blaze. *Bob Tronolone*

soundly blew off, but still couldn't quite handle Cotati's joker entry, Davey MacDonald's and Thanks a Million's *Simpson Special*.

Davey, driving like Davey, at one point surrendered his lead by disappearing down an escape road and had to hang a Louie to get back in the race. He and the *Simpson* clobbered us right at the finish strip, where Don blew the engine. That wasn't the worst news. Because our crew had given him an illegal push-start, Don was disqualified and on Sunday would be relegated to the back row.

Sunday morning all of us were hollow-eyed from working all night repairing the mill, but so were Davey and Thanks a Million, who'd worked alongside us all night helping out. They said it seemed the sporting thing to do. And in that same spirit of insane sportsmanship, Davey waived his right to start from pole position and then joined Don, his only competition, at the race's rump. Then Davey defeated Don and won again.

To off-the-wall personalities go off-the-wall race cars. Following an extra-smooth job of buttering up its female owner, Don gained entrance to the clapped-out Lister-Corvette fate had waiting for him. Here, at long last, was the life raft that was going to float him onto the cover of *Car and Driver*.

The configuration of an oversized Lister forced a lay-down driving posture. Hulette issued dire warnings that he couldn't see behind, only in front, and in a *Los Angeles Times* GP at Riverside raced like it, particularly while attacking blind switchback hell in heavy traffic conducting an impossible series of outrageous passes.

At last his Lister ran amok, dashed itself against a ditch, its somersaulting gasoline-soaked wreckage flaming into a fireball. A photographer caught the fire and black smoke and obliterating heat . . . and Don casually walking to safety between walls of flame. *Car and Driver* published the picture, though not on its cover.

A couple of seasons afterward, Riverside tensed at the sight of a second fireball—it was the switchbacks getting hammered all over again. This time a beast called the *Sorrell Special* missed Turn 1, overturned, and crash-landed, burning. Its driver safely bailed out. But firemen who had faced Hulette's earlier conflagration didn't fool around. They called for a skip loader to bury the blazing *Sorrell* on the spot.

The explanation was odd. It was the *Sorrell*'s magnesium wheels and fuel tank that wouldn't stop flaming; but the rest of its components had been salvaged off what had remained of Hulette's own earlier burned-out Lister.

More piano pounding followed.

Don unexpectedly lost interest in racing and vanished during the 1960s. He didn't, however, go quietly. Resurrecting his awful *Pickford Special* and pit crew, he improbably captured the Pacific Coast seasonal championship. Then he acquired his last patronage. A man with a Lotus sports coupe employed him to race the flyweight bugger at Sebring in the 12 Hours—a gig far more dangerous than piloting the Lister, especially when Hulette passed the nighttime hours being bombarded by Ferraris and Maseratis blazing into his mirrors going 100 miles per hour faster. Bruce Burness, my friend from motorcycle racing and the mad station-wagon dash towing a Shelby King Cobra, was one of the wretched mechanics on this particular caper.

And what remains of Hulette's Lister and the toxic *Sorrell Special* continue leading a subterranean existence, contaminating the ground under the forlorn tract houses standing where Riverside Raceway used to be.

CHAPTER NINE

BALLYHOO MERCHANTS

Los Angeles . . . it's the plastic asshole of the world.

—William Faulkner, cracker scribbler

"While I'm fastest," Hurricane declared, "I'm going to prove I'm fastest." And, well, he did, over and over and over, until fractures from a brutal water-skiing wipeout caught up to him. *M Focus, Joe Scalzo collection*

"Let the spectator be king!" Michael Goodwin seemed to be roaring all those seasons ago when he was ballyhooing his radical new invention, the Superbowl of Motocross. Thanks to him, classic motorbike motocross got moved from the great outdoors and into the Los Angeles Coliseum, formerly a stadium for jockstraps only. And there inside the Coliseum, the wisdom of the Goodwin formula for success was preached and perfectly executed over and over. Its essence was really very simple: never ever bore, confuse, or stretch beyond endurance the attention span of the rube, paying public.

Opposite: Wild child of the wild desert Bob "Hurricane" Hannah helped make Mike Goodwin and his Superbowl of Motocross a fortune with his ultra-airborne jumps and licks. Hurricane was all the buzz. And though he didn't plan it that way, he's a trailblazer. Free-style X-Games motocross was actually invented by Hurricane 20 years ago out on the far sand canyons of the Mojave. *M Focus, Joe Scalzo collection*

After getting his spectators seated and making them extra comfy, Mike breathtakingly messed over decades and decades of history and tradition by junking motocross' two tactical 40-minute moto format, and mutating the Superbowl into a simple, devouring, 20-minute sprint. His dandy little racetrack laid out down on the Coliseum floor was sadistic and claustrophobic. Hondas, Yamahas, Kawasakis, and Suzukis faced gravity-defying brews of rollercoastering whoops, hellish hairpins, and demonic bumps, plus stutter steps and rhythm steps combined with double and triple jumps. All these activities annually filled the Superbowl to its 80,000 capacity, making Mike rich. And purists realized too late that wild Mike hadn't merely messed with traditional motocross. He'd obliterated it.

MIKE AND HURRICANE

Every ballyhoo merchant needs a star. During a previous life as razzle-dazzle rock concert impresario, Mike's had been Janis Joplin. But Janis went the way of rock stars. So, at the Superbowl, out of the huge yearly cast of highly visible riders aboard their jumping motorcycles, Mike's new lodestar became an untamed hero/villain piece of merchandise called Bobby "Hurricane" Hannah.

Thousands of Aggie photos exist, but only one captures him minus sombrero. At the White House in September 1971, during an incredible soiree thrown in tribute to car racing, he gives an earful to Tricky Dick. *Joe Scalzo collection*

Aggie and the preternatural Troy Ruttman, first Okie race driver champion. Aggie hauled Rutt out of a hardscrabble chunk of L.A. real estate known as Billy Goat Acres and put him smack into the winner's circle of the Indy 500. *Joe Scalzo collection*

One sunny, clear morning in November 1979, I found myself deep in the Mojave Desert, standing outside a house trailer at the end of a dead-end dirt road, and listening to Hurricane Hannah daring bird, beast—and perhaps even human being—to appear so that he might blast them into eternity with the pellet gun clenched in his right fist. I had never seen him in such a terrible mood. But it was understandable, because his right foot, ankle, knee, and thigh were trapped inside a blindingly white plaster-of-paris prison. Glancing down suddenly, Hurricane swore loudly upon discovering he was standing on top of a red ant hill. Some were even making their way inside the cast. "Go on, get that little bastard, hurry," Hurricane implored as I bent down, using my hands to crush as many as I could.

Afterward, he gimped off down the dirt road, still brandishing the gun but finding nothing to fire on. Randomly, he took aim at a distant mailbox. Ka-wang! Bull's eye. It appeared to make him no happier.

Disaster not at the Superbowl but on the water had overtaken the Hurricane. Just two months earlier, on the Arizona side of the Colorado River near Blythe, while water skiing in the exact manner he did motocross—showing off to the hilt—he had gotten careless and crashed headlong into the rocky shoreline, absorbing a maiming.

Until that accident spoiled it, the saga of Hurricane Hannah was one of L.A.'s most choice: a wild and antisocial teenager off the Mojave Desert who flunked out as a dishwasher, chicken-truck driver, gas station attendant, and grunt laborer learned he could race the Superbowl of Motocross faster than anybody else, and found loving sponsors like Yamaha International Corporation, who smothered him with gifts that included a Ferrari 308.

Hurricane recuperated and returned to the Superbowl, the event he starred in, but oddly never won. Residual fallout from the injuries cost him his edge, and he could no longer race the Superbowl in the manner he once had, the Craig Breedlove manner, doing everything but setting himself afire.

At his pre-injuries peak, he'd been eye-popping. One year at the Superbowl I watched him make an absurdly poor start, putting him at the butt end of the pack. But that was where he liked to be, boiling through traffic to the front. Making things happen.

Catching up, Hurricane was jumping, springing, and bounding into the Coliseum night, brilliantly flicking handlebars this way and that, while soaring, diving, and making crash-landings without crashing. But while in the mad process of overtaking everything in front of him, traffic forced him completely off the track. Fanning and firing the hair-trigger hand throttle, and going on

What would it be this time? A chemical explosion that drops flaming detritus into the pits and ships Parnelli Jones to the burn ward? A flying Dzus fastener that hits P. J. dead-bang in the face and covers his melon with gore? A pin-hole puncture taking out the brakes? A leak in the oil reservoir to spray slippery black 50-weight onto all the opponent race cars? Meet the No. 98 Agajanian-Willard Battery Special, most bedeviled Indy 500 big cucumber of them all. *Bob Tronolone*

the attack all over again, he swung wide to the outside of wolf packs of Hondas, Suzukis, and Kawaskis, exposed to knock-off specialists. But this time nobody tried up-ending him, so he let fly another roundhouse pass, this time getting blocked into a welter of colliding bikes and bodies. Smashing right over the tops of them he rocketed on, still playing the scale on the hand throttle.

Back he came again to re-pass almost everyone who had passed him; he was passing some of them for the third time. His tactics did everything but win the Superbowl, and he was runner-up by one second. Hurricane was loved for his riding but hated for refusing to sign autographs, and as he left the Coliseum through one of the tunnels, fans were chanting, "You suck, you suck, you suck."

The very next morning we made a nonstop motor trip together. Starting from his trailer, we streaked through the High Sierra clear to Lake Tahoe to look at real estate, followed by a pell-mell journey back again the

same afternoon and night. Just before dawn we rolled into my driveway. Hurricane sprang out of the car (not his Ferrari) to take a long tinkle on my lawn, then he went roaring off into the sunrise bound now for San Diego, I think he said. He never said goodbye.

A few hours afterward, the telephone shook me. It was Hurricane. "Get up," he commanded, "we're going jet-skiing at Castaic Lake!"

Having long since bolted L.A., Hurricane is now living somewhere in Idaho where, as I understand, he brokers aircraft. Try Hurricane if you want to purchase anything from a Cessna to a DC-10.

Like it or hate it, the face-lifting Mike Goodwin forced on motocross stuck. His various Superbowls were enormous financial successes. In the typical L.A. manner, he exported them to Pittsburgh, Washington D.C, New Orleans; Dallas, and Houston. Mike started that whole X-sport biz.

Against all odds, mean-tempered old No. 98 did win an Indy 500 for Aggie and Parnelli, that of 1963. Then 29 years later in 1992, as part of the pre-500 hoopla, No. 98 looked great in its 1964 livery as it took a slow nostalgic lap of the Brickyard. Parnelli was again its wary pilot. Sure enough, the hex was still in. No. 98 proceeded to make another spectacle of itself by throwing two separate fits of mechanical temper. The old beast barely condescended to complete the lap at all. *Bob Tronolone*

Until he split the scene rather suddenly in the late 1980s, Mike was totally hands-on. He did everything. One night the announcer on the public address caught laryngitis or something, and instead of finding a replacement, Mike went on the air to bark his Superbowl.

Another year, on the weekend before the Superbowl, Mike drove to Riverside to enter a motorbike road race. He fell off and broke his keister. Against all medic orders, he still showed up to take charge of the Superbowl as usual. Prostrate on his belly on the back of a gurney, his bare ass covered by a towel, he was receiving nourishment from an IV drip-feed. And while pushed around on the gurney by some of his stooges, he could be heard letting loose his annual tirade, railing against his riders, his sponsors, and even the Superbowl's television cameras.

AGGIE

Unlike Mike, who had Hurricane for a star, Aggie Agajanian never required a star. He needed no star. He was his own star. In half a century of ballyhooing Agajanian

extravaganzas all over L.A., filled with Indy 500 winners, national champions, and the whole blasting lot, the only mug he used on his promotion pictures was his own. Aggie so loved getting his own picture taken, he could be shameless. When his discovery, Parnelli Jones, won a *Times* Grand Prix, Aggie—resplendent as ever—elbowed his way into victory circle at Riverside to be photographed with P. J. as if Aggie, instead of Ol' Shel Shelby, was owner of the winning King Cobra.

Other things Aggie truly loved were speaking Armenian back and forth with his big loving family, all his racing promotions, his Indy car team—twice winner of the 500—and its ill-tempered big cucumber roadster No. 98, the *Agajanian Willard Battery Special*, and winning gin-rummy marathons when gin rummy was the game of Indianapolis.

Aggie had much to be proud of; he was one smart cookie. Before adding race-promoting to his successes, he had coupled a family rubbish collection business with a most profitable hog farm and become a millionaire.

Above and right: A J. C. Agajanian extravaganza, the *Examiner* Grand Prix at Pomona, got off to a red-blooded beginning with a touring of the racetrack by a braless Jayne Mansfield. The shocks went right on when everybody dropped clutches and the blunderbuss Mickey Thompson Cad-Kurtis, raced by an Albuquerque hill-climber of destiny, careened into Turn 3 leading. Other shocks were soon to come. *Bob Tronolone*

Nobody screwed Aggie out of money, whether it was in gin-rummy duels or pitching pennies. Of all people, Colin Chapman once tried to with the same buccaneering spirit he unleashed on his various Yankee distributors. But when he attempted to rip off Aggie, Chapman immediately got landed on with a lawsuit, dragged before a magistrate, and told to pay up *now*.

Troy Ruttman and Parnelli Jones were Aggie's two great, blue-collar, L.A. discoveries. Troy, out of hardscrabble Billy Goat Acres, was the first Okie champion of Indy (1952). Parnelli, of course, was the only Jalopy Derby grad to ace the 500 (1963).

Without Aggie and his ballyhooing, L.A. racing might not have amounted to much: no Indy winners flown in to Ascot Park for local sprint car drivers to take batting practice on; no Ascot Park flat-track Friday nights; and no *Examiner* Grand Prix at Pomona, one of Aggie's and L.A.'s most ludicrous productions.

Thanks to Aggie flimflam and legerdemain, a patch of flat and barren parking lot real estate outside the Los Angeles County Fairgrounds got jury-rigged into a supposedly world-class venue of 2 miles and 11 corners, hosting hot dogs ranging from Max Balchowsky to Ol' Shel.

Race day dawned sunny and fine. Matters got off to a hot-blooded start when a red Elva sports car set off on a slow hypnotic lap carrying on its deck Jayne Mansfield, who was dressed in a mesmerizingly tight costume, without a bra.

An instant later, the pack of 37 angrily dropped clutches and began a journey of 150 ultra-hostile miles.

It never hurt to stimulate an Aggie promotion with some cheesecake, 1961-style. No. 3 is ill-starred Ascot flat-track hero Prince Albert Gunter. *Joe Scalzo collection*

Matters promptly took a dramatic turn when Max's big nailhead decided to have one of its big Buick connecting rods take the scenic route and blow bullet holes through the block.

An enormous lake of black *Ol' Yeller* blood slicked down the front straightaway, yet the first dozen drivers safely navigated it. But the 13th, a Beverly Hills swashbuckler heir to a swimming suit empire, Bruce Kessler, began spinning like a top. Deciding that the contraction of his sphincter was an augury that he was going to overturn, Bruce decided to act on his curious theory that *jumping out of the cockpit onto the racetrack* might be a life-enhancing act. Landing splat on the pavement, he awoke suffering road burns, cracked ribs, and a well-earned concussion.

And Bruce hadn't needed to jump at all, for his driverless race car never overturned. Instead, it invaded the race car pits at better than 100. After smashing through some straw bales, it next bashed around various human beings, among them a priapic 18-year-old male driven out

of his mind by the earlier vista of Miss Mansfield. He'd stolen into the pits for a closer taste and his horniness got him laid low.

Besides wrecking itself, Kessler's vacant automobile also did quite a job on a pretty, parked Cadillac town car, Aggie's personal transport.

HARRY

In l994, I drove out to the San Bernardino Fairgrounds and Victorville Speedway, which for some reason had just defaulted on a debt of $100,000. This was the written explanation of Harry Schooler, track promoter:

> My name is Harry Schooler. I am a promoter. I put on attractions and sell tickets. Usually I will sell more tickets than it costs to pay for the show. And there will be a profit.
>
> I promoted Culver City Stadium. I financed and built Gardena Stadium. I financed and built Ascot Park. I entered into a multi-year lease with the San

Aggie's archrival, Harry Schooler, worked his employee race drivers hard, causing them to occasionally double as mud wrestlers. Scotty Cain is in there somewhere. *Joe Scalzo collection*

Bernardino Fairgrounds to build/operate a motor stadium. . . . I laid out and built Victorville Speedway . . . I arranged the financing and credit using my personal reputation for success as collateral.

The stadium is a big success! It fills a need. Thousands of fans came each night. We took in well over $100,000. Many creditors and race drivers now want to know what happened to that money. So do I. . . .

Victorville will again have the stadium it needs and deserves! Additional financing is being arranged and I hope to reopen the facility soon to promote professional auto racing. With insurance premiums and all purses put up in cash prior to racing!

Reading this, in the manner of Dashiell Hammett's bulldog, the Continental Op, I wondered how many intended or unintended falsehoods were in those words. I came up with nine and was sure, with a little research, I might uncover more.

Harry was himself a pioneer ballyhooing promoter, but at first not racing. Dancing was his racket: 10-cents-a-dance dancing, marathon dancing, swing-shift dancing. He operated out of the old Aragon and Lick Pier ballrooms.

Scotty Cain absorbs another boot to the butt. Scotty was Harry Schooler's star attraction. *Joe Scalzo collection*

Harry (left) happily lets Scotty, rag hanging out of his back pocket, give the works to Miss Brew 102. Harry was less amused when Scott arrived at a second Schooler production escorting Harry's own missus. *Joe Scalzo collection*

His great racing contributions, all of them vaguely sleazy, included demolition derby, figure-eights, and Jalopy Derby from Gardena Stadium on Sunday-afternoon TV, for which he deserves a merit badge. Harry additionally was drawn to the doll faces: cheesecake derby, perfume derby, original lady lead-foots. If a program was dragging, he might throw on a tournament of infield mud wrestling.

Just like Mike Goodwin and Hurricane Hannah, Harry required a star, and often it was Scotty Cain. Harry, however, parted with dough only under severe duress, so he and Scotty frequently were sideways with each other.

Their relationship never fully recovered from Scotty's decision to blow Harry's mind by showing up for a Jalopy Derby with a celebrity date—this statuesque lovely who happened to be Harry's own wife. Harry swiftly ordered Scotty removed from the premises, but there were difficulties. Should security cops be called upon to order Scotty to leave, Scotty would not be able to stop himself from taking out six or eight of them. Additionally, the other drivers were in support of Scotty and threatening to boycott. Then the grandstands got into it with a near-riot and made ready to pelt Harry with bottles of the heavy Pepsi and Coke variety.

Scotty was permitted to race.

MICKEY

Jan Opperman cut his hair!

Mickey Thompson was nearing 60, but still was going strong in the 1980s. In terms of accomplishments of one type or another, he may well still have been racing the strongest of any freak in the village. But although his eyes

Both of them a long way from the L.A. homeland, Mickey Thompson and Aggie have a heart-to-heart at Indy. Mickey's 1988 gangland-style slaying convulsed and plunged into deep mourning the City of Speed. *Greg Sharp collection*

still blazed, Mickey was at last tired. He was also for the first time starting to feel the effects of all the wounds he'd absorbed everywhere and in everything, from a crashing taxicab in the Mexican Road Race, a berserk streamliner on the dry lakes, and a flipping speedboat across Lake Mead, plus the emotional wear and tear of the Davey MacDonald and Eddie Sachs business.

So, Mickey decided to go the Jan Opperman route. Opp, to get a ride in the Indy 500, chose to go from a hippie long-hair to an establishment short-hair, thereby proving that everybody is free to change. Equally as radical a change, in the opinion of many, was Mickey's break from the tradition of being a racer to his new tradition of becoming ballyhooing promoter of racing events. First he went desert off-road, and then, aping

Mike Goodwin's Superbowl of Motocross, Mickey went stadium racing, but with off-road four-wheelers instead of motorcycles.

This proved to be a huge financial success. And Mickey became world-class capitalist. He began dressing in expensive clothing, driving expensive cars. He'd never previously worn his hair in anything but a racer's crew cut; now he got it styled into a poof. And he took up residence among the pricey compounds of chic Bradbury, an exclusive millionaires' colony, gated by high walls to keep out the peasants.

Only a few miles to the west, but light years apart from Bradbury in dollars and drag, is my own woebegone, isolated, mountainous stomping grounds—the tiny and forgotten community of Sierra Madre. An

Above and left: A great proponent of the theory that if one engine is good, two are better, the unstoppable Mick blasts off at the drags then prepares to do the same on the Bonnie salt. *Greg Sharp collection*

and pilot Engine 41—the big pumper—code three to the big blaze. Providing it wasn't a false alarm.

Against all odds, this sink of Babbittry that I love more than any place on earth has a racing heritage. Belohlavek's Garage, the best in town, had a Sierra Madre race car at Legion Ascot. Frank Arciero once tried to subdivide our scraggly foothills with blocks of expensive homes, but was repelled by our city council and to this day curses me for living in such a dumb-cluck outpost. Tony Settember, who went from Corvette racing to Formula 1, once was in residence here; and the sanitarium where crazy Wally Reid got locked up was in Sierra Madre.

So, downtown on dull weekdays, I used to gaze east to Bradbury, thinking of Mickey living the sweet life out there and existing in elegance. And maybe counting the ways it beat sleeping all night long on the salt of Bonneville, or racing and crashing and massacring in the Mexican Road Race, or acquiring still more clobberings on the water . . .

But there was an epilogue. Somebody introduced Mickey and Mike Goodwin, and out of this came a stadium racing partnership combining two wheels and four wheels. In something like three months, Mickey and

unlikely chunk of midsection Babbitt U.S.A. pasted right on the foothills of the San Gabriels, where the coyotes yip and Santa Anas howl, Sierra Madre is utterly unique to the rest of L.A. Additionally, Sierra Madreans are so tight with a roll that out of the entire megalopolis, we're the only settlement refusing to pay for a professional fire department. Instead, it depended on a mad corps of volunteer vigilantes, of which I once was one, and quite a scene it was: awake at two o'clock in the morning to the beguiling song of the ancient air raid siren downtown wheezing to life; drag on the protective turnouts; pile into the family sled; roar full tilt four blocks to the fire station; and first arrival gets to turn on the siren, hook up the red lights,

Mike were already at each other's throats. The inevitable ugly lawsuit that followed was for a lot of money and was decided in Mickey's favor.

Then came 1988 and the wildly apocalyptic ending. Gunned down with his peppy young wife, Trudy, at dawn outside their swanky Bradbury digs, Mickey died a Mafia capo's death, his two murderers escaping on a pair of bicycles.

The Sheriff's department unleashed a piteous investigation, ransacking Mickey's racing life for suspects. They even re-opened the raw wound of the Davey MacDonald disaster, visiting the MacDonald household to determine if George MacDonald, Davey's bereaved father, held a grudge toward the man whose Indy monstrosity with go-kart tires and gasoline sidesaddles had destroyed his son. But the senior MacDonald, victim of a cerebral hemorrhage, had checked out long years before.

Following years of footwork, the Sheriff's department decided that the murderer must be . . . Mike Goodwin, Mickey's ex-partner. Despite profusely pleading his innocence, Mike has been chilling in the hoosegow for the past five years. As I write this in autumn 2006, Mike's trial, after endless legal delays, is beginning.

Mickey left a trace of history on every vehicle he touched. The Ford push vehicle here getting his saltmobile moving became the deadly lightweight-turned-stocker Mickey raced in the Mexican road race. It careened into a mob of spectators, many were killed, and Mickey was initially reported dead himself. *Greg Sharp collection*

$$$$$$$$$

CHAPTER TEN

Los Angeles, it should be understood, is not a mere city.

—Morrow Mayo, rabble-rousing radical

Mickey Thompson, who in his line of work needed one, was a Bell helmet proponent. And so was many-time California Racing Association seasonal sprint car champion Billy Wilkerson, a sharp wit, who notably credited the Bell "with saving more heads than a psychiatrist." *Greg Sharp collection*

Like almost everything else, the whole speed-shop business pretty much began in Los Angeles. And then, much like city racetracks, nearly all the famous old performance houses went the way of the brontosaurs, variously destroyed by old age, incorporation, the fantastic property values of the real-estate market, pain-in-the-ass L.A. right-to-work laws, and the blandishing of other interior cities and states offering sweetheart deals to those fools willing to move. Incredibly, out of the original gaudy roster of hundreds of prewar hop-up huts, just six remain: Edelbrock Corporation, the resurrected So-Cal Speed Shop, Grant Piston Rings, Bell Auto Parts, the minuscule and amazing Blair's Speed Shop, and Iskenderian Racing Cams, whose namesake grinder Isky, now headed toward 90, is still going strong.

Post–World War II was when the game really got started. With more bomber aircraft and fighter hardware having been produced in L.A. than any other location in the world, huge war surplus stores began springing up on the boulevards following the armistice. It turned out that appliances of mass destruction selling at cut-rate prices converted nicely for racing purposes. Simultaneously,

the racers of L.A. tapped into their benefits from the G.I. Bill of Rights, and the most ambitious ones hit the surplus lots, stocking up on everything from military nuts and bolts to pumps and tube fittings to belly tanks. They became seat-of-the-pants entrepreneurs. Opening their own emporiums, they ginned up products, including high-compression pistons, stroker connecting rods, flamethrower camshafts, heavy-duty cranks, six-pack carburetion, nitro valves, aluminum mag wheels, cherry bomb exhausts. . . .

Then they carried products and inventions to the racetracks and lakes to show them off and generate word-of-mouth sales. Many a business took off, none better and bigger than Edelbrock, still the colossus today.

Paterfamilias Vic Edelbrock began life as a completely brilliant dry lakes kid who, at Muroc and El Mirage, did speed tricks—tricks nobody else could imagine, let alone carry out—with the high-boy Ford roadster. Yet another big breakthrough for Vic and his fledging Edelbrock Equipment Company involved Henry's old V8-60.

The engine was the ugly duckling of thoroughbred 1940s midget-car racing on Wednesday nights at glamorous Gilmore Stadium, kingdom of the out-of-this-world 110 Offy. The Offy was a homeboy mill. Fred Offenhauser had invented it in L.A. Six-toed Louie and Dale Drake were marketing it here. The little Offy was about as Los Angeles as you could get.

Opposite: Bell Auto Parts, creator and manufacturer of landmark goods ranging from Cragar wheels to Bell crash hats, is popularly regarded as L.A.'s original speed shop. *Art Bagnall*

The father and son Edelbrocks, Vic and Vic Jr., at their Edelbrock Equipment Co. Edlebrock is an empire in the twenty-first century. *Greg Sharp collection*

Vic, meantime, continued marching to the jazz beat of L.A.'s two other blue-collar mavericks, Eddie Winfield and Max Balchowsky: hot summer Wednesday night after hot summer Wednesday night he carried, fearlessly, his underdog Edlebrock bent eight—all tricked-out and juiced to the hilt with the most volatile fuels—to Gilmore. And lost every time. August 10, 1950, at last brought the inevitable. The Edelbrock was killer hot and its regular chauffeur Rodger Ward was in searing form. And Vic's maverick V8-60 became the only non-Offy to win a postwar Gilmore main event.

Bolstered by the acclaim, the young Edelbrock concern—any modest diagnostic tune-up center today is vastly better equipped—was on the path to become a high-profile institution.

Gilmore, unfortunately, was on its way to collapse. Just a couple of months after Rodger's win, the stadium shuttered. No more Gilmore wins for Vic's rebel V8-60.

ISKY AND OSIECKI

In 1961, Daytona Beach's intimidating new International Speedway was barely three seasons old—a mere infant compared to Indianapolis, whose Brickyard was nearing its golden anniversary. To give Daytona some legend of its own, Bill France, dictator of taxicabs, decreed that his high-banked emporium must host racing's original 180-mile-per-hour lap. The very first race car to bounce, swerve, and sail across Daytona's vast banking at 3 miles a minute was to be rewarded with a $10,000 prize—a fortune in 1961, if the car could be brought back alive.

Following a bloodbath race there in 1959, Indianapolis had banned all its cucumbers and personalities from racing anymore on the big D. So candidates for the 10 grand were, for the most part, reckless mercenaries who viewed this as their big, and perhaps only, rendezvous with riches and glory. Many of them were complete nut jobs, and easily the most relentless was Bob

The modern tune-up shop at the average gas station offers a far wider range of diagnostic equipment than anything L.A.'s early speed cats enjoyed. Edlebrock brains Bobby Meeks and Fran Hernandez flesh out the ground-shaking Edlebrock V-8-60, the only postwar Ford to beat the glam Offy 110s of Gilmore Stadium. *Greg Sharp collection*

Osiecki, proprietor of his own speed igloo in Charlotte, North Carolina, and a drag strip in Chester, South Carolina. Osiecki was regarded by the racing community at large as a bizarre personality and wild promoter, although Osiecki considered himself an engineer. Originally, Bob went after Daytona's 10 Gs with his own cars. He designed three, all failures. Then, in 1961, he discovered a discarded Indy big cucumber, a worn-out Kurtis-Kraft that had blitzed its driver and afterward become a tire-testing mule for Firestone.

It had no engine, so Bob did the same thing anybody would in his position and flew into L.A. for a powwow with "Isky" Iskenderian, who had supplanted Eddie Winfield and Clay Smith as village cam-grinder supreme. Via drag racing, Isky knew lots about supercharging, in particular supercharging oversize and vicious Chrysler and Dodge merchandise.

Following the powwow, Isky created a 413-cubic-inch, fuel-injected, 15:1 compression wedge Dodge V-8, then bolted a blower on top. Bob somehow made it fit in the cucumber. It developed almost 1,000 horsepower, nearly three times that of a Meyer-Drake. It gorged 8 gallons of methanol per lap. Started up, the Isky could be heard in downtown Daytona Beach, several miles distant.

Being that it was his fourth, and with luck final, record-effort car, Bob called it *Mad Dog IV*. The name was

apposite. As someone wrote, *Mad Dog IV* looked and sounded like something only a madman would drive.

It was the spring of 1961. A lot of different crazies were in and out of the thing. All of them agreed that *Mad Dog IV*, with its Isky pedigree, could beat 3 miles a minute; the *Dog*, in fact, was already exceeding 200 on the straights, so its problem wasn't that it lacked go. The problem was control. So Bob and Isky cogitated further and decided to fine-tune the chassis and, during the inspection, discovered that the torsion bar bushings were rusted and frozen shut. Not a happy sign.

March passed, and part of April. Nothing much was happening. One guinea pig driver became impatient and decided to uncoil his throttle foot. He informed Isky and Bob that he was "going to see the tach standing on end," or go home. "The tach standing on end" meant that the cockpit tachometer was going to be pegged at 6,000 rpm, more engine revolutions than ever turned before.

The ride that followed lasted for 2,100 feet and included seven full spinouts. While performing them, *Mad Dog IV* hit things. It clobbered its nose and split open the radiator, and its starter shaft sliced a guardrail post in half. The driver felt every impact, counted every spin, yet was unharmed.

Bob took the damaged vehicle back to Charlotte. It returned in July with three new and eye-catching

appendages. One was a tall dorsal fin on the tail, and the two others were a pair of airplane wings sprouting from each side of the cockpit. They were supposed to add stability and prevent further spinouts. An engineer from Douglas Aircraft and Georgia Tech had developed them. The guinea pig driver looked at *Mad Dog IV*'s wings with suspicion. They were at jugular heights, which was to say, if they ever snapped off and came back into the cockpit, the driver would have to search for a new skull.

Undaunted and still enthusiastic, Isky and Bob found a new guinea pig candidate, and went for "high-tech" by repeating the trick that Hep Hepburn played on the original overpowered Novi at Indy. To prevent the throttle from going to the floor, they put a 2x4 board under the pedal. Even at three-quarters power, *Mad Dog IV*'s lap speeds rose to l70, then l72, and even blew past 175.

At that speed, a complete set of Firestones was wearing out in only four laps. They were hard, stiff, Monza eight-plys, and the supply was diminishing rapidly. *Mad Dog IV* was showing signs of wear itself. Its Isky began

losing oil pressure, and then its clutch, a multi-disc unit meant for a Meyer-Drake, began slipping.

On August 5, Isky had oil pressure restored by moving the pump to the rear of the oil pan. Daytona timing clocks caught *Mad Dog IV* at 177.79 miles per hour. On August 21 matters got faster still—178.25 miles per hour. The $10,000 reward was less than 2 miles per hour away. Two days later came the longest *Mad Dog IV* skid yet. On August 28, while a 12-knot wind gusted, *Mad Dog IV* took three warming laps, followed by a fourth careening one. As *Dog* swerved into the front straightway bulge, where clocks for measuring trap speed were located, Isky, from the engine sound, estimated its velocity at better than 220 miles per hour.

Safely past the traps, *Mad Dog IV* jumped completely sideways and almost crashed. The clocks said the lap time was 49.57 seconds. A moment later, a telephone rang, and the call was from the official timing tower to the track's infield. Dictator France, who'd come out to observe *Mad Dog IV*'s run, answered it. "Mr. France," the

It wasn't all speed shop business. The U.S. Department of Transportation contracted Halibrand Engineering to come up with a 240-mile-per-hour train, then wouldn't fund the project. *Bob Falcon*

chief timer told him, "that last lap just cost you 10 grand." The velocity was 181.51.

As if prematurely worn out by all the 3-mile-a-minute stress, Bob Osiecki scarcely got to enjoy his prize, succumbing to exhaustion just two years later.

Isky Iskenderian basked in the glory and, afterward, counted it one of the successes that really got chez Iskenderian up and running.

BIG ANDY

Worshipping multi-million dollars, making multi-million dollars, blowing multi-million dollars is what good Babbitt Americans love to do, or dream of doing. Being abnormal and superior, L.A. racers did not. Racing, you lost your ass, plus it could ruin your mental and physical well-being. Still, there was nothing like racing. Racing was what you did for delivering kicks. It became the conceit of Anthony "Big Andy" Granatelli, an L.A. racing entrepreneur and speed shop boss, to shatter this mold and make racing earn him multi-millions.

Andy became Big Andy not because he was merely fat, but obese. He had one of those bellies from the gilded age. He used to stick it out with pride, as if saying: Look at this mother. I grew it *myself* and I'm *proud* of it.

Immediately after World War II, in his Chi-town stomping grounds, he very early got in on something that was on the verge of making him filthy wealthy. It was his own lawless Hurricane Racing Association, a thuggish reform school of raw hot-rodding—T-boning, short-braking, slide-jobbing, crooked scoring, and rooked results that made L.A. Jalopy Derby and Corvette racing look like child's play. Soldier's Field played to standing-room-only nighttime mobs, and if only television hadn't come along to make everyone a TV dummy—and the mobs disappeared—Hurricane might be playing yet.

During the 1950s, Big Andy gathered up his brothers to migrate west to L.A. and paradise, where he opened a razzle-dazzle Granatelli speed house in Santa Monica, converting street chugs to supercharging. But he'd also let

Halibrand Engineering's Ted Halibrand, right, with the cooperation of the great Vince Conze, perfected racing's quick-change rear-end and introduced some of the earliest disc brakes. Here he shows them to perennial Indy car customer Ernie Ruiz. *Greg Sharp collection*

the Studebaker-Packard Corporation name him president of its chemical additive division and fortuitously assigned him to hawk a lubricant named STP.

STP is today, on record, admitting that all three once-big automakers in Detroit regard its product as, perhaps, patent medicine. So, better than 40 springs ago in the 1960s, Big Andy vowed to overcome the libel by promoting STP via racing. What's more, having earlier acquired at a fire sale what was left of the team of famously loud-yodeling and hexed blown Novis, he was in possession of what seemed the perfect marketing tool. He sprayed them STP orange, slapped STP decals all over them, and then carried them back to six Memorial Days 500s.

Unfortunately, no matter how much STP got pumped into a Novi, the monster went right on crashing, exploding, and stubbornly refusing to finish.

Fed up at last, Big Andy in 1966 happened to bump into Colin Chapman, and, in effect, pleaded, "I don't know what to do with this SOB. Will you take it?"

Chapman was warming to the idea of slapping the bull Novi inside one of his flyweight coffins-on-wheels, and only Allah knows how many lives got saved when he didn't get to. Something else happened.

Everybody had been racing their Meyer-Drakes around Indy for so long that it had been years since anybody had read the 500's rulebook regarding alternate powerplants to internal combustion. Per his wildly controversial memoirs, Big Andrew now did: he made the

Halibrand wheels enhance the contours of this mild-custom T-Bird. *Bob Falcon*

Above and left:
SoCal Speed Shop promoted its vaunted name on the flanks of Alex Xydias' gorgeous, flathead-powered belly-tanker. The original shop closed in 1961 but was reincarnated in 1997 by top hot rodder Pete Chapouris. *Greg Sharp collection*

Smile, Andy. *Bob Tronolone*

huge decision to take a swing at the avant garde and conquer the Brickyard with a gas turbine out of Canada, a creation that depended on expanding exhaust gases for motivating the helicopters of the country's Air Force.

Despite the fact that it doesn't get much, if any, credit in Andy's memoirs, a fantastic L.A. talent bank was responsible for the creation of the STP turbine. Its leader was none other than icon Parnelli Jones, who, before consenting to chauffeur the thing, had to be assured constantly that its output shaft, chugging along at a hard 70,000 rpm, wouldn't blow him full of shrapnel à la a Top Fuel digger.

Nat the Glass Man and Thongs Burrell did the fiberglassing and shaping. The task of putting together the 20,000-rivet aluminum boxed spine fell to the wizard fabricator and drag-racer Jim Lytle, previously celebrated for his Quad Al, the 12,000-horsepower terror of Lions flung by four V-12 Allison airplane engines.

The gentleman who turned out to be the most important member of the squad also was the most anonymous, just as public relation flacks are supposed to be. He was William C. Dredge. Parts of Dredge's subsequent PR blitz were flashy and crude, a circus of red and white STP stickers and polka-dot STP publicity uniforms and blazers with Andy and his gut well in the lead.

Andy-the-dandy ripped the Indianapolis Motor Speedway and its 500 a new one with his smoke-and-mirrors STP Turbine.
Bob Tronolone

Happy Jean Marcenac, right, the French-ancestored technician of speed, went clear back to the age of Frank Lockhart and Frank's deadly LSR run of 1928. Then M Jean had mechanical custody of the intimidating Novi for decades. In Andy's memoirs, poor Jean gets slammed as a retard who couldn't properly time the monster V-8. *Greg Sharp collection*

Andy spent years chasing the Indy 500 grail, always missing it despite such can't-miss sponsorships as this STP pairing of Colin Chapman and the peerless Scot, Jim Clark. *Bob Tronolone*

The Granatellis were a loving family of hopelessly obsessed racers, left to right, Joe, Andy, and Vince. *Greg Sharp collection*

The unequalled Parnelli Jones caught the chair in the STP Turbine, and it was a good thing, because probably nobody else had the chops to handle it. Tempermental buggy. Its idle speed was too high for cornering, so it had to be checked with the brakes on all 800 Brickyard corners. The throttle lag was insane. Parnelli was counting one thousand, two thousand, three thousand, and then *boom!*, one thousand or so turbine horsepower hit the bloodstream and Parnelli exploded forward. *Bob Tronolone*

But Bill Dredge realized that the drama of the STP turbine had something for everybody. For mainstream news reporters, the story had the buzz they liked. And who would know this better than Bill, formerly the car editor of the *Times*? For the credulous, it was a gizmo story to fire hearts and interest. And for end-of-the-world, save-the-planet environmentalists, the STP turbine carried startling implications extending far beyond racing, running as it did on renewable fuel producing no hydrocarbons and thereby offering a happy alternative to the noxious old internal combustion mill.

Sounds wonderful. What you have to know, however, is that crap was the coin of the realm. Far from being mankind's salvation, the legend of the STP turbine was a huge hoax. For one reason or another, no turbine ever made it onto the freeways or interstates.

Nor did the STP turbine live up to its advanced billing and capture the 1967 500, Parnelli falling out late with a reported failed transmission bearing. P. J. had, however, shattered some dozen speed records, which caused the forward-thinking brains of the Indianapolis

Speedway to react. With the internal combustion mob cheering it on, Indy slashed the turbine power.

Big Andy didn't think that fair and brought a lawsuit to overturn the rules. He lost, of course. You don't bring suit against Indianapolis in Indianapolis. But Andy also won, because Andy came across in the national press as progressive and the Speedway reactionary. STP also attained vats of ink, and sales skyrocketed. Andy was a popular late-night guest on Joey Bishop and also on Johnny Carson. At its peak, STP reported $50 million sales seasons. Andy returned in 1968 with smaller turbines, Pratt & Whitneys with the first two axial stage compressors removed and the annulus reduced. Parnelli in the meantime had retired, so Andy had to scare up driving and engineering talent outside L.A. He went with a chassis made by Lotus, and after the regular human sacrifice—a fine Brit driver named Spence—the other STP turbines set speed records starting on the front row, and again led early and broke late.

Trying to salvage the season, Big Andy took them to the other champ car tracks, and after no wins in eight

starts, they appeared at the season finale at ornery old Riverside. Both of them lost their brakes on friendly Turn 9, and its familiar wall said, "Hello, my beauties!"

Big Andy got out of the turbine business afterward, instead choosing to have STP sponsor the conventional, dependable turbocharged Fords and Drakes of other teams, and collected two 500s over the next four seasons.

Sometime after this, he surrendered the STP presidency and, with a reported $400 million in his jeans, ceased racing. Without Big Andy and the fantastic Dredge endorsing it, STP slipped from sales leadership.

Andy, in this twenty-first century, looks down upon the rest of us L.A. peasants from his mansion—the mansion that STP syrup built—in ritzy Santa Barbara's Montecito district, where a medium-priced shanty goes for $2 mil. His neighbors have included the French chef Julia Child, the trendy quill T. Coraghessan Boyle, and Oprah and her $70 million digs.

Give credit to Big Andy: he has staying power and continues to get toasted at honorary banquets. And at one of the most recent, the host introduced Andy with the confession that he always used STP because Andy said to, but that he, the host, still didn't know what STP did.

"I'll tell you what STP did," Big Andy merrily responded, sidestepping the question. "It made me a multi-millionaire."

Exactly what he always wanted to be. Mission accomplished.

CHAPTER ELEVEN

SCHMOOZIN' AND BOOZIN'

Los Angeles offers the hope of being one of the rottenest cities in the country.

—Edward M. Davis, police chief

The vanishing alumni of Gilmore Stadium's grand old mob of L.A. midget racers used to regularly assemble for eats and booze and gab at another "Gilmore Roars Again" fete. Glamorous Gilmore—which enjoyed the widest fame and reputation of all the mini-arenas hosting the midget racing boom—fell in 1950 to make space for CBS Television City. But until the grim reaper got the last of them, Gilmorians went right on gathering every summer at the adobe villa of track potentate Earl Gilmore, celebrating the sweet L.A. past. *Neil Nissing*

We're just a few seasons into the twenty-first century, and already the L.A. racing family no longer behaves, talks, constructs the same type of race cars, or even races as it did during the twentieth. But left over from the dead century are lots of lively ghosts, many of whom can be found in the 8000 block of Beverly Boulevard. Today the site is a joyless power station, but during the late 1950s and early 1960s it was the Grand Prix Restaurant. Nothing glitzy, but it was a racing caravansary enjoying a short but jumping history for its alcoholic refreshment and banter.

Opposite: Pasadena's Fletcher Aviation, on Green and Delacy Street, sponsored a Porsche in the Mexican Road Race and, as the premier tank manufacturer on the planet, stamped out the original aviation belly tankage for the P-38, P-47, P-51, F-47, and F-51 aircraft. Those that survived World War II found fresh hot rod lives on the lakes. Evans Special at speed here at El Mirage, 1952. *Greg Sharp collection*

One of the Grand Prix's owners was a merry matriculate of the vino-doll-face-melody academy, a funny and happy man named Bobby Drake, who used to casually flip everybody the bird while racing. He was a disheveled, totally irreverent character who once supposedly ran a fishing boat, or wandered the floor of the Pacific as a professional deep-sea diver, yet had somehow became a restaurateur. He was astonishing. Just as fast as—and frequently faster than—L.A.'s more famous types, he scored the victory of his life in a broken-down Cooper Climax in the nationals at Palm Springs, then took no prisoners in a terrific Birdcage Maserati. At one point he got caught in a fuel-doping scandal. That particular hornets' nest led to Bobby's brief unemployment.

But about then his friends the Balchowskys arrived, advising Bobby to quit putting on the Ritz with all those high-toned foreign jobs and to get down and dirty with 400 righteous cubic inches of nailhead Buick, handing Bobby the keys to Ol' Yeller.

Grand Prix restaurant major-domo Bobby Drake, No. 49
Cooper-Climax dwarf, prepares to do a "Ken Miles" and
swarm all over the bloated heavy metal in front of him.
Bob Tronolone

Being smart, Bobby sailed for the deal. Many monster moments followed. Then, courtesy of Max's friend Haskell (*Who's Afraid of Virginia Woolf?*) Wexler, they got out of racing and into the movies together, performing stunt jobs as well as turning Ol' Yellers into camera chase cars. And it was more laughs and hot times until the 1990s, when Bobby unexpectedly succumbed in the old actors' home.

Hotheads, short-fusers, sugar daddies, power brokers, worthless kibitizers, star race drivers and hacks, assorted lovers and current and former spouses, plus doll babies of all shapes and sizes comprised the clientele of the Grand Prix. All of them always got well eyeballed by Gus Vignolle, Gus and his booze-smoked brain debating who among them *Motoracing* might savagely libel in its next number.

Racing movies hit the screen on Tuesday and Thursday evenings, and I helped close down the bar many a night, with two nights in particular, both involving doll faces, leading the pack.

In addition to the dwarf Climax, Bobby's racing assignment including this Birdcage Maser. It was fast as a .357 magnum cartridge, and mercifully minus all that showoffish high-revving rigmarole of some Ferraris. If anything, it sounded like a big cucumber Meyer-Drake roadster. *Bob Tronolone*

Alas, not only did Bobby's Birdcage sound like a Meyer-Drake, it smelled like one. So right after Bobby had won big at Memorial Day Santa Barbara, the Birdcage got spiked when somebody protested it was burning illegal doped fuel. With a suspension hanging over his head, the Birdcage's owner, grumpy Joe Lubin, pedaled it to another team. Bobby was suddenly unemployed.
Bob Tronolone

RIP RON

I had never seen Ron O'Dell happier. Ron was one good-looking stud as well as a soldier of the Porsche Carrera, so expert at winning checkers and cups in production car skirmishes that he occasionally spooked Ronnie Bucknum. Maybe Ron was as fast a driver as Ronnie, but he never caught the same breaks. He'd also read way too much of Kenny Purdy's dreamy claptrap about hero drivers and Ferrari 4.9s and dreamy doll faces. So when Ron finally did get to go to Riverside and take a spin in one of the last moldy 4.9s—the old crate locked up in first gear in just one lap—he was forever hooked. And just like in *Appointment in Samarra*—that penny-dreadful tome about suicide and death, where a single tossed drink triggers a conflagration—that one lap was going to unravel Ron's life.

As a newspaper distributor barely squeezing out a paycheck, he was earning a living but hardly enough of one to support a Ferrari habit. Ron needed a sugar daddy. But the closest thing he could find was a twice-married doll face, who was ex-restaurant carhop, ex-telephone operator, and proprietress of her own small salon that was dragging down $150 a week. A lot of heads would have to be cut to pay for a Ferrari, but for Ron it was a beginning.

Also, Ron's end. The lady barber was a firecracker and, per later court testimony, she and Ron "maintained a disposition to be quarrelsome with one another." Early one a.m., the O'Dells decided to engage in another of their rip-roarers. Upon exhausting themselves, they at

last broke off the quarrel, with Ron retiring to bed and the lady barber to the living room to iron some clothing. Then Ron awoke and decided to resume the quarrel. It was a dumb mistake, because the lady barber kept a blue-steel .357 magnum around the house, and after missing Ron with the first round, finished him with the second.

I can still see Ron beaming, and the lady barber (who was a knock-out) flashing her assassin's eyes. It was a Wednesday night one week after their wedding, and one week prior to Ron's eclipse: at the Grand Prix he was showing off his new bride, also who he expected to be his new Ferrari sugar daddy, when the only place she really was going was into the lockup for homicide in the second degree.

There's no genteel way of putting this, and I don't necessarily mean it critically, but set an L.A. driver—and it doesn't matter if he's sports car, Indy car, drag race, or taxicab issue—set him in front of a stack of stones, and he will seduce the entire stack on the off chance that there's a Gila monster lurking inside. Love those doll faces! Wives, mothers, girlfriend's sister, grandmothers—they all are at risk when L.A. race drivers are on the prowl.

So, one lusty night at the Grand Prix, I happened to be in attendance with a pole position date, "Carol," a siren of international racing and normally the consort of race drivers instead of some common scribbler.

Carol was stunning. I could feel the libido of every race driver in the place revving up. After we were seated

CERTIFICATION OF VITAL RECORD

COUNTY OF LOS ANGELES • REGISTRAR-RECORDER/COUNTY CLERK

CERTIFICATE OF DEATH
STATE OF CALIFORNIA—DEPARTMENT OF PUBLIC HEALTH

LOCAL REGISTRATION DISTRICT AND 7040 — CERTIFICATE NUMBER — 14646

1A. NAME OF DECEASED—FIRST NAME: Ronald
1B. MIDDLE NAME: Keith
1C. LAST NAME: O'Dell
2A. DATE OF DEATH—MONTH, DAY, YEAR: August 11, 1961
2B. HOUR: 2:40 A.M.

3. SEX: Male
4. COLOR OR RACE: Caucasian
5. BIRTHPLACE: Washington
6. DATE OF BIRTH: Dec. 23, 1927
7. AGE (LAST BIRTHDAY): 33 YEARS

8. NAME AND BIRTHPLACE OF FATHER: David J. O'Dell, Michigan
9. MAIDEN NAME AND BIRTHPLACE OF MOTHER: Gladys E. Stevenson, Washington
10. CITIZEN OF WHAT COUNTRY: U.S.A.
11. SOCIAL SECURITY NUMBER: 568-28-9252

12. LAST OCCUPATION: Newspaper Distributor
13. NUMBER OF YEARS IN THIS OCCUPATION: 4
14. NAME OF LAST EMPLOYING COMPANY OR FIRM: Self Employed
15. KIND OF INDUSTRY OR BUSINESS: Newspaper Distribution

16. IF DECEASED WAS EVER IN U.S. ARMED FORCES, GIVE WAR OR DATES OF SERVICE: WW II
17. SPECIFY MARRIED, NEVER MARRIED, WIDOWED, DIVORCED: Married
18A. NAME OF PRESENT SPOUSE: Mary Ellen O'Dell
18B. PRESENT OR LAST OCCUPATION OF SPOUSE: Beauty Operator

19A. PLACE OF DEATH—NAME OF HOSPITAL: (None)
19B. STREET ADDRESS: 6069 Riverside Ave.
19C. CITY OR TOWN: Huntington Park
19D. COUNTY: Los Angeles
19E. LENGTH OF STAY IN COUNTY OF DEATH: 14 YEARS
19F. LENGTH OF STAY IN CALIFORNIA: 28 YEARS

20A. LAST USUAL RESIDENCE—STREET ADDRESS: 6069 Riverside Ave.
20C. CITY OR TOWN: Huntington Park
20D. COUNTY: Los Angeles
20E. STATE: California
21A. NAME OF INFORMANT: Father: David J. O'Dell
21B. ADDRESS OF INFORMANT: Ephrata, Washington

22B. CORONER: Autopsy
22E. DATE SIGNED: 8-17-61

23. SPECIFY BURIAL, ENTOMBMENT, OR CREMATION: Burial
24. DATE: Aug. 16, 1961
25. NAME OF CEMETERY OR CREMATORY: Rose Hills Memorial Park
27. NAME OF FUNERAL DIRECTOR: Rose Hills Mortuary
28. DATE ACCEPTED FOR REGISTRATION: AUG 21 1961

30. CAUSE OF DEATH
PART I. DEATH WAS CAUSED BY: IMMEDIATE CAUSE (A): Gunshot wound of chest with laceration of heart and massive intrathoracic hemorrhage

34A. SPECIFY ACCIDENT, SUICIDE OR HOMICIDE: Homicide
34B. DESCRIBE HOW INJURY OCCURRED: As above by known person.

35A. TIME OF INJURY: 2:17 A.M. August 11, 1961
35B. INJURY OCCURRED: ☑ NOT WHILE AT WORK
35C. PLACE OF INJURY: Home
35D. CITY, TOWN, OR LOCATION: Huntington Park — COUNTY: LA — STATE: Calif.

This is to certify that this document is a true copy of the official record filed with the Registrar-Recorder/County Clerk.

CONNY B. McCORMACK
Registrar-Recorder/County Clerk

JAN 31 1997
19-505770

This copy not valid unless prepared on engraved border displaying the Seal and Signature of the Registrar-Recorder/County Clerk.

ANY ALTERATION OR ERASURE VOIDS THIS CERTIFICATE

RIP, Ron, you poor SOB. One life-altering lap in a Ferrari led to his termination by gunfire. *Joe Scalzo collection*

182

What a waste! Team Cunningham brought these three sumptuous Birdcage Masers to Riverside for another *Times* GP all ready to mow down L.A. cars and cowboys. Instead, we kicked the dog crap out of them and sent 'em home beaten and miserably disgraced. *Bob Tronolone*

for dinner, I knew it was only a matter of time before some race driver would be arriving at our table, saying "Hi, Scoop! Who's your cute little friend?"

"Hi, Scoop! Who's your cute little friend?"

It was old Eric Hauser, creator of Riverside Turn 1 notoriety, and he had already shifted gears into God's-gift-to-women mode. He'd even put on his toupee.

Without invitation, he sat down at our table and joined us. Also without invitation, he began talking. This was the worst thing that could happen. He was going to lecture on high finance. And sure enough—uttering the edicts in a strange, fantastic stock market patois—he was off and running about inflation, deflation, portfolios, hedge funds, offshore funds, and the bear market.

I wanted to call him out of order, but he was in rare stupendous form, barricading every utterance against possible verbal onslaughts. There was just no shutting the guy up.

In frustration, I excused myself and when I got back to the table, as I expected, all the stock market baboonery was gone and at full speed Eric was trying to talk his way into Carol's bloomers. He never made it. Yet scribblers, too, can chase doll faces and get their ashes hauled. I did.

MR. CORVETTE

Ventura Boulevard, that 9-mile-long passageway connecting the San Fernando Valley from east to west, contains more booze dives per square mile than even 16th Street, Indianapolis. Visiting it again in 2006, I found Ventura as busy and boozy as ever. But the parking lot in Sherman Oaks, where Cal Bailey used to deposit his red Corvette, was missing, and so was Cal's favorite house of spirits, the Tender Trap. Here it was where Cal, called "Mr. Corvette," used to joke, curse, threaten, and knock back the loudmouth till the wee hours. Poor palooka Cal has himself been among the missing for 40 years, or since 1966. This was the mad season when he at last forsook his cult status as Mr. Corvette to achieve far greater notoriety with his photograph on the front page of the *Times*. There he was, Mr. Corvette—muscular shoulders, bull neck, baleful face, and straining, slightly crazy eyes. When the photograph was published, some

Bobby Drake wasn't unemployed for long. Iconoclast Max Balchowsky, a friend and admirer, advised Bobby to get down and dirty with 400 righteous cubic inches of nailhead Buick. Max was offering Bobby the wheelhouse of L.A.'s, ultimate backyard bomb, Ol' Yeller. Many monster moments followed for himself, Max, and Ol' Yeller, none bigger than at a Riverside Grand Prix, when Bobby whipped a Scarab but took runner-up to a high-falutin' Birdcage belonging to the Maserati importers of Beverly Hills. Afterward, the champion Birdcage had to visit the hospital; and the Scarab got loaded inside its custom hauler. Legend suggests that Bobby and Max put Ol' Yeller on the freeway and drove home to L.A. giggling all the way. *Bob Tronolone*

of us wondered whether the picture was taken after he was shot.

At the beginning of another recreational evening at the Tender Trap, big Cal tended to be jovial, with belligerence gaining the upper hand as the night wore on. Chug-a-lugging suds not out of a glass but a bottle, for additional show-boating he'd whip out a $100 bill to wrap around the neck of the bottle. Sometimes, too, you'd listen to him lying like a psychopath about all the burglaries and bank heists and stickups he secretly pulled off without getting caught. And if you disagreed with him, he'd inquire if you'd like to have your head stuffed inside a cement mixer.

So far as all of us knew, there were two things Cal Bailey truly loved: one being his wife and family, and the other his collection of Corvettes. Despite her husband's wild and reckless character, and all the saturnalias at the Tender Trap, Cal's long-suffering bride—she was a ravishing beauty 15 years Cal's junior—regarded him as

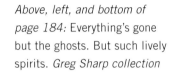

Above, left, and bottom of page 184: Everything's gone but the ghosts. But such lively spirits. *Greg Sharp collection*

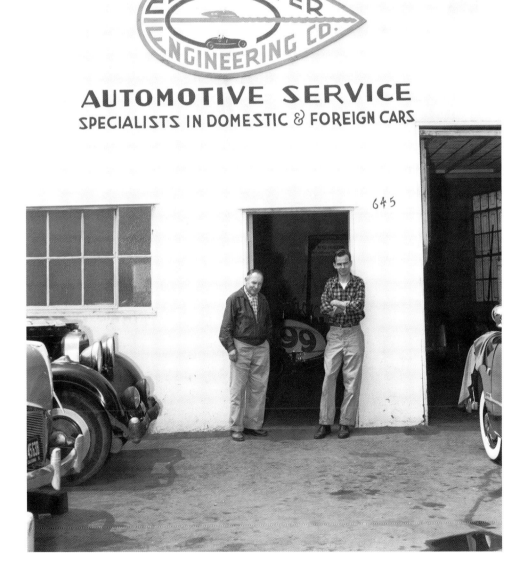

Most embarrassing defeat ever for Los Angeles warriors came in 1957, again at Riverside. Ricardo Rodriguez—here a couple seasons later—was a mad little gunner, still four months shy of his 16th birthday and just up from bicycles and motorbikes, when he arrived with a silver RS Porsche with MEXICO emblazoned on its hood. Some of L.A.'s fastest Porsche, Lotus, and Cooper-Climax heroes—Bobby Drake and Ken Miles among them—were Ricardo's opponents. Our L.A. cowboys fired on him and he fired back. Hurtling right past them, he led all of them on a merry chase, winning so devastatingly that he lapped everything but second, third, and fourth places. *Bob Tronolone*

the most gentle and mildest of men. Or so she said. The Baileys lived in a big house in the San Fernando Valley, and the man known as Mr. Corvette was a member of the PTA who chauffeured the kids to church on Sundays.

Cal was not always Mr. Corvette. When he first got into amateur sports car racing, he tooled a gullwing 300SL, one purchased from none other than Lance Reventlow. But after Wild Billy Mitchell and Eddie Cole's V-8 hit big, he wisely made the big switch to plastic.

He came to own a pair of Corvettes, perhaps more. One was a red road sleeper, innocently licensed for the avenues. It paid regular visits to Hollywood Motors, where Max Balchowsky tweaked it into becoming, arguably, L.A.'s fastest street 'Vette. Cal knew what speed was. Saying so long to Max, he'd scald north on Mulholland, cross the top of the Hollywood Hills, then plunge down the other side to faithfully skid his red bomb to a halt in the parking lot of the Tender Trap for the start of cocktail hour.

His second Corvette was a still faster black one, No. 4, so raging it could not set wheels on the street at all. This was Cal's road racer, and at every sports car track, from Palm Springs to Paramount Ranch, he pitched in,

defending the honor of the tribe of L.A. Corvettes. But he was erratic, got No. 4 off the pavement a lot, and lacked the cool temperament demanded of a winner.

Naturally enough, gossip soon spread about bad, black No. 4's immense power. Dan Gurney, then unknown and penniless, had just flunked out of a Ferrari-chauffeuring seminar at Tony Parravano U, Willow Springs. He was still on the make for a sugar daddy and hit up Cal at length. Cal at last gave Dan the okay for Riverside International Raceway's inaugural.

With what was obviously shattering ease, Gurney and No. 4 won. Won huge. The victory, in fact, became the talk of L.A. sports car racing, leading to Frank Arciero hooking up Dan to the same Ferrari 4.9 that would later bring nothing but grief to Ron O'Dell. And Dan's stature grew so enormous that he was being petitioned by Enzo Ferrari himself, asking Dan to join the Formula 1 squad.

Cal Bailey, in the meanwhile, basked briefly in his honorable new image as the sugar daddy responsible for launching Dan Gurney. But then Cal proceeded to lose his shirt in a truly hair-frying business venture involving a bowling alley. And following this, he embarked on the

UNFAIR ADVANTAGE

All of us in L.A. yawned with boredom when, at the 1994 Indy 500, Unfair Advantage Roger Penske stood on its head a statute intended to create less-expensive stock-block engines and instead had his fat friends at Mercedes tool up a purebred Benz Panzer, which devastated all opposition by 100 horsepower or so, winning easily. Out in L.A., however, we'd already been there, done that. Decades earlier, in 1962, Unfair Advantage had attended Riverside and looted the rule book by showing up for the sports car Grand Prix with a single-seater Formula One car with coachwork; and then successfully railroaded the mutant right past the brain-dead technical scrutineers to capture the GP. Even if they'd been smart enough to think of it, L.A.'s happy-go-lucky sugar daddies of yore never would have countenanced so sneaky a maneuver. They were rivals yet fond buddies. They kept no secrets and all were onto each other. Many of them even ran unsuccessful teams—yet the laughs never stopped. Racing was joy. Nonetheless, Unfair Advantage discovered his now-familiar *modus operandi* at Riverside: nail the racing rule book of any ambiguity; then get hold of the one exotic gizmo nobody else has thought of or

Bob Tronolone

can afford. Following his Benz Panzer trickery of 1994, the Indy 500 attempted to stop Roger, and knock off at last that deadly "unfair advantage" business of his, by disbanding its existing sanctioning body and forming a new, anti-Penske, one. But in the twenty-first century, the ever-rampaging Roger continues shocking the Hoosiers by winning their 500 anyway.

caper of his career, whose objective was to kidnap for ransom one of L.A.'s big tire and rubber rajahs.

That little trick got him killed, and also confirmed the worst suspicions of his rattled drinking buddies at the Tender Trap, who suddenly came to understand the source of Mr. Corvette's gangster talk and his flauntings of hundred dollar bills. Cal's ravishing spouse—herself belatedly revealing her late husband's secret life—described an odd domestic episode that revolved around Cal's creating an enormous hole in the floor of their kitchen. Deliberately discharging a sawed-off shotgun will do that. But the prize for receiving the biggest jolt of all went to Lance Reventlow. When he'd sold Cal his

300SL, Lance had neglected to realize that Cal was marking him down as a future snatch victim himself.

The total denigration of Cal's character achieved its peak when the police went public and pronounced him a compulsive, lifelong, wholly inept thug, whom the constabularies of two nations had stuck behind bars in the 1940s and early 1950s. But they couldn't hunt down and deliver the capital punishment they believed he deserved until he dressed up in a Halloween mask and undertook the kidnapping of Leonard Firestone 16 years later.

Cal Bailey was born in Texas in 1922 and, by the time he reached our city a generation later, he had indeed seen the inside of penitentiaries in the United States and

Canada, attesting to his unsoundness as a car thief, robber, and bungling burglar. But thanks to the salutary influences of Los Angeles, for a brief period he remained reasonably clean.

It didn't last. Cal's troubles began when, in trade for some range land he'd managed to acquire in Oregon, he came into possession of a bowling alley out in the middle of the Mojave Desert. This became an unmitigated disaster. The bowling alley piled up thousands in debts, and Cal, who suddenly had litigious investors after him, decided to torch the place for insurance.

But his midnight arson party went awry because all the gasoline fuses Cal had set refused to ignite. Opening a door to investigate what was wrong, he unwittingly supplied the fire scene with the last ingredient it was missing: air. The following backdraft and violent explosion lifted the roof off the structure and hurled Cal out into the street, as well as back to the attention of his friends the bulls. Cal, however, could not be prosecuted for burning down his own property. Encouraged, he next set out to sue the insurance company for refusing to pay off, and of course was soundly defeated.

Life became dull, especially since he was out of racing, having sold No. 4. And Cal's bankroll was now as deficient as his smarts. Having earlier become casually acquainted with Leonard Firestone, and having had a long conversation with him on the subject of Corvettes, Cal concluded he might as well shanghai him for ransom.

Following weeks of vacillation about the amount of restitution ($8 million? $2 million?), Cal and his henchman, one George Skalla, at last initiated the abduction by motoring toward Firestone's Beverly Hills estate high in secluded Coldwater Canyon.

For once, Cal was not driving a Corvette. He was the driver of a passenger car he had earlier charged goon Skalla to borrow via midnight auto parts. The two morons stopped so that Cal could telephone Firestone's. A maid provided the information that Mr. Firestone was home but indisposed.

Cal garbled the message. "Firestone's working on the garbage disposal," he explained to Skalla. "Guess he's throwing Coke bottles down there."

Moments later, Cal and Skalla, crook and accomplice, pulled onto Firestone's semicircular drive. Dressed up in a ghoul's mask for Halloween and flourishing a big revolver, Cal identified himself as the parcel post delivery man, then opened Firestone's front door to confidently waltz inside.

He was hit immediately by a cannonade of gunfire discharged by three barricaded homicide dicks, who had been patiently waiting inside to fill Mr. Corvette full of as much lead as they possibly could.

The maid who'd answered the phone had been an undercover police agent. Leonard Firestone wasn't at home and hadn't been ever since George Skalla had run to the police to rat out Cal with news of his plans. Cal could not have possibly chosen a more lethal accomplice. Himself an ex-jailbird about to be returned to prison, Skalla—who had absolutely believed Cal's threats about "sticking your head into a cement mixer" and consequently was petrified of him—had sung and sung and sung. A stool pigeon magnificent.

As a result, the coppers had known more about the kidnapping than Bailey did; they even rented the getaway vehicle that Cal had instructed Skalla to steal. Skalla was furthermore wired for sound, and those detectives waiting to send him to eternity presumably got a good chuckle about Cal's "garbage disposal" remark.

As befits a Judas goat, Skalla perished with Cal in the fusillade. With life oozing out of him, he asked his policemen friends, who had become his assassins, what had gone wrong and was informed he'd neglected to duck. Some epitaph.

All its customers agreed that the Tender Trap became a far more peaceful joint without Cal threatening to jam skulls into cement mixers. A duller one too. It soon tanked.

In a last, bizarre twist, heirs of George Skalla tried, unsuccessfully, to sue the police for workman's compensation benefits. For, after all, hadn't stone-stupid Skalla been employed as a cop snitch instead of the fumbling associate of brigand Cal Bailey, Mr. Corvette?

FUMBLER

The old-money community of Pasadena, once a village of millionaires, used to be a village of racers. Wise old Art Sparks mortgaged his Pasadena home to secure the long green required to construct his Indianapolis Big and Little Six series; also in Pasadena, he founded his corporation, Forged True Pistons. Famous around the globe.

Frank Monise, a rare surviving top Lotus pilot, was based here. So were the Milne brothers, Jack and Cordy, world champions of international speedway motorbiking, spouses of stripper royalty like Madame Lili St. Cyr. They were also pioneer operators of one of the first sports car dealerships, whose lead salesman was Bob "Fearless" Feurhelm, a colleague of Thanks a Million Simpson and perhaps the funniest man in L.A. Blair's Speed Shop is still in Pasadena. Before quitting the country to complete the task of drinking himself to oblivion in rural Mexico, Gus Vignolle was briefly a Pasadenan. He turned his apartment into a 24-hour wet bar, and every time I'd go visit I got burned to the ground.

Pasadena's racing saloon of note was the Peppertree restaurant on Walnut Avenue, where I used to share lots of laughs and Seagrams VO with Fearless Feurhelm before he had his last adventure in Baja, which culminated with his taking square in the face the ax end of a low-diving Piper Cherokee. George Follmer, the dapper insurance salesman/tire dealer with the wild gleam in his eye who knew just what to do with a race car's loud pedal, was still another Peppertree denizen.

In 1998, when L.A. expatriate Georgie came down from his home near Coeur d'Alene, Idaho, trying to sell a Formula 1 Shadow he owned, we made the Peppertree—since torn down—our meeting place.

The Chablis was chilled, the reminiscences worth repeating. Along with Parnelli, George was perhaps L.A.'s most versatile shoe. Fast in anything, something in George prohibited him from putting down roots anywhere. So he recalled what it was like being a sporty car guy with a low-buck, iron-block stovebolt confronting the reigning Indy guys with their turbo Drakes and Fords . . . and blowing their butts sideways by a margin of 2 miles. From there he segued into war stories of Formula 1, Indy, and Daytona 500s, Can-Ams, Trans-Ams, Formula 5000s, and the International Race of Champions. On taxicab bullrings he raced the 409 Impala of Nat Reeder, and we talked about the Glass

Man. He won the United States Road Racing Championship series and throttled the Chaparrals of Jim Hall in an amazing Porsche prepped by Bruce Burness, and we talked about Bruce.

I love bad boys, and Follmer always was one of the worst. Penske once named him "Fumbler," and it stuck because George could be an incorrigible employee, and not just with Team Penske. Messes Georgie brought on included a dandy riot in the victory circle of a Trans-Am pony car meet. Evading security Georgie inveigled his way in, strolled up to the race winner, and, under the pretext of extending congrats, instead began swinging on him. The guy had nudged him off the road, causing Georgie to blow. He's kin to Scotty Cain and Dickie Rathmann; their problem solving was hands-on—on your nose, your chin, your ribs, your gut . . .

All the vino was gone, it was time to go, yet George had a last action vignette. He recalled a Cam-Am contest the strange season when he'd had to go at top speed to wrap up a main event in under 45 minutes. His main opponent was internal—a shot of lidocaine holding off the hurts from his torn-up rib cage. If he exceeded 45 minutes, pain would stab him like a razor, negative reinforcement in pure form. He succeeded.

I took a last look around the Peppertree for Fearless Feurhelm, but couldn't find him anywhere.

GILMORE ROARS AGAIN

Like the playing of "Taps," L.A., throughout its closing decades, threw many a last, all-sales-final, farewell party. It took lots of work to put on such jamborees, and most of them were pretty bad, or at least so they seemed to me. Rather than blowouts energizing the lost past, too often they were slobbery melancholy wakes mourning its end. Too much freaking nostalgia. Too many maudlin old-times.

One heavily attended L.A. reunion that used to never sentimentalize but invigorate, was the annual Gilmore Roars Again fete honoring Gilmore Stadium and its grand old mob of doodlebug racers. Glamorous Gilmore—it enjoyed the widest fame and reputation of all the mini-arenas hosting the midget car racing boom of the 1930s and 1940s. It fell decades ago to make room for CBS Television City. But after Gilmore was missing for half a century, and most of its proud racer tribe had gone the way of the world and disappeared, Gilmore celebrations grew from all-midget clambakes to embrace sounds, race cars, and potentates from the L.A. canon in general.

Down on the Earl Gilmore adobe villa at Beverly and Fairfax, under the August sun, I noticed with appreciation a 1940s belly tanker prepped by famed nitro-mixologist Barney Navarro, a shimmering replica of a Bill Stroppe Lincoln from the Mexican Road Race, and the sensational Ford V8-60 midget used by Knothead Heath to conquer a Riverside 500-miler. I said hello to Parnelli, who never misses such parties, and also visited with the L.A. expatriate from the old Culver City gang of race mechanics, Herbie Porter (the undertaker got him less than a month later), who contributed to my education with a yarn about the seething argument he and Colin Chapman had once engaged in. Herbie insisted that the dumbest race drivers in the world came from L.A., and Chapman argued back, no, it wasn't true, no race drivers could be more stupid than those of the United Kingdom.

During one Gilmore reunion, Mr. Smokey Yunick himself journeyed clear from Daytona Beach, and everybody in attendance fortunate enough to have taken part in the Indy 500's era of big cucumber Meyer-Drakes was well pleased to welcome him. Though not truly L.A.-crazy, Smokey, during those golden times, could function like he was. Most Mays at the Brickyard, he remembered to carry along his Florida notary public's ticket for convincing willing Hoosier doll faces that he was licensed to bring happy couples together in weekend-long wedlock—ceremonies not conducted at the courthouse, naturally, but as often as not in the romantic atmosphere of motel shower stalls.

Gilmorians were not xenophobic; we heartily welcomed as guests any out-of-state racers who'd ever had the guts to race in L.A. and be beaten and fiercely humiliated. Guts is exactly what it took to come to Los Angeles and risk getting told off by Crabby Travers, or having Scotty Cain lock you up in a full-nelson, or feel the bite of Riverside Raceway taking a hunk of your posterior—which is what happened to this famous Midwest hero with the hot Corvette I ran into at a 1998 Gilmore.

The year was 1959. All summer this individual had been bushwhacking the plastic pachyderm competition east of the Rockies. But L.A. was way out of his jurisdiction. We had, after all, really fast Corvettes out here. So when the hero and his hot Chicago Corvette arrived with much fanfare at Riverside, our guys were ready for him.

They ran a tag-team, physical comedy routine on him that was unrelenting. On the first lap into the switchback esses, one of our lads went broadside in front of the visiting hero, but also swerved off the switchbacks and out into the dirt where he began performing endos. Then, at Turn 9, a second L.A. Corvette struck from behind a third, sending it splintering into the boilerplate.

And as one ambulance was departing from the switchbacks with the wounded endo guy, and a second was getting dispatched to Turn 9, Riverside's third and last meat wagon was on its way back to the switchbacks where a fourth L.A. Corvette had turned turtle. The race was won by a fifth L.A. Corvette, manhandled by Bobby Bondurant, later to form one of the first race car driving academies. Well behind was the by-now-shaken Midwest hero. Had Davey been there, he'd have lapped him. Afterward, there'd been nothing for him to do but turn and run for Chicago.

I said hello and tried talking to this loser anyway. Which I immediately regretted, because he proceeded to give me a totally screwed and wildly inaccurate account of how he'd completely annihilated all our L.A. Corvettes at Riverside long ago.

In your dreams, I thought. To paraphrase a song, I wanted to blast him with a Gus Vignolle shot. But I was there to celebrate the twentieth century, not bury it. So the Sal Scarpitta in me came through.

"Yes," I replied, brightly smiling and meaning it, "those used to be some great times out here, didn't they?"

INDEX

24 Hours of Daytona, 43
Adamic, Louis, 166
Adams, Clyde, 142
Agajanian, J. C., 70, 94, 98, 155, 156, 158–161, 163
All-American Racers, 25, 28
Allison, Bobby, 86
Alten, Frank, 114
American Honda, 29
Andretti, Mario, 115
Arciero, Frank, 117–119, 121, 149, 164
Arfons, Art , 134–137, 139
Arfons, Walt, 134
Ascari, Alberto, 19
Ascot Park, 79, 80, 82, 97, 106, 117, 160
Atlantic Speedway, 107
Avant, Kirby, 43, 65, 102
Ayulo, Manual "Yo Yo," 22, 23, 76
Bailey, Cal, 58, 183, 184, 186–188
Balchowsky, Ina, 13, 51–57, 126, 152, 179
Balchowsky, Max, 13, 49–58, 61, 63, 86, 102, 110, 114, 122, 126, 152, 159, 160, 179, 184
Bell Auto Parts, 167
Belohlavek's Garage, 164
Beverly Hills racetrack, 10, 83
Biennale di Venezia, 25, 142
Bignotti, George, 26, 31, 33, 147, 151
Black, Keith, 39, 44
Blair's Speed Shop, 167, 188
Bondurant, Bobby, 57, 93, 104, 111, 190
Bonneville Salt Flats, 36, 42, 129, 132, 134–136, 164
Borgeson, Griff, 8, 15
Boyle, Mike, 13, 15
Breedlove, Craig, 129, 130, 132–139
Breedlove, Lee, 136, 137, 139
Brock, Peter, 57
Brown, Don, 147
Brown, Travis, 103
Bucknum, Ronnie, 53, 57, 94, 109–111, 114, 115, 181
Bugatti, Ettore, 11
Bullitt, 114
Burness, Bruce, 65–67, 121, 153, 189
Burrell, Jim "Thongs," 120, 147, 174
Cain, Ralph "Scotty," 71, 97–100, 161, 162, 167, 189, 190
California Racing Association, 119
California Speedway, 79
Campbell, Donald, 147
Capone, Al, 100
Cars
 Agajanian-Willard Battery Special, 157, 158
 Batmobile, 71
 Belond, 63
 Bill Forbes, 62
 Blue Crown Special, 14, 35, 149
 Blue Flame, 139
 Bluebird III, 147
Campbell Special, 123

Challenger, 132, 133
Chromolite Special, 15
Clark Gable Special, 99
Eliminator, 71, 73, 74
Ernie Triplett No. 12, 142
Evans Special, 179
Fike Plumbing Special, 153
Fuel Injection Special, 24, 35
Gilmore Special No. 2, 33
Green Monster, 134–137
Hinkle Special, 143
Johnny Lightning Special, 73
Mad Dog IV, 169
Ol' Yeller, 49–57, 61, 63, 71, 81, 86, 102, 110, 126, 152, 179, 184
Parnelli, 73
Pickford Special, 152, 153
Poison Lil, 16
Purple People Eater, The, 99
Reynolds Wrap Special, 71
Shrike, 65
Simpson Special, 117, 120, 122–127, 147, 153
Sorrell Special, 13, 153
Spirit of America, 129, 132–139
Tamale Wagon, 69
Thompson Special, 71
Vestris, 15
Weinberger Homes, 62
Winfield Special, 33, 35–38, 46, 57
Car and Driver, 152, 153
Caravan Inn, 121
Carillo, 33
Carrell Speedway, 82
Casner, Lloyd, 88
Castilli, Leo, 142
Champ Car tournament, 29
Chapman, Colin, 65, 71, 72, 93, 95, 103, 115, 121, 159, 172, 175, 190
Chapouris, Pete, 173
Chinatown, 32
Clark, Jimmy, 65, 103
Clinton, Bill, 98
Club Rendezvous, 16
Cohen, Mickey, 83
Cole, Eddie, 42, 43, 50, 125, 186
Collins, Emory, 19
Conze, Vince, 38, 172
Coon, Frank, 22, 35, 37, 42, 43, 50, 51
Coon, Jim, 77
Cosworth Engineering, 26, 29, 31, 33, 45, 47
Culleton, Jim, 65–67, 95, 121
Culver City Speedway, 10, 42, 83, 160
Daddy's Body Shop, 147
Daigh, Chuck "Charlie," 50, 51, 54, 58, 88
Daigh, Harold, 54
Davis, Eward M., 178
Daytona 500, 10, 21
Daytona Speedway, 20, 84, 88, 168
de Kooning, Willem, 141

de Portago, Fon, 122, 127
Dean, Jimmy, 114, 121
DeBischop, Bob, 24, 27
Dees, Mark, 8, 31
Deidt, Emil, 142
Diedt, Emile, 50
Dillinger, Johnny, 36
Doheny, Eddie, 124
Drake Engineering, 46
Drake, Bobby, 74, 94, 110, 179, 180, 181, 184, 186
Drake, Dale, 21, 24, 66, 167
Dredge, William C., 174, 176, 177
Du Quoin racetrack, 22, 77
Duesenberg, Augie and Fred, 8, 15
Durant, Billy, 13, 15
Duray, Leon, 11, 13
Dutch, Von, 50, 70, 151
East African Safari Rally, 77
Edelbrock Corporatoin, 167, 168
Edelbrock, Vic Jr., 168
Edelbrock, Vic, 167, 168
Eisele, Harry E., 99
Ekins, Bud, 114
El Mirage, 54, 167, 179
Ellico, Ron "Yo Yo," 82
Epperly, Quin, 23, 26, 59, 70, 134
Europe Grand Prix, 7
Ewing, Wayne, 149
Examiner Grand Prix, 93, 95, 159
Examiner, 81, 134
Fante, John, 128
Faulkner, Walt, 33, 44, 76, 77, 109
Faulkner, William, 140
Ferrari, Enzo, 186
Feurhelm, Bob, 188, 189
Field, Ted, 123
Firestone, Leonard, 187, 188
Fletcher Aviation, 179
Follmer, George, 94, 148, 149, 189
Ford Motor Company, 23–25, 35, 36, 42, 43, 46, 54, 56, 64, 66, 71, 93, 94, 104, 111
Ford, Henry "Hank the Deuce" II, 23, 63, 71, 76
Ford, Henry, 8, 11, 19, 21, 36, 38, 40
Foyt, A. J., 42, 43, 94, 124, 147, 149, 150
France, Bill, 168
Freitas, Joe, 103, 104
Fromm, Paul, 33, 34
Gabelich, Gary, 139
Gardena Stadium, 97, 160, 162
Geddes, H. Dean, 104
Gemsa, Joe, 38, 99, 100, 108
General Motors, 11, 42
Giles, Herman, 107
Gilmore Roars Again, 190
Gilmore Stadium, 84, 169, 179, 190
Gilmore, Earl, 179, 190
Ginther, Richie, 94, 111
Goodwin, Michael, 155, 157, 158, 162–165

Goossen, Leo, 6, 9, 11, 13, 16, 18, 21, 31, 36, 51, 129
Gordon, Al, 16–19, 143
Granatelli brothers, 147, 175
Granatelli, Anthony, 171, 172, 174–177
Grant Piston Rings, 167
Grant, Gerry, 22
Great Escape, The, 114
Gunter, Albert, 119, 160
Gurney, Dan, 25, 28, 57, 66, 73, 83, 94, 102, 111, 117, 121, 186
Halibrand Engineering, 65, 171, 172
Halibrand, Ted, 172
Hall of Fame Museum of Indianapolis, 144
Hall, Jim, 72
Hannah, Bob, 155–158, 162
Harris, Bobby, 123
Harry A. Miller Inc. Products Company, 8, 9
Hassler, Peter, 93
Hauser, Eric, 183
Hawley, Don, 82
Hearst, William Randolph, 81
Heath, Allen, 40, 82, 99, 114, 190
Hepburn, Ralph "Hep," 18, 21, 41, 123, 170
Hernandez, Fran, 169
Hilborn, Stu, 22, 43
Hill, Graham, 65
Hill, Phil, 65, 66, 94, 111, 122, 127
Hirashima, Takeo "Chickie," 14, 16, 20, 21, 24, 31, 74, 129
Hollywood Motors, 57
Holman Moody, 111
Hooper, Doug, 104
Houlgate, Deke, 83
Howard, Kenny, 37, 46
Hughes, Howard, 21, 75, 129, 139
Hulette, Don, 74, 87, 152, 153
Hunt, Joe, 70
Hurricane Racing Association, 100, 171
Hurtubise, Herk, 177
Hutton, Barbara, 50
Indianapolis 500, 6–14. 16, 18, 20, 22, 24–31, 33–35, 41, 43, 45, 47, 61, 65, 71–74, 76, 93, 97, 100, 101, 124, 134, 156
Indianapolis Motor Speedway, 15, 17, 31, 39, 46, 59, 63, 70, 174
Indianapolis Racing League, 29
International Race of Champions, 80
Irwindale Speedway, 84
Iskenderian Racing Cams, 167
Iskenderian, Eddie, 13, 33, 37, 73, 170, 171
Jack, Rajo, 13, 35, 107, 108
Jeffries, Dean, 70, 147, 151s
Johncock, Gordn, 27
Johnson, Bob, 86
Jones, Mike, 94
Jones, Parnelli, 24, 26, 45, 65, 70, 71, 73,

77, 80, 93, 97–100, 149, 157–159, 174, 176
Kaiser Steel Mill, 80
Keck, Howard, 35, 43, 77
Keen, Neil, 117, 119
Kessler, Bruce, 160
Kimble, David, 144
Kimbrough, Willie, 80, 106–108
Knoxville Nationals, 52, 53
Kurtis, Frank, 64
Kuzma, Eddie, 23, 26, 60, 70, 147
Laguna Seca Raceway, 58, 61, 66, 67, 105, 141
Land Speed Record, 7, 15, 129, 130, 132–139, 147
Le Mans, 114, 115
Lee Castle, 18
Lee, Tommy, 18
Legion Ascot Speedway, 12, 16–18, 33–37, 41, 43, 46, 47, 67, 69, 81, 141–143, 164
Lerner, Stanford Jay, 86, 87
Lesovsky, Lujie, 23, 26, 30, 61, 70, 141, 147, 150
Leverett, Bayless, 37
Lewis, Harry, 147, 149
Lions Drag Strip, 79, 80
Livingston, Frank, 73
Lockhart, Frank, 8, 10, 14, 15, 84, 109, 129, 132
Long Beach MG Club, 103
Los Angeles Times Grand Prix, 43, 58, 81, 88, 93, 95, 104, 122, 153, 158, 183
Louie Unser Racing Engines, 33
Lovely, Pete, 93
Lubin, Joe, 181
Lytle, Jim, 174
MacDonald, Davey, 58, 65–67, 72, 94, 101–106, 115, 117, 120, 123–127, 133, 149, 153, 163, 165, 190
MacDonald, George, 165
MacDonald, Sherry, 105, 107, 124
Mansfield, Jayne, 159, 160
Mantz, Johnny, 76, 77, 109
Manzanar Relocation Camp, 21
Marcenac, Jean, 175
Mate's White Front, 71, 74
Matlock, Spyder, 16, 18, 19
Mayo, Morrow, 48
Mays, Rex, 34, 37, 46, 74
McAfee, Ernie, 124
McCone, John, 95
McGrath, Jack, 76, 77, 109, 143
McQueen, Neile (Toffel), 115
McQueen, Steve, 114, 115
McWilliams, Carey, 154
Mears, Rick, 118
Meeks, Bobby, 169
Mencken, H. L., 78, 116
Mexican Road Race, 50, 57, 61, 75, 109, 121, 124, 163–165, 179, 190
Meyer, Louie, 9, 14, 15, 17, 19, 21, 24, 30, 31, 46, 66, 167
Michigan International Raceway, 111
Miles, Ken, 93–95, 111, 186
Miletich, Vel, 65, 73
Miller Dynasty, The, 31
Miller Manufacturing Company, 13

Miller, Ak, 76
Miller, Chet, 40
Miller, Harry Armenius "Father," 5–7, 11–20, 23, 24, 31, 33, 35, 36, 50, 66, 129, 132, 146
Miller, John, 24, 28
Millermania, 141, 144
Millican, Howard and Anita, 31
Milne, Jack and Cordy, 188
Milton, Tommy, 11–13, 23, 84
Mitchell, Billy, 186
Monise, Frank, 115, 188
Monterey Grand Prix, 58
Monterey Historic Automobile Races, 144
Montlhéry racetrack, 11
Monza Grand Prix, 11
Moore, Lou, 14
Morton, John, 109
Mosley, Mike, 112
Motoracing, 49, 58–60, 110, 180
Mudersbach, Lefty, 44
Mueller, Butch, 103
Mulligan, Johnny, 44, 45
Murphy, Jimmy, 7, 12, 15
Musso, Luigi, 122, 127
Nancy, Tony, 50
Nash, Ogden, 96
Nassau Speed Weeks, 51
Navarro, Barney, 33, 41, 190
Nehamkin, Lester, 56
Neumeyer, Leroy, 108
Newall, Dickybird, 119
Nicholson, Jack, 32
Nissing, Neil, 147
O'Dell, Ron, 117, 181, 182, 186
O'Neil, Kitty, 139
Offenhauser, Fred, 13, 18, 21, 66, 167
Oldfield, Barney, 8
Ongais, Danny, 123
Ontario Motor Speedway, 25, 79, 80
Opperman, Jan, 45, 46, 162, 163
Osiecki, Bob, 168–171
Panch, Marvin, 88
Parravano, Tony, 60, 118, 119, 121
Pearson, David, 86, 186
Pebble Beach racetrack, 94, 124
Penske, Roger, 83, 111, 114, 121, 187, 189
Peter DePaolo Engineering, 43
Petillo, Kelly, 13, 18, 24, 25, 37, 46, 74, 108, 147
Petrali, Joe, 21, 75, 129, 134–136, 139
Phoenix 200, 65
Piggot, Pat, 95
Pink, Ed, 33, 39, 44
Pittman, Tom, 114
Porter, Herbert, 22, 27, 190
Porterfield, Andy, 104
Pritchard, Pete, 53
Purdy, Kenny, 8, 61, 97, 181
Race of Two Worlds, 122
Rail Duster, 142
Rajo Jack, 142
Rathmann, Dickie, 100, 101, 103, 189
Reeder, Nat, 147, 148, 150, 174, 189
Reid, Wally, 114, 164
Renay, Liz, 83, 84
Reventlow Automotive, 50, 51, 54, 60, 64

Reventlow, Lance, 49–52, 55, 57–60, 81, 187
Richter, Les, 82, 83, 86, 95
Riverside Grand Prix, 74, 83, 99, 100, 102, 127
Riverside International Raceway, 40, 58, 67, 71, 74, 79–84, 86–88, 92, 95, 98, 104, 105, 121–123, 126, 153, 181, 183, 186, 190
Road America, 63
Rodriguez, Ricardo, 95, 186
Rose, Mauri, 35
Roth, Ed "Big Daddy," 147
Ruby, Lloyd, 94
Ruttman, Troy, 101, 156, 159
Ryan, Peter, 95
Sachs, Eddie, 72, 102, 107, 115, 124, 127, 133, 163
Salem racetrack, 20
Salih, George, 63
Savage, Swede, 26
Scarpitta, Salvatore, 12, 17, 25, 114, 141, 143, 190
Schooler, Harry, 106, 160–162
Senter, Louie, 82
Settember, Tony, 104, 117, 164
Shaver Specialties, 45, 47
Shaver, Ronnie, 33, 34
Shaw, Wilbur, 19
Shelby American, 64–66, 102, 105, 111, 121
Shelby, Carroll, 13, 56–58, 60, 61, 63, 64, 70, 76, 88, 92–94, 104, 111, 117, 121, 126, 159
Sheldon, Jack, 4
Silverstone, 51
Simpson, Jim, 104, 117, 124, 126, 127, 149, 151, 153, 188
Sirokin, Mike, 44
Skalla, George, 188
Sloan, J. Alexander, 11
Slutter, Larry, 46, 47
Smith, Blaine, 33
Smith, Clay, 22, 23, 44, 54, 76, 77, 109, 169
Smithsonian, 14
SoCal Speed Shop, 68, 167, 173
Sorrell, Bob, 13, 88
Sparks, Art, 16, 20, 22, 31, 37
Sports Car Club of America, 64, 67
St. Cyr, Lili, 188
Stapp, Egbert, 81
Steele, Johnny, 148, 149
Stevens, Myron, 142
Stevenson, Chuck, 109
Stroppe, Bill, 13, 54, 75, 77, 109, 110, 190
Stutz Motor Company, 132
Sutton, Frank "Willie," 117
Sutton, Jack "Willie," 121, 147
Syracuse racetrack, 12
Team Cunningham, 183
Team Lincoln, 76, 77
Thomas, Bill, 104
Thompson, Mickey, 36, 38, 65, 72, 75, 101, 106, 124, 126, 130, 132, 133, 159, 162–165, 167
Thompson, Trudy, 165

Thorgrimson, Rich, 104
Thorne, Joel Wolfe, 16, 51, 55
Timbs, Norman, 35
Titus, Jerry, 67
To Please a Lady, 99
Toyota Racing Development, 29, 47
Traco, 33, 42, 43
Travers, Jim, 22, 35, 37, 42, 43, 50, 51, 77, 190
Triplett, Ernie, 17, 25, 143
Union Jack, 74
Unser, Louie, 33
Utzman, Willie, 33, 41
Valenta, 99
Victorville Speedway, 160
Victory Circle, 31
Vignolle, Gus V., 49, 52, 58–60, 110, 180, 188, 190
von Dorey, Pedro, 93
von Neuman, Eleanor, 124
von Neuman, Johnny, 58, 122, 124
Vukovich, Billy, 22, 43, 76, 77
Ward, Rodger, 71, 168
Watson, A. J., 23, 26, 30, 33, 70
Weatherly, Joe, 92
Wetteroth, Curly, 19
Wexler, Haskell, 180
Wilkerson, Billy, 167
Williams Grove, 43
Willow Springs Raceway, 118
Winchell, Walter, 123
Winchester racetrack, 20
Winfield, Bud, 38, 41, 42, 47, 123
Winfield, Eddie, 33–36, 38, 46, 56, 57, 169
Wirth, Eddie, 119
World of Outlaws, 34, 52
World War II, 18, 20, 68, 107, 125, 143, 147, 167, 171, 179
Worth, Kenny, 69
Wright brothers, 13
Xydias, Alex, 68, 173
Yunick, Smokey, 43, 190